CHRISTIANITY & LEISURE

ISSUES IN A PLURALISTIC SOCIETY

CHRISTIANITY & LEISURE

ISSUES IN A PLURALISTIC SOCIETY

REVISED EDITION

EDITED BY: PAUL HEINTZMAN, GLEN A. VAN ANDEL, THOMAS L. VISKER

Dordt College Press

Dordt College Press   www.dordt.edu/dordt_press
498 Fourth Avenue NE
Sioux Center, Iowa 51250
United States of America

ISBN: 978-0-932914-66-8

The Library of Congress Cataloging-in-Publication Data
is on file with the Library of Congress, Washington, D.C.
Library of Congress Control Number: 2006929691

Contents

Section Four: Play, Sport, and Athletics

Section Five: Leisure and Culture

Preface

After several years of deliberation, a number of Christian professionals who work as practitioners and educators in the fields of theology, philosophy, English, communications, camping, church education, business, leisure studies, and physical education met at Calvin College in Grand Rapids, Michigan in the summer of 1989 to share and discuss theoretical and practical concepts and ideas on leisure and related topics. Our vision was to create a forum for Christians to present papers that were relevant to our culture and to stimulate discussion on important professional issues. With the success of the initial event, conferences were organized in successive years.

The papers presented in this volume represent the proceedings from the first four annual conferences. Readers will be challenged by the wide variety of topics and the thoughtful ideas presented by the authors. We are grateful to all the authors for their significant contributions to this book, but more importantly to the body of knowledge of which this work is now a part. We trust that it may be used by many students and others to develop a Christian perspective on these disciplines and provide new insights into our culture as we face the challenge of living a life that is consistent with our faith.

The editors would also like to make special note of the untimely deaths of two of the authors, Dr. Gordon Dahl and Dr. Gordon Spykman, both early contributors to the conference. Professor Spykman was noted for his ability to articulate a worldview that recognized and celebrated the Lordship of Jesus Christ in every area of God's creation. Gordon Dahl's presentation was the last professional paper written by this prophetic author who called the Christian church to respond to the challenges of the leisure revolution. It is our hope that this volume will help sustain their legacies.

Paul Heintzman
Glen Van Andel
Tom Visker

Contributors

JOHN BYL received his Ph.D. from SUNY at Buffalo. He is currently a professor in the Physical Education Department at Redeemer University College. Dr. Byl has written numerous articles and published several books including *Intramural Recreation: A Step-by Step Guide to Creating an Effective Program, Organizing Successful Tournaments, 101 Fun Warm-up and Cool-down Games, an Co-ed Recreational Games*. He is also the co-editor of *Physical Education, Sport and Wellness: Looking to God as We Look at Ourselves*. His research interests lie in the nature of tournament organization and the history of sports, particularly Canadian women's experience before 1950.

GORDON DAHL is the author of *Work, Play, and Worship in a Leisure-Oriented Society* as well as numerous articles published in a variety of religious and professional publications. He was the founder of "494 Ministries" which served persons who frequented bars and other establishments along Highway 494 near St. Paul, Minnesota. He also formed the Mall of America Citizens Committee which worked with the developer of the Mall of America to secure space for local arts, religious, and social groups to perform and hold religious services. He was the campus pastor at the University of Minnesota and the founder of Leisure Studies, Incorporated. Dr. Dahl passed away in 1990.

DON DEGRAAF received his Ph.D. from the University of Oregon. He is currently a professor of Recreation at Calvin College, were he teaches recreation leadership and programming. Dr. DeGraaf has authored or c-authored several articles and numerous books including *Leisure and Life Satisfaction,* and *Programming for Parks and Recreation: A Servant Leadership Approach*. His scholarly interests lie in the areas of work motivation, benefits of organized camping, and Christianity and the environment.

MURRAY W. HALL received his B.Ed. from Queens University and a B.P.H.E from Laurentian University. He is presently an associate professor of Human Kinetics at Trinity Western University in Langley, British Columbia. Mr. Hall also holds the title of Director of Athletics. Mr. Hall's research interests lie in the areas of Circadian Dysrhythmia and ethics in sports.

RUSSELL HEDDENDORF received his Ph.D. in Sociology from the University of Pittsburgh. He is currently a professor emeritus of Sociology at Covenant College. He served as Chair for the Global Trends in the 21st Century Core Curriculum Committee. He is also a member of the MacLellan Scholars Committee. Dr. Heddendorf has written an article entitled *Hidden Threads: Social Thought for Christians*. Dr. Heddendoorf's scholarly interests lie in the areas of sociology of humor, sociology of religion, and Christian worldview and sociology.

PAUL HEINTZMAN is an assistant professor in the Leisure Studies program at the University of Ottawa where he completed his undergraduate degree. He holds a Master of Christian Studies degree, with a thesis on the philosophy of leisure, from Regent College in Vancouver. Paul held a variety of positions in the recreation field before completing his PhD in Recreation and Leisure Studies, with a thesis on leisure and spiritual well-being, at the University of Waterloo. In 2003 he received the Society of Park and Recreation Educator's Innovation in Teaching Award for the experiential exercises he developed to teach about leisure and spirituality. His areas of research include: leisure and spirituality/religion/Christianity; philosophy and ethics of leisure; and recreation and the environment. In 2005 he was a Visiting Scholar at Regent College.

SHIRL J. HOFFMAN received his Ed.D. from Columbia University Teachers College. He is professor and former administrator of the undergraduate and graduate programs in the Department of Exercise and Sport Science at the University of North Carolina at Greensboro. Dr. Hoffman has been a leader in examining the relationship between sport and religion and sport ethics. He has written extensively in this area including *Sport and Religion*. His scholarly interests lie in the areas of sports and religion, sport philosophy and ethics, and motor learning and control.

ROBERT K. JOHNSTON received his Ph.D. from Duke University. He is professor, and former provost, of Theology and Culture at Fuller Theological Seminary. He is the author of the book *The Christian at Play*. His scholarly interests lie in the areas of evangelical theology, theological hermeneutics, Old Testament, wisdom literature, theology and contemporary literature, and aims and purposes of theological education.

KIMBERLY A. KELLER is a graduate of Trinity Western University and

Western Washington University with degrees in Psychology and Physical Education. She was the recipient of the Outstanding Major Student Award at Western Washington University in 1993. Her academic interest is in the effects of competition on elementary and secondary school students.

JAMES A. MATHISEN received his Ph.D. from Northwestern University/Garrett-Evangelical Theological Seminary. He is currently an associate professor of Sociology at Wheaton College. He also has been Wheaton's faculty representative to the National Collegiate Athletic Association and to the College Conference of Illinois and Wisconsin. Dr. Mathisen has contributed significantly to the sociology of sport literature including a co-authored book entitled *Muscular Christianity: Evangelical Protestants and the Development of American Sport.* His scholarly interests lie in the areas of institutional religion and American civil religion, in sport as an American folk religion, and in the history and development of modern muscular Christianity.

GARY H. NAYLOR is sessional associate professor of Human Kinetics at Trinity Western University. He received his M.A. in Physical Education at the University of Alberta. His professional interest is in sports ministries, and he is the coordinator of sports ministry at Trinity Western University.

CATHY O'KEEFE received her M.Ed. in Therapeutic Recreation from the University of South Alabama. She is currently an instructor of Therapeutic Recreation and Leisure Studies at the University of South Alabama. She also coordinates clinical placements for therapeutic recreation students. Her scholarly interests include the relationship between leisure and spirituality, therapeutic recreation applications to all populations, and issues related to death and dying.

LELAND RYKEN received his Ph.D. from the University of Oregon. He is currently the Clyde S. Kilby professor of English and former chair of the English Department at Wheaton College. Dr. Ryken has written several books including *Work and Leisure in Christian Perspective* and *Redeeming the Time: A Christian Approach to Work and Leisure.* Dr. Ryken's scholarly interests lie in the areas of work and leisure, literary criticism, and Puritanism.

QUENTIN J. SCHULTZE received his Ph.D. in communications from the University of Illinois. He is currently a professor of Communication Arts and Sciences at Calvin College. His five books include: *Television: Manna From Hollywood?*; *American Evangelicals and the Mass Media; Dancing in the Dark: Youth, Popular Culture and the Electronic Media; Televangelism and American Culture: the Business of Popular Religion*; and *Redeeming Television*. Dr. Schultze is former president of the Religious Speech Communication Association.

GORDON SPYKMAN received his Th.D. from the Free Reformed University of Amsterdam. He was a professor of Religion and Theology, emeritus at Calvin College. Dr. Spykman was a member of the governing board for the Calvin Center for Christian Scholarship and a member of the Karl Barth Society. Dr. Spykman's scholarly interests were in topics of theology, culture, and worldviews. Dr. Spykman died in 1993.

DAVID R. STIRLING received his Ph.D. from the University of Saskatchewan. He was an associate professor of Physical Education and director of research and grants at Trinity Western University. He also held the position of adjunct professor of Physical Education at Simon Fraser University and was a member of the Sport Science Clinic at the University of Alberta.

JOSEPH D. TEAFF received his Ed.D. in Leisure Education from Columbia University and is a professor of Recreation emeritus, at Southern Illinois University. From 1960–1965, he was a student for the Roman Catholic priesthood, completing his undergraduate degree in philosophy as a part of the seminary program. Dr. Teaff has written several articles on therapeutic recreation and one book entitled, *Leisure Services with the Elderly*. His scholarly interests lie in the areas of leisure and aging, therapeutic recreation management, travel and tourism, and the philosophy of leisure.

GLEN VAN ANDEL received his Re.D. in Recreation from Indiana University. He is currently a professor of Recreation at Calvin College. Dr. Van Andel has co-authored an introductory textbook in therapeutic recreation entitled *Therapeutic Recreation: A Practical Approach* and published several articles including a co-authored article on, "Christian Spirituality and Therapeutic Recreation". Dr. Van Andel's scholarly interests lie in the areas of therapeutic recreation, philosophy of leisure, and Christian perspectives on play and leisure.

THOMAS L. VISKER received his P.E.D. from Indiana University. He is currently professor of Physical Education at Bethel College in Mishawaka, IN. Dr. Visker has written several articles on Christian sport participation and is the co-editor of *Physical Education, Sport and Wellness: Looking to God as We Look at Ourselves*. He has coached baseball at many different levels including 25 years as the head baseball coach at Dordt College, Sioux Center, IA. His scholarly interests include the philosophy of sport, the psychosocial dimension of physical activity, and Christianity and sports participation.

GWEN WRIGHT received her Ed.D. in religious studies and counseling psychology from the University of Northern Colorado. She is currently Spiritual Director and Retreat Leader at St. Andrew Presbyterian Church, Boulder, Colorado Her M.A. is in drama from San Francisco State University. She is a member of the American Academy of Religion and the College Theological Society. Her interests include leading Christian spiritual growth retreats and integrating experiential learning into college teaching. Dr. Wright's scholarly focus is a study of the connection between Christian spiritual development and the development of creativity.

MARVIN A. ZUIDEMA received his P.E.D. from Indiana University. He is professor emeritus of Physical Education at Calvin College where he served as department chair, athletic director and soccer coach. Dr. Zuidema has published a series of Physical Education teacher-education manuals for Christian Schools International. His scholarly interests lie in the area of philosophy of physical education and sport, curriculum and programs, and methods of instruction.

SECTION ONE

Biblical and Historical Perspectives

While leisure is not a unique phenomenon of the twentieth century, the last few decades have witnessed a tremendous growth in the field of leisure studies and research. While Christians, particularly since the Reformation, have produced a large body of theological literature to provide ethical guidance with respect to work, there has been a paucity of theological and ethical reflection, from a Christian perspective, on leisure. We are still confronted with what Robert Lee (1964), some twenty-five years ago, called a "theological lag" in which theological and ethical thinking lags behind social and technological change.

It is true that in recent years Christians have begun to reflect theologically about leisure. Foundational work was done by Josef Pieper (1963) who viewed leisure as an attitude of mind, a condition of the soul which is rooted in divine worship. Lee (1964) illustrated how man's time and God's eternity are connected in the Christian use of leisure. Rudolf Norden (1965) argued that Christian vocation encompassed both God's call to leisure and to work. Gordon Dahl (1972) conceived of leisure as a qualitative aspect of human life; a Christian experiences leisure when one comes into complete awareness of the freedom one has in Christ. David Spence (1973, iv–v) suggested that "leisure is the opportunity and capacity to experience the eternal, to sense the grace and peace which lifts us beyond our daily schedules." Harold Lehman (1974) saw leisure as God's gift which takes on many difference dimensions. Robert K. Johnston (1983) suggested that the style of life God intended for us includes both work and play in a crucial balance and creative rhythm. Leland Ryken (1987) argued that work and leisure belong together; they are complementary parts of a God-ordained whole, which although they have many similarities, also balance each other in the rhythm of work and leisure.

The above-mentioned writers have made an important contribution to the development of Christian thinking on leisure. However, as Ryken notes, many books claim to present a Christian theology of leisure, but most of them are "notably vague and insubstantial, with almost no attempt to root an author's personal (and sometimes fanciful) opinions in the Bible" (1987, 182). No doubt the theological task is a difficult one as it *"consists of an ongoing dialogue between biblical, traditional and contemporary sources"* (Johnston 1983, 5). This task is no small one as it involves the systematic hermeneutical task of searching the biblical record for principles that relate to leisure, reviewing the twenty centuries of Christian history and tradition as well as interacting with the leisure realities and leisure ideas of our contemporary pluralistic society.

This section of the book is concerned with continuing to clarify and develop a fuller Christian understanding of leisure through an examination of biblical and historical sources. The section begins with Robert K. Johnston examining work and play from a Biblical perspective, in particular, identifying the wealth of biblical material available to develop a biblical understanding of play. Following this overview, Paul Heintzman focuses on the biblical concepts of sabbath and rest, and through a systematic exegetical and hermeneutical process, fleshes out an understanding of leisure which involves both qualitative and quantitative dimensions. The final article in this section is a historical one. Leland Ryken explores some of the fallacies that are commonly but erroneously associated with the Puritan Ethic, and notes that much good teaching of the Puritans on moderation in work and the need for leisure has been overlooked.

Paul Heintzman

References

Dahl, G. 1972. *Work, play and worship in a leisure-oriented society.* Minneapolis: Augsburg.

Johnston, R.K. 1983. *The Christian at play.* Grand Rapids: Eerdmans.

Lee, R. 1964. *Religion and leisure in America: A study in four dimensions.* New York: Abingdon Press.

Lehman, H. 1974. *In praise of leisure.* Kitchener, ON: Herald Press.

Norden, R. 1965. *The Christian encounters the new leisure.* St. Louis: Concordia.

Pieper, J. 1963. *Leisure: The basis of culture.* New York: Random House.

Ryken, L. 1987. *Work and leisure in Christian perspective.* Portland, OR: Multnomah.

Spence, D. 1973. *Towards a theology of leisure with special reference to creativity.* Ottawa, ON: Canadian Parks/Recreation Association.

Chapter One

Work and Play: A Biblical Perspective

ROBERT K. JOHNSTON

Our Context: Work

We are to work. Most Christians have no trouble believing this. When I was a child, one of the songs in our hymnal was "Be strong! We are not here to play." The words of the song were as follows: "Be strong! We are not here to play, to dream, to drift; we have hard work to do, and loads to lift. Shun not the struggle, face it, 'tis God's gift. Be strong, be strong!" According to most observers, Christianity and the work ethic go hand in hand. It did not take Max Weber to convince us of this truth. We learned it alongside our mother's milk.

The Christian's commitment to work is rooted in God's work of creation. We read in Genesis 2: "Thus the heavens and the earth were finished, and all their multitude. And on the seventh day God finished his work that He had done. . . ." Not only was God a worker in creation, but we were created to be God's co-workers. In Genesis 1:28 we read: "God blessed them, and God said to them, 'Be fruitful and multiply, and fill the earth and subdue it; and have dominion over the fish of the sea and over the birds of the air and over every living thing that moves upon the earth.'"

Moving to the New Testament, John records Jesus saying, "We must work the works of Him who sent me while it is day; night is coming when no one can work" (John 9:4). In a complimentary way, Paul writes to the people in Colossi: "Whatever your task, put yourselves into it, as done for the Lord and not for your masters, since you know that from the Lord you will receive the inheritance as your reward; you serve the Lord Christ" (Colossians 3:23–24). And in one of Paul's better-known admonitions, 2 Thessalonians 3:10–13, we read:

> . . . Anyone unwilling to work should not eat. For we hear that some of you are living in idleness, mere busybodies, not doing any work. Now such persons

we command and exhort in the Lord Jesus Christ to do their work quietly and to earn their own living. Brothers and sisters, do not be weary in doing what is right.

From beginning to end there is a steady note of work sounded throughout the pages of Scripture, and Christians have responded accordingly. We know we are to work and our American culture, itself influenced by the Christian work ethic, has reinforced this ideal. Walter Kerr, writing in the *Decline of Pleasure*, comments humorously:

> We are all of us compelled to read for profit, party for contacts, lunch for contracts, bowl for unity, drive for mileage, gamble for charity, go out for the evening for the greater glory of the municipality, and stay home for the weekend to rebuild the house. . . . In a contrary and perhaps rather cruel way the twentieth century has relieved us of labor without, at the same time, relieving us of the conviction that only labor is meaningful. (1962, 40, 48)

In an advertisement which appeared in the *New Yorker* (1983, March 21, 95), Fortune magazine showed the picture of a vintage Rolls Royce with a chauffeur. Underneath the picture was a caption, "Drive yourself today and tomorrow you may not have to." The advertising copy said,

> There's a lot to be said for hard work. To start with it's the straightest route to the top and all the perks that go along with success.
> And it can be downright fun when you're out there testing yourself against the best and the brightest. The nice thing is, you don't have to hide your ambition under a bushel. . . .
> If you're driving hard for success, your basic business reading has to start with *Fortune*.

What *Fortune* magazine was counting on was a wide cultural acceptance of the value and importance of work. It is okay to be ambitious, even at the expense of others, or so some in our society think.

In his humorous but pointed work, *Confessions of a Workaholic*, Wayne Oates summarizes much of our modern American attitude in these words: "The Workaholic's way of life is considered in America to be at one and the same time a religious virtue, a form of patriotism, the way to win friends and influence people, and the way to be healthy, wealthy and wise" (1971, 12).

The pressures in society to push harder, to keep up with others, and to work ever longer hours were documented in a series of surveys reported by *The New York Times* (1990, June 3). For example, among all people 16 years of age and older who were employed full-time in 1989, 23.5 percent of these workers worked 49 or more hours a week. This percentage rose to 29.4 percent for professionals, 33.9 percent for sales workers, and 36.5 percent for executives, administrators, and managers. These percentages had consistently increased over the last decade. In 1980, only 17 percent of all Americans worked a 50-hour or more week. In a similar vein, moonlighting has risen from 4.9 percent in 1980 to 6.2 percent in 1989.

As one might suspect, as Americans are working longer hours, the median number of leisure hours for adults has continued to drop. Whereas the typical American had 26.2 hours of leisure in 1973 and 19.2 hours in 1980, in 1987 that figure had fallen to 16.6 hours. In the analysis of these trends, *The New York Times* commented that extra work does no more good for the economy than it does for the health. Working longer and harder is not the same as working smarter. In short, it is not clear that the economy is benefiting from increased frenetic activity. It is clear that we, as a people, are playing less and enjoying our work less.

Our Longing: Play

Yet when we do play, we sense play's value. Many have read C.S. Lewis's autobiography, *Surprised By Joy* (1955). In that book, Lewis describes those moments of play which were somehow more primary or basic than most of the rest of life. Although he was a typical English lad who studied Greek and Latin before his teens and excelled in his studies, it was not his work that provided Lewis fundamental experiences. Lewis speaks of smelling a flowering currant bush, of listening to Wagner's music, of reading Norse mythology, of having his mother read Beatrix Potter's *Squirrel Nutkin* to him, of reading *Hyppolytus* (the Greek play), and most particularly, of reading George MacDonald's *Phantastes*. Each of these experiences of play Lewis labeled a "surprise of joy." In these "play" events, Lewis felt himself to be ushered into a reality that was more basic, more primary, than everyday living. In fact, as an adult, Lewis came to the conclusion that these experiences had been divine encounters. The God of creation had become known to Lewis through His creation in all its goodness.

A second example of the innate goodness of play that all of us sense from time to time comes from an essay in the *New Yorker* (1972, July 29) by John Updike. He comments, "There is a goodness in the experience of golf that may well be a place where something breaks into our workaday world and bothers us for evermore with the hints it gives" (76). Those familiar with Updike's other writings will also think of the conversation between Rabbit (Harry) and Eccles, as the liberal protestant minister cynically probes after what Rabbit seeks in life: "What is it? What is it? Is it hard or soft, Harry? Is it blue? Is it red? Does it have polka-dots?" (1960, 112). Eccles is belittling Rabbit's quest for transcendence, and Rabbit has no answer until he steps to the tee and for the first time that day hits a perfect drive. "'That's it!' Rabbit cries and, turning to Eccles with the smile of aggrandizement, repeats, 'That's it!'" (1960, 113).

What Lewis and Updike have intuitively recognized is now beginning to be argued by social scientists as well. Some are suggesting that there is a wholeness, and intrinsic value, to play. George Vaillant's book, *Adaptation to Life*, for example, reports on the findings of his study of several-hundred Harvard University graduates. They were interviewed over a forty-year period spanning their undergraduate days into later life. Vaillant said his interest was in "the kind of people who do well and are well." His conclusion: Being a good businessman (there were no women at Harvard at the time) goes hand in hand with being a good tennis player and husband. Contrary to common mythology, the very men who enjoyed the best marriages and the richest friendships tended also to become the company presidents. "Inner happiness, external play, objective vocational success, mature inner defenses, good outward marriage, all correlate highly—not perfectly, but at least as powerfully as height correlates with weight" (1977, 373). Similar findings have been made by Jay Rohrlich, a practicing psychiatrist with an office on Wall Street. In his book, *Work and Love: The Crucial Balance*, Rohrlich argues from a Freudian perspective that, "Working and loving [which is for him the essence of play] are states of mind. The quality of our lives depends on a healthy balance between them" (1980, 23).

The same conclusion has been reached by Charles Garfield, a psychologist at the University of California Medical School in San Francisco. In the late 1960s, Garfield launched a nationwide study to find out why some people were very successful workers and others were not. Although the workaholic might initially out-distance the others, Garfield discovered such a person not be the "optimal performer," the one making the major contribution to any group, profession, or business. In analyzing five major groups (athletes, educators, health-care workers, creative artists, and people in business and industry), Garfield discovered that the high performers (those recognized as being in the forefront by their colleagues) had a work style that could be characterized by "intention and delight." In contrast with others who typically worked "with determination and for relief," high-level performers had a sense of joy with regard to their activities. Moreover, almost without exception, the most successful not only worked hard, but they played with equal intensity. If their work was chiefly physical, furthermore, they turned in their play to something cerebral (for example, athletes often enjoyed meditation or reading). If their work was of a managerial nature where they sought to control the various elements, they enjoyed in their play something that required an acceptance of life as it presented itself, such as bird watching or sail boating (very few optimal performers in business had motorboats). Garfield's conclusion: "There is a kind of reflexive balancing, or equilibrium, around which the optimal performer launches his or her efforts. There is a centeredness, if you will" (personal communication, April 1981).

Our Ideological Background

What are we to make of this "counter witness"? Do these personal testimonies and these reflections by social scientists, these minority reports in our culture with regard to the value of play and leisure, have something to say to the Christian? What is a Christian understanding of play? (Let me use leisure and play as synonyms at this point.) Does not our play need some justification? Should not play be understood for our edification, our exercise, or even our escape (we all need 10 percent time off from being productive)? Is it not a form of work in disguise ("working out")?

The Bible speaks throughout its pages of the value of play, but we have failed to hear it. Ecclesiastes talks of the joy of food, drink, and the person we love. Song of Songs envisions a healthy sexuality. The sabbath at its most basic to be a time of "non-work." Sprinkled throughout the Old Testament are festivals, dances, and examples of the practice of hospitality which bring a wholeness to life. Turning to the New Testament, we see in Jesus' own life a rhythm of work and play. His friendships with others, particularly Mary, Martha, and Lazarus, show us that play, as well as work, was important to our Lord.

Yet we have systematically misinterpreted these texts having to do with the other side of work. Christians have often asked how Ecclesiastes got into the canon, and have concluded awkwardly that it tells us only about "life under the sun" (that is, secular existence). We have tried to reduce the Song of Songs to an allegory about God's love for the church. We have turned the sabbath ordinance into an injunction with regard to worship. We have understood Old Testament practices of hospitality only in their ethical and not their aesthetic dimensions. We have failed to see these times as occasions for a party. We have viewed Jesus' friendships as a way of his proclaiming his messiahship, not as expressions of his basic humanity. In these and other ways, we have failed to let Scripture speak to us on its own terms with regard to a necessary, God-intended rhythm of work and play, play and work. Instead, we have allowed an undialectical commitment to work become our ideology.

A Biblical Perspective

Genesis 1 and 2 present two stories of creation. God is said to have worked and then rested. His rest included enjoying his creatures and fellowshipping with them. Here is the primary paradigm for humankind. Created in God's image, we are creatures who are to work and to play.

The sabbath ordinance picks up this basic rhythm, this God-given shape to human life.

> Six days you shall work, but on the seventh day you shall rest; even in plowing time and in harvest time you shall rest. You shall observe the festival of weeks, the first fruits of wheat harvest, and the festival of ingathering at the turn of the year. (Exodus 34:21–22)

For the twentieth–century Christian, the sabbath is inextricably associated with worship and cult. This, however, is a secondary association. The sabbath was originally not a time for the cult. Sacrifices were, after all, a daily event. It was first and foremost a time for abstinence from work (compare Exodus 16:22ff.). The sabbath was intended to be that parenthesis in life which had no outside or wider purposes. It was viewed, in broad terms, to be an instance of "play." By regularly resting from their efforts, the Israelites found themselves refreshed and were able to renew themselves and to recall their God.

In Deuteronomy 5, where the ten commandments are restated by Moses at the end of his life, the justification for the sabbath practice is referenced with regard to the needs of others. There should be a sabbath for the sake of one's male and female slave. This is a secondary, but nonetheless important, rationale: an ethical dimension to play needs to be recognized. Play is what allows work to be humane. But, prior to this teaching, an aesthetic dimension to play was affirmed in Exodus. Play was thought to have its own value and purposes independent of work. Thus, the sabbath ordinance in Exodus 20 refers not to the need for refreshment from work, but rather references the sabbath to God himself. In our play we are given the opportunity to recall that life is a gift as well as a task. As

Karl Barth suggests, "The aim of the sabbath commandment is that man (and woman) shall give and allow the omnipotent grace of God to have the first and last word at every point" (1961 iii, 4). In our play, we are both reminded of our God and sensitized to the needs of our co-workers. We are not only to work, but to refrain from work.

The God-intended rhythm of work and play is picked up by the writer of Ecclesiastes as well. Our "lot" in life, he writes, is to enjoy our work and our play. He writes:

> Go, eat your bread with enjoyment, and drink your wine with a merry heart; for God has long ago approved what you do. Let your garments always be white; do not let oil be lacking on your head. Enjoy life with the wife whom you love, all the days of your vain life that are given you under the sun, because that is your portion in life and in your toil at which you toil under the sun. Whatever your hand finds to do, do with your might; for there is not work or thought or knowledge or wisdom in Sheol, to which you are going. (Ecclesiastes 9:7–10)

How can Qoheleth say this? Where has God already approved our work and our leisure? Surely in creation. As Qoheleth mounts a frontal assault on our workaholism throughout the chapters of this book, the writer quotes from and alludes to Genesis 1–11. Without having the ultimate assurance that Christ's further revelation brings, that is, without knowledge of our re-creation, Qoheleth can still argue that we are created to play and to work. It should be perhaps easier for Christians, who know that the Creator is also the Redeemer, to rest in this reality. Sadly, this assurance does not seem to be the case empirically. More than ever, Christians today need to hear what Qoheleth preached.

Although most of scripture concerns God's work and our work in response, there is also sufficient textual support for valuing human play. Not wanting to believe the Song of Songs to be so human in its focus, Christians through the centuries have attempted to explain the text away. Jerome can be seen as proto-typical, offering the following advice to Laeta about her daughter: "Let her never look upon her own nakedness." "She should not read the Song of Songs until she has read Chronicles and Kings, for otherwise she might not observe that the book refers only to spiritual love" (Schonfield 1959, 12). It was not until the Enlightenment that the vitality and passion of this love song was recognized freely for what it was. But even now, the sheer enjoyment of human love which this song celebrates is too often ignored or too quickly allegorized. What we miss in the process is a window into the wholeness and beauty of sexual relationships.

As the Psalmist recognizes, it is God who has created us to work and to play. "You cause the grass to grow for the cattle, and plants for people to use, to bring forth food from the earth, and wine to gladden the human heart, oil to make the shine, and bread to strengthen the human heart" (Psalms 104:14–15). We are to cultivate the earth in order that there might be bread to eat, but also so that there might be oil to make our face shine and wine to make our heart glad. As the apex of God's creation, men and women are encouraged to adopt a human lifestyle not only of work, but of play.

Biblical discussions of play, though rooted in creation theology, are not limited to these creational perspectives. If one reads the biblical record carefully, one will observe the importance of play even within the more dominant biblical discussion of God's saving activity on behalf of his people. The teaching is present, that is, even in the books of the law and of the prophets. In particular, Israel's God-intended play is evident in descriptions of her festivals and of her love for dance. It is basic to the importance attached to feasting. It is even central to her practice of hospitality.

Many of the texts having to do with such play have other intentions than to instruct us concerning play. That is why it is perhaps best to begin a biblical overview of play with the creation-centered text. But a description of Israel's lifestyle is nonetheless instructive, for it models, in a cultural-specific way, a more general pattern that views play as an important component in life. Even if the customs of hospitality might change, or even if such rites of passage as weaning might no longer be celebrated, the larger issue—the importance of play—remains evident. A comment on two of play's motifs will need to suffice in this regard—a comment stemming from the strong importance attached both to the acts of hospitality and to the role of friendship in the salvation history narratives.

The clearest Old Testament example of the cultural importance of hospitality as an occasion for play is the description in Genesis 18 and 19 of the visits to Abraham and Lot by the divine messengers. These visitors came offering salvation from the impending judgment of Sodom. But neither Abraham nor Lot knew of the secret identity of the heavenly visitors when they initially opened their houses to them. Both men went up to greet these total strangers, bowing to the ground, as was the custom. Abraham, as the gracious host, tried to minimize his involvement. He asked if he could provide a "morsel of bread" and "a little water." In actuality a feast was ordered and conversation developed naturally. For the bread, only the best flour was used and in abundance. Milk in a form of yogurt was served, as was meat from a choice calf which was slaughtered for the occasion. And then conversation ensued. Everything came to a halt during the meal; it was an occasion for play.

Another example of Old Testament hospitality is found in Psalm 23. In his time of crisis, the psalmist sings a song of trust to his Lord. He goes back to his youth and finds effective analogies for his God in his shepherding experiences and in the Near Eastern customs of hospitality practiced by his family. Wanting not to argue the truth, but to sing it, he seeks to fill his readers' minds with the wonder and glory of God. God is that good shepherd who provides, leads, and protects. He is also a gracious host offering abundant hospitality.

Turning to the importance of friendship, we can observe the model of Jesus' own life. In Luke 7, for example, Jesus contrasts his convivial lifestyle with John the Baptist's ascetic approach. John's life was a living parable of the need to repent, even if his critics rejected him as demon-possessed. Jesus' style, on the other hand, embodied the future kingdom of joy. While John withdrew, Jesus enjoyed the company of others so much that his critics scolded: "Look, a glutton and a drunkard, a friend of tax collectors and sinners!" (Luke 7:34).

Perhaps the classic account concerning Jesus' conviviality involves his meal with Mary and Martha at their home. Martha meant to honor her friend by preparing an elaborate meal. Mary instead chose to sit at his feet and to listen to him. In a culture in which women had little significance beyond the kitchen, Mary's action was radical indeed. Moreover, as the larger context of the dinner was Jesus' travels, Martha was correct in seeking to be hospitable. But it was the very need to provide hospitality that prevented Martha from listening to Jesus, from being truly hospitable. Jesus' correction of Martha is pointed, even if somewhat ambiguous. His reply might be "Few things are needful," that is, "Keep the meal simple." In other words, listening to him should take priority. Although the latter interpretation is usually adopted, it is too often spiritualized. To sit at Jesus' feet is said by Christians today to be the only thing we need. Such an interpretation misses the point, however, for it fails to see the importance to Jesus of friendly conversation. Hospitality should be the occasion for enjoyment—for play—and not merely a duty.

The friendship of Mary, like the friendly act of the woman who poured perfume over Jesus (Mark 4), cannot be compared with the obligation to prepare food for one's guests or to help the poor. The obligation to work for justice remained paramount to Jesus. But alongside Christ's work was his play. Like God himself, Jesus both worked and rested.

Conclusion

The evidence for "play" in the Bible is extensive. Yet we have, for the most failed to recognize it or act upon it, for our work-dominated culture has our interpretation. There is an intended human lifestyle of work and play is mirrored throughout the pages of Scripture. Neither needs justification. Their meaning comes with creation itself and is reinforced through Jesus' re-creation message.

The academy award-winning film, "Chariots of Fire" (Hudson, 1981), illustrated well the value of both play and work. The movie tells the story of two runners in the 1924 Olympics, Harold Abrahams and Eric Liddell. Abrahams, a Jew among Gentiles, runs for his country in order to prove his worth to others. Only by being a success can he overcome the anti-Semitism directed at him. When his girlfriend asks him if he loves his running, he responds, "I'm more an addict. It's a compulsion. A weapon." As he waits for the finals of the 100-yard dash, he tells his friend that he is scared: "Ten lonely seconds to justify my existence." Abrahams does just that; he wins the gold medal. Having proven his worth through running, Harold Abrahams can give it up, and he does. His job has been completed.

Eric Liddell, on the other hand, runs for the sheer pleasure of it, so much so that his austere religious sister is led to criticize him. "I don't want his work spoiled with all this running talk," she says. In a poignant moment in the film, Liddell tells his sister: "I have decided to go back to China for missionary service." She is overjoyed until he adds, "I've got a lot of running to do first. Jenny, you've got to understand it. I believe God made me for a purpose—for China. But he also made me fast. And when I run I feel his pleasure . . . it's not just fun. To win is to honor Him." Liddell does win the 400-meter dash and it does bring honor to his Lord.

As the film ends, we are told that after the Olympics Eric Liddell returned to China for missionary work. His primary season of play completed, he is able to find a similar joy in his work, knowing it, too, is a part of God's purpose for his life. While in China, moreover, Liddell continued to run occasionally. His play, like his work, continued to fit into a larger rhythm. Eric Liddell understood what many Christians do not: we are called not only to work, but to play.

References

Barth, K. 1961. *Church dogmatics.* Vol. 3. Edinburgh: T. and T. Clark.

Fortune advertisement. 1983. *The New Yorker*, March 21, 95.

Hudson, H. (Director). 1981. Chariots of Fire (Film). New York: Warner Bros.

Kerr, W. 1962. *The decline of pleasure.* New York: Simon and Schuster.

Kilborn, P.T. 1990. The work week grows: Tales from the digital treadmill. *The New York Times*, June 3.

Lewis, C.S. 1955. *Surprised by joy: The shape of my early life.* New York: Harcourt, Brace and World, Harvest Books.

Qates. W. 1971. *Confessions of a workaholic.* New York: World.

Rohrlich, J. 1980. *Work and love: The crucial balance.* New York: Summit Books.

Schonfield, H.J. 1959. *The Song of Songs.* New York: New York American Library, Mentor Book.

Updike, J. 1960. *Rabbit run.* Greenwich, CT: Fawcett Books.

Updike, J. 1972. Is there life after golf? *The New Yorker*, July 29.

Vaillant, G. 1977. *Adaptation to Life.* Boston: Little, Brown.

Chapter Two

Implications for Leisure from a Review of the Biblical Concepts of Sabbath and Rest

PAUL HEINTZMAN

> The Bible knows nothing of "a problem of leisure." ... The general standpoint of the Bible is that it is "folly" (i.e. sinful) to be idle between daybreak and sunset.... Hence we must not expect to derive from the Bible any explicit guidance upon the right use of leisure. (Richardson 1952, 51)

I believe Alan Richardson is correct in stating that the Bible does not provide us with explicit guidance concerning leisure. However, I believe he is wrong in depicting the life of the person living in the biblical world as one preoccupied with work. The Hebraic lifestyle, which included Sabbath observance and the notion of a blessed life in the land, suggests that there was more to life than work. And, although there is not a fully developed theology of leisure in the Bible, there are numerous biblical elements which may guide us in our understanding of leisure.

This paper will focus on two biblical elements relevant to a biblical understanding of leisure: the principle of the Sabbath and the concept of rest. These biblical elements cannot be equated with leisure; however, they provide material to flesh out a Christian understanding of leisure. The elements of sabbath and rest will be developed to illustrate that a biblical understanding of leisure encompasses both a rhythm to life (which includes a quantitative dimension of leisure) and the quality of life which God offers us (a qualitative dimension of leisure).

The Sabbath

The principle of the Sabbath is more central to Israelite life than any of the other Old Testament instructions. Not only is the Sabbath Commandment longer than any of the other commandments in the Decalogue, but the principle of the Sabbath is reformulated and discussed throughout scripture. My discussion of the Sabbath will start with the creation account and then trace through Scripture the teaching on this principle. From this material I will attempt to extract some general principles which are applicable and relevant to leisure.

The Creation Account

In the Genesis account of creation the work of creation took six days; then God rested from His labor on the seventh day. There is a distinction between six days of labor and the seventh day of rest.

In the creation account the word "sabbath" (*sabbat*) does not occur, but the root (*sbt*) from which sabbath is derived is found at the end of the creation account in Genesis 2:2,3.

> By the seventh day God had finished the work he had been doing; so on the seventh day he rested from all his work. And God blessed the seventh day and made it holy, because on it he rested from all the work of creating that he had done.

The creation account ends with a focus on God: God blessing the seventh day, God making the seventh day holy, and God resting from his work. What is the significance of God resting? Commentary on God's resting in Gen. 2:2,3 is supplied by Exodus 31:17 where we read: ". . . for in six days the Lord made the heavens and the earth, and on the seventh day he abstained from work and rested." The important point here is that God stopped and rested. God is a God whose very nature is one of rest.

The creation account suggests that not only is God a God whose nature is one of rest but rest is also an essential component of human nature. The creation account depicts the first complete day of humanity's life as a day of rest, a day to rest with God and reflect upon God's work of creation. Only after this first full day of rest do humans turn to their work. Claus Westermann writes: "The work which has been laid upon man is not his goal. His goal is the eternal rest which has been suggested by the rest of the seventh day" (1974, 65). Not only does the divine rest on the seventh day indicate the goal of creation, but, as Karl Barth has suggested, it is the summons to humanity to enter upon history and to enter life participating in this rest:

> The goal of creation, and at the same time the beginning of all that follows, is the event of God's Sabbath freedom, Sabbath rest and Sabbath joy, in which man, too, has been summoned to participate. It is the event of divine rest in the face of the cosmos completed with the creation of man—a rest which takes precedence over all of man's eagerness and zeal to enter upon his task. Man is created to participate in this rest. (1958, 98)

Thus from God's resting on the seventh day we see not only a rhythm to life in which there is one day's break in seven, but also a quality of life characterized by rest.

Exodus 16

There is no further mention of the word "Sabbath" in the Bible, nor explicit reference made to Sabbath-keeping until Exodus 16 which outlines regulations for the Israelites to gather and prepare the manna while they were wandering in the wilderness. Each day, while the Israelites were in the wilderness, God provided a fresh supply of manna; each day it had to be collected afresh, for the manna from the previous day would rot and smell. But on the sixth day God sent a double supply of manna. Obeying the instruction of the Lord, Moses instructed the people, "This is what the Lord commanded: 'Tomorrow is to be a day of rest, a holy Sabbath to the Lord. So bake what you want to bake and boil what you want to boil. Save whatever is left and keep it until morning," (16:23). What was saved for the seventh day "did not stink or get maggots in it" (16:24).

Yet some of the people went out on the seventh day to gather their manna, but we are told "they found none" (16:27). This comment, writes Hans Walter Wolff, is "an almost humorous criticism of our restless, over-zealousness for work . . ." (1972, 73). Work on the seventh day is ridiculed as foolish, for its results are nil; it fails to acknowledge that God supplies what is needed. Exodus 16, then, relativizes humanity's work—one day in seven is to be set aside for rest. This is possible because it is God who provides what is needed to live.

The Mosaic Law and the Sabbath Commandment

The Sabbath Commandment is found in all accounts of the Mosaic Law (Exodus 20:8–11, 23:12, 31:12–17, 34:21, 35:1–3, Leviticus 19:3, 23:1–3, 26:2, Deuteronomy 5:12–15). In my examination of this material two questions need to be considered. First, what reasons are given for observing the Sabbath? Second, how is the Sabbath to be observed?

Why is the Sabbath to be observed?

In his article on "Sabbath" in the *Theological Wordbook of the Old Testament*, Hamilton (1980) identifies four motives given in the Mosaic Law for observing the Sabbath. Let us examine each one of these motivations.

The analogy of God resting

In Exodus 20:8–11 we encounter the first reason provided for observing the Sabbath day: the analogy of God resting at the end of the creation account.

> Remember the Sabbath day by keeping it holy. Six days you shall labour and
> do all your work, but the seventh day is a Sabbath to the LORD your God. On
> it you shall not do any work, neither you, nor your son or daughter, nor your
> manservant or maidservant, nor your animals, nor the alien within your gates.
> For in six days the LORD made the heavens and the earth, the sea and all that
> is in them, but he rested on the seventh day. Therefore the Lord blessed the
> Sabbath day and made it holy.

On the basis of His own rhythm of six days of activity and one of rest,
God blesses and hallows the Sabbath day for Israel; the model is six days
of work and a seventh day Sabbath (see v.9). What is the significance of
this motivation for Sabbath observance? First, the appeal to the creation
account in the Sabbath commandment demonstrates that the rhythm of
God's six days of activity and one of rest is to be the pattern for a rhythm
of six days of work and one of rest in human life. Richardson writes,
"Our human rhythm of work and rest is a refraction of that image of
God, in which we were made" (1952, 53–54).

Second, the appeal to the creation account suggests that Sabbath observance is to be characterized by a certain attitude or posture before
God. By recalling that God rested on the seventh day, the Israelite, in the
act of Sabbath rest, "experienced his God as a God whose very nature
was one of rest" (Johnston 1983, 95). Furthermore, the Sabbath, as out-
lined here in Exodus 20:11, "is an invitation to rejoice in God's creation,
and recognize God's sovereignty over time" (Hamilton 1980, 903). Abram
Heschel writes:

> To observe the seventh day . . . is to celebrate the creation of the world and to
> create the seventh day all over again, the majesty of holiness in time, "a day of
> rest, a day of freedom," a day which is like "a lord and king of all other days."
> (1966, 19–20)

Thus the Sabbath was not primarily for restorative purposes but time
to be seen simply as God's time, a time to consider God and his purposes. The Sabbath was a time for the Israelites to recognize that life
was a gift from God and not just the result of human work. As such the
Sabbath qualified the Israelite's workaday world by putting one's six days
of work into proper perspective. Exodus 20:11 suggests that the day of
rest forcefully reminds humans, once every seven days, that they live in a
world which contains not only all one needs but also many other things
to enjoy. "So the Sabbath, which brings to an end the week, becomes for
Israel an invitation to enter into, and rejoice in the blessings of creation"

(Dumbrell 1984, 35).

In summary, the appeal to creation theology in Exodus 20:11 suggests two dimensions to Sabbath observance. Quantitatively the Sabbath is to be a one-day break from the other six days of work. Qualitatively the Sabbath is an invitation to experience God as a God whose very nature is one of rest and also to rejoice and celebrate in God's creation.

The remembrance of deliverance from Egypt

Although the Ten Commandments as recorded in Exodus 20 are almost the same as the account of them in Deuteronomy 5, the Sabbath commandment is a noticeable exception. A different motive for observance of the Sabbath is found in the Deuteronomic account of the Decalogue where the Sabbath command is linked with God's deliverance of the Israelites from bondage in Egypt:

> Observe the Sabbath day by keeping it holy, as the LORD your God has commanded you. Six days you shall labour and do all your work, but the seventh day is a Sabbath to the Lord your God. On it you shall not do any work, neither you, nor your son or daughter, nor your manservant and maidservant, nor your ox, your donkey or any of your animals, nor the alien within your gates, so that your manservant and maidservant may rest, as you do. Remember that you were slaves in Egypt and that the LORD your God brought you out of there with a mighty hand and an outstretched arm. Therefore the LORD your God has commanded you to observe the Sabbath day. (Deuteronomy 5:12–15)

In this account the reason for keeping the Sabbath day is the affirmation that Yahweh had liberated and delivered Israel from bondage in Egypt. As such, the "Sabbath was a remembrance that Israel rested ultimately in God's graciousness" (Johnston 1983, 89). It is the Exodus redemption which makes possible the new life in the land, and thereby Edenic rest. Without the redemptive activity of God, the original notion of Sabbath rest is impossible. Yet the expectation of "rest" was not realized in Israel's experience, and finally Israel was exiled from the land. The Epistle to the Hebrews (4:8–10) reminds us that although Israel did not enter this rest, there still exists a Sabbath rest for believers which is a fulfillment of creation's purpose.

In light of the fact that Israel did not enter the promised rest, it is interesting to note, as Johnston points out, that the later Deuteronomic account shifts "from a focus on God to a stronger emphasis on the human need for relief from the oppressive reality of much work" (1983, 90). The Hebrew word *shamor* ("observe the Sabbath day") has a definite ethical connotation as compared with the Hebrew word *zachor* ("remembering the Sabbath") which is found in Exodus 20:11. Furthermore, the Deuteronomic version of the fourth commandment includes the ethical justification "that your manservant and maidservant may rest, as you do" (5:14). Here is a humanitarian emphasis. The necessity to abstain from human toil on the Sabbath for human benefit is emphasized in the phrase "may rest, as you do." As such the Sabbath is also for human rest, restoration, and recreation.

The Sabbath as a humanitarian ordinance

A third motivation for observing the Sabbath, a humanitarian one which we have already noted in Deuteronomy 5:14–15, is more clearly stated in Exodus 23:12: "Six days do your work, but on the seventh day do not work, so that your ox and your donkey may rest and the slave born in your household, and the alien as well, may be refreshed." In this verse the only purpose given for the day of rest is that the dependent laborers and domestic animals experience rest and recuperation. The word "refreshed," which is used to describe the alien or the slave born into an Israelite household is the exact same word which is used to describe God's rest on the seventh day in Exodus 31:17. According to Exodus 23:12, then, the Sabbath was especially for the benefit of those who were severely burdened with work and were under the orders of others.

The implication of this humanitarian motive for observance of the Sabbath is that all members of society should both work and rest. As Gerhard Hasel points out, the Sabbath reminds us of "the social emphasis on equality of all human beings (free persons and servants) under God" (1983, 194). Thus the biblical view does not lend support to a social structuring of society such as in the Greece of Aristotle's day when slaves made it possible for a few to have a life of leisure, nor does it support a leisure class who live a life of conspicuous consumption at the expense of a working class such as is described in Thorstein Veblen's *The Theory of the Leisure Class* (1934). The humanitarian motivation for the Sabbath suggests that all are entitled to a break from work, and therefore leisure, in at least a quantitative sense.

The Sabbath as a sign of the covenant

The fourth motivation for observance of the Sabbath is that it is a sign of the covenant:

> The Israelites are to observe the Sabbath, celebrating it for the generations to come as a lasting covenant. It will be a sign between me and the Israelites forever, for in six days the Lord made the heavens and the earth, and on the

seventh day he abstained from work and rested. (Exodus 31:16,17)

In this passage the Sabbath is not only a sign of the covenant but is itself called a covenant. Sabbath observance is also claimed to be the sign of Israel's allegiance to God in Exodus 31:13. The Sabbath was to be observed not only within the context of a relationship with God, but it was a sign of the relationship.

What implications does this covenant motivation for Sabbath observance have for our study of leisure? While some benefits may accrue from observance of one day's rest in seven, leisure like the Sabbath may find its true meaning and reach its fullest potential when one lives in relationship with God.

How is the Sabbath to be observed?

In the Mosaic covenant, the Sabbath rest is a matter of detailed regulations. All work is forbidden and what constituted work is delineated with great precision. The Sabbath was to be kept by all on every seventh day. The references to the family, servants, and all other members of the Hebrew household, animals, and sojourners listed in Exodus 20:10 and Deuteronomy 5:14 guarantee that no one over whom the male Israelite had authority would have to work; therefore, everyone would be able to rest from work.

It is not only laborious work that is prohibited, as is the case on many of the holy days; on the Sabbath "you are not to do any work" (Leviticus 23:3 compare to "do no *regular* work" of Leviticus 23:7,8,21,23,35,36; Numbers 28:18,25,26; 29:1,12,35). The gathering of food, the lighting of fires and the collecting of firewood are all forbidden (Exodus 16:25–30; 35:1–3; Numbers 15:32–26). The phrase in Exodus 34:21, "even during ploughing season and harvest you must rest," stresses that even at the busiest time of the year in an agricultural society the Sabbath was to be kept. Especially in such busy times humans need a day of rest.

How the Sabbath was to be observed is summarized in Exodus 34:21a: "Six days you shall work, but on the seventh day you shall cease work!" (NEB). The sabbatical legislation declared that life was best lived in a rhythm wherein all people both worked and then refrained from work. In this sense the Sabbath was a quantity of time in which no work was performed. Likewise, leisure may be understood quantitatively as a period of time in which no work is performed.

But was the Sabbath only a quantity of time in which no work was performed? The Sabbath is enumerated among the sacred festivals, "the appointed feasts of the Lord" (Leviticus 23:1–3). The Sabbath and worship are linked together by the joint command given both in Leviticus 19:30 and in 26:2: "Observe my Sabbaths and have reverence for my sanctuary." The Sabbath was a day of worship as well as a day of rest from labor. However, rest was itself an expression of worship; no distinction was made between rest and worship—resting was worship. Thus the Old Testament taught that the Sabbath was to be observed not only by a cessation from work but also by a rest which was of the nature of worship.

The Prophets and the Sabbath

The prophets' utterances concerning the Sabbath only apply what has already been revealed in the Pentateuch. Although the prophets spoke critically of the practices that occurred on the Sabbath, they did not condemn the Sabbath itself but rather a misuse of the Sabbath. The prophets also pointed to the blessings which follow from a correct observance of the Sabbath.

For example, Isaiah decried the ritualistic Sabbath observance of his day (Isaiah 1:12, 13) and in a classic passage outlines what will follow from a true observance of the Sabbath:

> If you keep your feet from breaking the Sabbath and from doing as you please on my holy day, if you call the Sabbath a delight and the LORD's holy day honourable, and if you honour it by not going your own way and not doing as you please or speaking idle words, then you will find your joy in the LORD. (Isaiah 58:13,14)

Amos, who passionately contended against the many abuses in the sacrificial cult (4:4ff.; 5:21ff.), brought down judgment upon the grain dealers who could not wait for the Sabbath to be over so they could sell their wheat and deceive the people through "skimping the measure, boosting the price, and cheating with dishonest scales" (8:5). The misuse of the Sabbath was also condemned by other prophets who interpreted the destruction of Jerusalem and subsequent exile of the Israelites to be partly the result of the desecration of the Sabbath (Jeremiah 17:27; Ezekiel 20:23–25).

In conclusion, the prophets' words contradict humanity's inclination to make life secure or add to life's abundance by nonstop, uninterrupted work. Yet the Sabbath suggests that "human life has a higher significance than being merely a struggle for existence" (Wolff 1972, 73). Work is only to occupy six days of the week. Work on the seventh day is not only unnecessary but prohibited. So there is a rhythm to life—six days of work and one of rest.

Jesus and the Sabbath

Jesus demonstrated a rhythm of work and rest and taught his disciples to take rest: "Come with me by yourselves to a quiet place and get some rest" (Mark 6:31). Furthermore, Jesus' teaching on the Sabbath upheld the authority and validity of the Old Testament law. But, on several occasions (Matthew 12:1–14; Mark 2:23–28, 3:1–5; Luke 6:1–11, 13:10–17, 14:1–6; John 5:9–18, 9:1–14), he reacted against the Pharisees who stifled the spirit of the sabbatical teaching with their restrictive oral and written tradition. On these occasions, Jesus put human need above formal external compliance with the Sabbath legislation. It was not wrong to pick and eat grain on the Sabbath nor was it unlawful to perform works of mercy or to heal on the Sabbath day. Yet Jesus never did or said anything to indicate that he intended to abolish the Sabbath along with the relaxation and other benefits such a day of rest offers. Jesus' emphasis was on keeping the spirit of the law and not only on an external observance of the law (Matthew 5:17–48). Jesus explained the true meaning of the Sabbath by teaching that it "was made for man, not man for the Sabbath" (Mark 2:27).

Jesus' teaching on the Sabbath suggests that leisure is more than quantitative; it also has a qualitative dimension to it. The Sabbath's one day of rest in seven is not just a day of inactivity. It is not just a time period, but a time set aside for humans, a time for bringing healing and wholeness. The same may be said about leisure. Leisure is not just a quantitative segment of life but a quality of life closely related to wholeness and fullness.

The New Testament Church and the Sabbath

The first Christians, as faithful Jews, worshipped each day in the temple at Jerusalem (Acts 2:46; 5:42), went to the synagogue (Acts 9:20; 13:14; 14:1; 17:1,2,10; 18:4), and respected the law (21:20). Very likely the early Jewish Christians also kept the Sabbath. In the epistle to the Colossians (2:16ff.), the Sabbath is to be understood as "a shadow of the things that were to come; the reality, however, is found in Christ." Romans 14:5,6 seems to imply that one day is no more sacred or special than any other. Thus Paul suggests that the Sabbath is not to be imposed on the Christian, rather the Christian is set free from the encumbrance of the law. The Spirit of Christ was understood as empowering one to fulfill God's will independently of the outward stipulations of the law.

Robert Banks summarizes the teaching of the New Testament on the Sabbath:

While Christians were no longer obliged to relax on a set day of the week (cf. Romans 14:5; Colossians 2:16–17), and believed that they had already begun to enter an eternal Sabbath (cf. Hebrews 4:3), the principle of taking proper physical and spiritual rest remained important. This was now taken, apparently, whenever the need or opportunity for it arose, rather than on a specified day (e.g. Mark 4:35ff., 6:30ff.). (1983, 185)

Summary on the Sabbath

In concluding our discussion of the biblical Sabbath, let us review three general principles that are applicable to our discussion of leisure. First, the Sabbath reminds us of the social equality of all human beings under God. All who work and labor, especially those burdened by work, are entitled to one day's rest in seven (Exodus 20:10; 23:12; Deuteronomy 5:14–15). Thus a society in which a few members enjoy a life of leisure based upon the endless work of the many is inconsistent with the teaching of Scripture. All are entitled to leisure at least in a quantitative or free-time sense. From a biblical point of view, the emphasis on social equality found in the Sabbath legislation would seem to negate any attempt to define leisure in terms of a leisure class.

Second, the Sabbath points to a rhythm in life—a rhythm of work and nonwork (leisure in a quantitative sense). This was evidenced in the creation account, the Exodus manna story, the Mosaic law, and the words of the prophets. So the Sabbath inculcated that Israel's life possessed the element of time free from work. The implication for our study is that the Sabbath suggests some rhythm or cycle of leisure (in a quantitative sense) and work is necessary for well-being and wholeness.

Whether or not we still see the Sabbath commandment as binding, it remains instructive regarding God's concern for the rest of humans. The rhythmic pattern to life, which the Sabbath suggests, may constantly serve as a model for us in shaping and scheduling life. The great benefit of a sabbatical structure to life is to provide special time each week for physical, mental, spiritual, and emotional renewal which leads to better health both for the individual and society,

Third, the Sabbath suggests that leisure may be defined in more than a quantitative sense, for the Sabbath is more than a time period, more than one day in seven. In the Old Testament, the Sabbath, as a day of abstaining from work, is not entirely for the purpose of restoring one's lost strength and enhancing the efficiency of one's future work. Rather than simply an interlude between periods of work, it is the climax of living. Heschel describes the Sabbath as "not a date but an atmosphere . . .

a taste of eternity—the world to come" (1966, 21, 31–30). The Sabbath suggests the attitude for humanity's basic posture in relation to God. I have argued from the creation account that rest is basic to the nature of humanity. In fact I stated that the divine intention to humanity is not work but the eternal rest symbolized by the rest of the seventh day. Thus humanity's chief end is not to labor but to enjoy God forever. The appeal to creation theology in the Exodus account of the Sabbath command-ment suggests that the Sabbath is an invitation to the Israelites, in the act of Sabbath rest, to experience their God as a God whose very nature is one of rest and to rejoice in and celebrate in God's gift of creation. The sabbatical legislation commanded a Sabbath rest which was of the nature of worship. The prophet Isaiah described the Sabbath as a delight. Jesus taught that the Sabbath was a time for bringing healing and wholeness. All this evidence conclusively suggests that the Sabbath, and likewise leisure, is more than a time of non-work; it has a qualitative dimension. I con-clude that the biblical Sabbath teaches us that leisure need not be merely an external cessation from work in the rhythm of human life, but that it may also be an internal spiritual attitude; leisure reaches its fullest poten-tial when our lives are lived in relationship with God.

The Biblical Concept of Rest

Leisure is frequently equated with the biblical concept of rest. Several writers (Dahl, 1972; Houston, 1981; Sherrow, 1984) draw parallels be-tween leisure and Christ's offer of rest in Matthew 11:28–30. Therefore, it should be fruitful to examine the biblical concept of rest and its implica-tions on our study of leisure.

Before proceeding to examine the biblical concept of rest, two intro-ductory comments can be made. First, it is natural that we should move from an examination of the Sabbath to a discussion of the theology of rest. Although the developed Old Testament theology of rest utilizes dif-ferent terminology than that used in Genesis 2:1–4, Dumbrell points out that the close link "between such 'rest' and the Sabbath which epitomized the concept was always maintained (see Exodus 20:11 where the two con-cepts of 'sabbath' and 'rest' are brought together)" (1984, 35). The close link between rest and Sabbath culminates, as will be explained, in the Sab-bath-rest of Hebrews 4:9.

Second, the belief is expressed throughout the Bible that God has giv-en, or will give, rest to His people. Yet Gerhard von Rad notes, "Among the many benefits of redemption offered to man by Holy Scripture, that of 'rest' has been almost overlooked in biblical theology" (1966, 94). Perhaps this overlooking of the biblical concept of rest partly explains the fact that Christians have a well-developed theology of work but not of leisure. Biblical theology has stressed Salvation History as something distinct from the earthly realm. It has ignored large portions of biblical revelation including the wisdom literature and the nature psalms. Salvation has been narrowed to mere deliverance while the significant themes of blessing, land, and rest have been ignored.

The Theological Uses of "Rest"

Let us now turn our attention to the biblical concept of rest, first by examining the Hebrew root for rest along with its major theological uses and then by tracing the development of the concept of rest through Scripture. According to Leonard J. Coppes, writing in the *Theological Wordbook of the Old Testament*, the Hebrew root of rest (*nuah*) "signifies not only absence of movement but being settled in a particular place (whether concrete or abstract) with overtones of finality, or (when speaking abstractly) of victory, salvation, etc." (1980, 562). At least three important theological uses are associated with this root: a psychological-spiritual (personal peace), a martial (rest from enemies), and a soteriological (salvation rest) use. If leisure includes a qualitative dimension, a condition of our being, then these uses of rest must have some relevance for our understanding of leisure.

The Deuteronomic Notion of Rest: Rest in the Land

We first meet the promise of rest in Deuteronomy:

> You have not yet reached the resting place and the inheritance the LORD your God is giving you. (Deuteronomy 12:9)

> When the LORD your God gives you rest from all the enemies around you in the land he is giving you to possess as an inheritance, you shall. . . . (Deuteronomy 25:19)

In Deuteronomy the concept of rest is grounded in and equivalent with possession of the land. Canaan as Israel's inheritance was to be a place of rest. Von Rad stresses that we must not spiritualize this concept of rest which was a direct gift from the hand of God: "[It] is not peace of mind, but the altogether tangible peace granted to a nation plagued by enemies and weary of wandering" (1966, 95).

The concept of rest to which Deuteronomy frequently refers is associated with the notion of a pleasant, secure, and blessed life in the land

(15:4; 23:20; 28:8; 30:16). Dumbrell connects this pleasant life in the land with the creation account:

> Israel will enjoy the gifts of creation in the way in which they had been meant to be used. In this theology of rest we are clearly returning to the purposes of creation set forth in Genesis 1:1–2,4A[check original source] and typified by the Eden narrative, namely that mankind was created to rejoice before the deity and to enjoy the blessing of creation in the divine presence. The notion of rest in both Genesis 2:2 and the book of Deuteronomy implies this. (1984, 121–122)

There is a sense in which the promise of rest was fulfilled in the Old Testament, in terms of rest in the land, and this fulfillment is first expressed in the book of Joshua:

> So the LORD gave Israel all the land he had sworn to give their forefathers, and they took possession of it and settled there. The LORD gave them rest on every side, just as he had sworn to their forefathers. Not one of their enemies withstood them; the LORD handed all their enemies over to them. Not one of all the LORD's good promises to the house of Israel had failed; every one was fulfilled. (Joshua 21:43–35, see also 1:13,15; 22:4)

Later in 2 Samuel, we read that the Lord had given rest in the land and will continue to do so during David's reign as king: "the king [David] had given him rest from all his enemies around him" (7:1). Then the word of the Lord came to Nathan instructing him to tell David that, among other things, the Lord Almighty "will also give you rest from all your enemies" (7:11b).

The fulfillment of the promise of rest may, even more clearly, be identified with the time of Solomon. In Solomon's blessing which followed his prayer of dedication for the temple he acknowledged the fulfillment of God's promise to give his people rest:

> Praise be to the LORD, who has given rest to his people Israel just as he promised. Not one word has failed of all the good promises he gave through his servant Moses. (1 Kings 8:56)

Thus it can be said that the divinely given rest was experienced by the nation of Israel during the times of Joshua, David, and Solomon. Yet, as we will see later in our discussion of Hebrews 3 and 4 there is a real sense in which the promise of rest was not fulfilled in the Old Testament.

The Chronicler's Notion of Rest:
The LORD God Resting Among His People

The Chronicler's notion of rest swings away from the deuteronomic conception of rest. "Rest from all your enemies" becomes a gift which God bestows periodically upon pious kings. Not only is Solomon a "man of peace," (1 Chronicles. 22:9), but God also grants rest during the reigns of King Asa (2 Chronicles 15:15) and King Jehoshaphat (2 Chronicles 20:30). In this same book, Solomon is now considered as a "man of peace, in an entirely new way, the fundamental characteristic is not that Israel obtains rest, but that God comes to rest in the midst of his people" (von Rad 1966, 97–98). Solomon ends his long prayer of dedication for the temple with the following exalted messianic invocation:

> Now arise, O LORD God, and come to your resting place, you and the ark of your might. May your priests. . . be clothed with salvation . . . O LORD God, do not reject your anointed one. Remember the kindnesses promised to David your servant. (2 Chronicles 6:41–42)

Now added to the promise that Israel as a nation would receive rest is the additional anticipation that God will finally come to rest among his people, Israel.

At this point let us summarize the strands in the complex of ideas about rest in the Old Testament. One strand is seen in Deuteronomy where the land is called Israel's resting place, for Israel was to obtain rest from all her enemies in the land she would inherit (12:9,10; 25:19; see also 3:20). A second strand of ideas concerning rest suggests that God has His resting place in the land and particularly in His sanctuary at Zion. This idea is especially evident in Psalm 132:7–8, 13–14 (compare to 2 Chronicles 6:41) and Isaiah 66:1. Elsewhere these two strands are joined so that the people's resting place is simultaneously God's resting place. An excellent example of this synthesis of the two motifs is recorded in 1 Chronicles 23:25, when David said, "The Lord, the God of Israel, has granted rest to his people and has come to dwell in Jerusalem forever."

Rest in Psalm 95

Another development in the concept of rest is found in Psalm 95 where the resting place of the people is not only the resting place of God but is God's rest itself.

> Today, if you hear his voice, do not harden your hearts as you did at Meribah, as you did that day at Massah in the desert, where your fathers tested and tried me, though they had seen what I did. For forty years I was angry with that generation; I said, "They are a people whose hearts go astray, and they have not known my ways." So I declared on oath in my anger, "They shall never enter my rest." (Psalm 95:7–11)

"Today" presents a new hope of salvation in contrast to the one forfeited by those who participated in the desert wanderings. This saying depends upon the concept of rest articulated in Deuteronomy in that the nation is still the subject of the rest. However the place of rest is now different. The Lord God says, "They shall never enter my rest." The resting place is God's rest. This refers to a gift of rest which Israel will only reach by a totally personal entering into her God. It is in this form that the Old Testament concept of rest is taken up by the writer to the Hebrews.

Rest in Hebrews 3 and 4

In Hebrews 3 and 4 the word "rest" (*katapausis*), which is first introduced in the quotation from Psalm 95 in 3:11, is repeated in 3:18, and is found six more times in chapter 4. We read:

> There remains, then, a Sabbath-rest for the people of God; for anyone who enters God's rest also rests from his own work, just as God did from his. (Hebrews 4:10,11)

Here the writer to the Hebrews refers to at least two distinct, but related, types of rest: (a) "a Sabbath-rest for the people of God," and (b) God's own rest on the seventh day of creation (see also Hebrews 4:4). The bringing together of these types of rest suggests that the Sabbath-rest, which remains for the people of God, is similar to God's resting from all His works at the end of creation (Genesis 2:3). The rest for the people of God is now viewed as the realization of God's intention in the creation to bestow such a rest on humanity. After the Fall, God's initial purposes for humanity's enjoyment of rest are made possible through His redemptive acts among His people. But the resting place in the promised land and in the temple at Jerusalem only aim towards the realization of God's purposes in creation. Now in Hebrews the final consummation is depicted as a heavenly rest, the antitype of the rest in the promised land alluded to in Psalm 95:11. There is no doubt that the final consummation of this rest is future, but it would be incorrect to view this Sabbath-rest as being totally in the future. The time frame of the rest in Hebrews is summed up by C. K. Barrett: "The rest, precisely because it is God's, is both present and future" (1956, 372).

What exactly is this Sabbath-rest? Biblical scholars describe it in a variety of ways. Jean Hering comments that this rest "must not invoke merely the notion of repose, but also those of peace, joy and concord" (1970, 32). Donald Hagner writes:

> the author has in mind the ideal qualities of the Sabbath-rest, namely peace,

well-being and security—that is, a frame of mind that by virtue of its confidence and trust in God possesses these qualities in contradiction to the surrounding circumstances. In short, the author may well have in mind that peace and sense of ultimate security "which is far beyond human understanding" (Philippians 4:7). (1983, 52)

Rest in Matthew 11:28–30

According to R. Hensel and C. Brown, "The concept of rest finds its ultimate and deepest development in Matthew 11:28ff" (1978, 256), when Jesus said:

> Come to me, all you who are weary and burdened, and I will give you rest. Take my yoke upon you and learn from me, for I am gentle and humble in heart, and you will find rest for your souls. For my yoke is easy and my burden is light. (Matthew 11:28–30)

How is the rest received? These verses, notes Edward Schweizer (1975), obviously imply that toil and labors do not lead to rest. Rather, it is through coming to Jesus that one will find rest. "The rest is identical with the yoke of discipleship" (Hill 1972, 208). From their union with Jesus, His disciples will receive refreshment and renewal that will enable them to carry their load without finding it heavy or burdensome (see also 2 Corinthians 4:16). W. Robertson Nicoll (1900, 155) points out that the literal translation is "I will rest you" which means more than "give you rest." The Christian finds rest for the soul through the assurance of the presence of the Risen Lord.

What is this rest? First, the rest is present. The future tense—"you will find rest"—indicates not a future hope, nor a rest in heaven, but a rest immediately available to all who follow Jesus. Second, the rest is not that of inactivity or idleness; it includes a yoke of discipleship. There is no discipleship without a task. Jesus does not promise freedom from work, toil, or burden, but a rest or relief which will make all burdens light. R.V.G. Tasker summarizes:

> Certainly Jesus does not promise His disciples a life of inactivity or repose, nor freedom from sorrow and struggle, but He does assure them that, if they keep close to Him, they will find relief from such crushing burdens as crippling anxiety, the sense of frustration and futility, and the misery of a sin-laden conscience. (1961, 122)

Third, H.L. Ellison (1969) points out that "rest for your souls" refers not merely to the inner being but to the whole person.

Summary on Rest

As we come to the end of this discussion of the biblical concept of rest, the question to be asked is what all this has to do with the concept of leisure? If we accept the classical conception of leisure which sees leisure as a condition of life and a state of being, then for the Christian the biblical concept of rest is very descriptive of what leisure may be. While we cannot derive an operational definition of leisure from our discussion of rest, our discussion supplies a wide variety of clues which are descriptive of leisure: a pleasant, secure, and blessed life in the land, for as Preece notes "We don't rest in a doctrine, we need a place to put our feet up, but a place in which God is personally present" (1981, 79); an entering into God's rest, a rest of completion, not inactivity, such as the Creator enjoyed when He had completed His works; a Sabbath rest of peace, joy, wellbeing, concord, and security; a relief and repose from labors and burdens; a peace and contentment of body, soul, and mind in God. While these elements of rest available through fellowship with God will be consummated in the heavenly rest, they are at least partially a present reality. These elements of rest are one way of describing the quality of life which may be seen as fleshing out the qualitative dimension of leisure.

Conclusion

A study of the biblical concepts of Sabbath and rest suggests that leisure may encompass two dimensions—a quantitative and a qualitative: one related to our doing and the other to our being. First, the Sabbath teaches a rhythm to life—six days of work and one of non-work. Second, the Sabbath inculcates a spiritual attitude for a person's basic posture in relation to God—one of rest, joy, freedom, and celebration in God and the gift of His creation. This qualitative dimension to life, descriptive of leisure, can also be seen in the biblical concept of rest which ranges from a pleasant, secure, and blessed life in the land to a peace and contentment of body, soul, and mind in God.

References

Banks, R. 1983. *The tyranny of time: When 24 hours is not enough.* Downers Grove: InterVarsity.

Barrett, C.K. 1956. The eschatology of the epistle to the Hebrews. In *The background of the New Testament and its eschatology,* edited by D. Daube and W. D. Davies. Cambridge: University Press.

Barth, K. 1958. *Church dogmatics.* Vol. 3/Part 1. Edinburgh: T. and T. Clark.

Coppes, L.J. 1980. In *Theological wordbook of the Old Testament,* edited by R.L. Harris, G.L. Archer, and B.K. Waltke. s.v. "nuab" (562–563). Chicago: Moody Press.

Dahl, G. 1972. *Work, play and worship in a leisure-oriented society.* Minneapolis: Augsburg.

Dumbrell, W.J. 1984. *Covenant and creation.* Exeter, Devon: Paternoster.

Ellison, H.L. 1969. *Matthew: A New Testament commentary.* London: Pickering and Inglis.

Hagner, D.A. 1983. *Hebrews: A good news commentary.* New York: Harper and Row.

Hamilton, V.P. 1980. In *Theological wordbook of the Old Testament,* edited by R.L. Harris, G.L. Archer, and B.K. Waltke. s.v. "shabat" (902–903). Chicago: Moody Press.

Hasel, G.F. 1983. Health and healing in the Old Testament. *Andrews University Seminary Studies.* 21(3): 191–202.

Hensel, R. and Brown, C. 1978. Rest. In *The new international dictionary of New Testament theology,* edited by C. Brown, 254–258. Grand Rapids: Zondervan.

Hering, J. 1970. *The Epistle to the Hebrews.* London: Epworth Press.

Heschel, A.J. 1966. *The Sabbath.* New York: Harper and Row.

Hill, D. 1972. *The Gospel of Matthew.* London: Oliphants.

Houston, J. 1981. The theology of work. In *Looking at lifestyles, professional priorities—A Christian perspective.* Proceedings from the Conference for Physicians and Dentists, Banff, Alberta, May 2–8, 1981: Christian and Dental Society of Canada.

Johnston, R.K. 1983. *The Christian at Play.* Grand Rapids: Eerdmans.

Nicoll, W.R. 1900. *St. Matthew: The expositor's Bible.* New York: Funk and Wagnalls.

Preece, G. 1981. Re-creation and recreation in the eighties. In *Faith active in love.* Proceedings of the 1980 Conference of the A.F.E.S. Fellowship, edited by J. Diesendorf. Sydney, Australia: A.F.E.S. Graduates Fellowship.

Richardson, A. 1952. *The Biblical doctrine of work.* Ecumenical Biblical Studies No. 1. London: S.C.M. Press.

Schweizer, E. 1975. *The Good News According to Matthew.* Atlanta: John Knox Press.

Sherrow, J.E. 1984. *It's about time.* Grand Rapids: Zondervan.

Tasker, R.V.G. 1961. *The Gospel According to St. Matthew.* The Tyndale New Testament Commentaries. London: The Tyndale Press.

Veblen, T. 1934. *The Theory of the Leisure Class.* New York: The Modem Library.

von Rad, G. 1966. There remains still a rest for the people of God. In *The Problem of the Hexateuch and other essays* (94–102). London: Oliver and Boyd.

Westersnmann, C. 1974. *Creation.* London: SPCK.

Wolff, H.W. 1972. The day of rest in the Old Testament. *Lexington Theological Quarterly* 7 (July): 65–76.

Chapter Three

The Puritan Ethic and Christian Leisure for Today

LELAND RYKEN

How often have you heard or read a sentence that begins with this lead-in: "We all know that the Puritans. . ." Given the popular stereotypes, we can fill in the blank in a dozen ways: we all "know" that the Puritans wore drab clothing, disliked sports, were sexually inhibited, never laughed, were the original workaholics, and so forth. As is often the case, the stereotype has not enough truth to be credible and sufficient falsehood to require refutation.

I should clarify at the outset that I am chiefly interested in the original Puritan ethic, as articulated by the English and American Puritans of the sixteenth and seventeenth centuries, who in turn were influenced by such Reformers as Luther and Calvin. What emerged after the seventeenth century is not rightly called Puritan or Protestant. It was instead a secularized perversion of the original Puritan ethic.

There are three reasons why we will profit from exploring the original Puritan ethic in a book that deals with leisure. First, it is always exhilarating to know the truth about a matter and to set the record straight, especially when someone has been unfairly maligned. Secondly, the Puritans posed the issues regarding work and leisure with unusual clarity, so we can emulate them where they were right and learn from them even when they were wrong. And thirdly, because the Puritans were evangelical Christians who accepted the authority of the Bible in matters of faith and practice, they can become for us a mirror in which to see the pressure points regarding work and leisure that we find in our own evangelical subculture. I am primarily interested not in defending the Puritans but in letting them speak for themselves. The Puritans, after all, are long gone. They will not benefit from what we say about them. It is our own house that we need to put in order.

As a point of departure, let us revisit the Weber thesis. It is part of the cultural consciousness of educated Westerners. We pick it up by intellectual osmosis during our college years. In reading the books and articles written by theorists of leisure, I find the Weber thesis simply taken for granted as a "given." The original Weber thesis was that there is a connection between the Protestant ethic and the spirit of modern capitalism. By making work a calling that glorified God, the Protestant ethic created an environment that made economic success possible. The early Protestants, claimed Weber, worked themselves incessantly to prove that they were saved; paradoxically they were also ascetic and rejected earthly enjoyments in deference to active work, and considered work to be "in itself the end of life" (1930, 159). According to Weber, the early Protestants regarded "private profitableness" as "the most important criterion" of one's calling (162).

By the time the Weber thesis became popularized, the Protestant ethic emerged as the convenient scapegoat for modern capitalistic tendencies, including the workaholic syndrome, unrestrained competitiveness, glorification of the success ethic, the belief that making money is the goal of life, the deification of work, and the eclipse of leisure. So pervasive is this popular equation of modern attitudes with the Puritans and Reformers that when *The Chicago Tribune* carried an article about workaholics who spend nearly half of their week—up to 70 hours—at their work, the writer entitled the article "The New Calvinists" (Phillips, 1986, 5–8). Having absorbed the Weber thesis in its popularized version, I remember how surprised I was when I first read Max Weber's book *The Protestant Ethic and the Spirit of Capitalism* while doing research for my book on the Puritans. Four things in particular leaped out at me: (1) the misleadingly selective quotation from Puritan sources, (2) the virtual absence of evidence for the cause-effect relationship that was claimed between the Protestant ethic and modern-capitalism, (3) a tendency to misunderstand the Christian worldview, and (4) how different the original Weber thesis was from the popularized version of it that prevails today. Overall, the picture that Weber painted of the original Puritans did not correspond to the picture that had emerged from my study of them, and the reason for the discrepancy was simply that Weber left too much data out of the picture and, in particular, ignored the primacy of the spiritual that was a hallmark of the Puritan movement.

Having thus paid my disrespects to Weber's book, I should add that compared to the popularized version of the Weber thesis, the book that gave rise to the movement strikes me as a relatively innocuous, if occasionally obnoxious and misleading, little book. I have been told that it is now a stock assignment to ask graduate students in history to shoot holes in the Weber thesis (for a brief list of published rebuttals, see Ryken 1987, 111). It is not an unjust fate for a book that has had an unjustifiable influence in the history of ideas. To me, the Weber thesis is a classic case of reading back into a movement features that arose two or three centuries later. Puritanism did not produce modern capitalism, though with its positive attitude toward work, moneymaking, and money lending for interest, it was certainly conducive to some form of capitalism.

As we know, symbolic truth is often more influential in a culture than the facts on which it is based. It is worth asking why the scholarly world, in general, and leisure theorists today so badly want to believe and perpetuate the Weber thesis. Why does Weber's book show up as a textbook even on Christian college campuses? Why, despite the scarcity of evidence in Weber's book, is our culture so eager to attribute some of its own worst tendencies to the Protestant ethic centuries after it was a dominant cultural force? These are questions worth pursuing.

I will make no attempt in this essay to cover all that the Puritans said about work and leisure. I refer readers who want more than I say here to my books (Ryken, 1986, 1987). I have selected the points that I consider most relevant to current Christian thinking about leisure, and I have arranged my remarks around the format of five fallacies that are commonly but erroneously associated with the Puritan ethic.

I

The first fallacy is that the original Puritans believed that work is the most important thing in life. Like most fallacies, this one is built around a core of truth that in this case has two main facets. One is the Puritans' scorn of idleness. Idleness was one of their most frequent themes in sermon and treatise. English Puritan Robert Bolton called idleness "the very rust and canker of the soul" (cited in George 1961, 171). Richard Baxter said that "it is swinish and sinful not to labor" (cited in Hill 1964, 139). "God doth allow none to live idly," wrote Arthur Dent (ibid).

Against whom were the Puritans directing their remarks in such statements? Recent theorists on leisure cite statements like these to support their claims that the Puritans were opposed to people who engaged in leisure pursuits. A look at the context in which these denunciations of idleness appear shows that this claim is untrue. The statements of the Puritans occur chiefly in contexts where they are talking about the aristocratic classes who did not work for a living, monks who retired from the world, and the Catholic proliferation of religious holy days. Here is an example of the tendency of some scholars and leisure theorists to transport Puritan statements out of their original context into a twentieth century context, where they are made to say something other than what the Puritans intended.

Along with this critique of idleness we find among the Puritans an equally hearty praise of the virtue of work and industriousness. Thomas Watson sounded the keynote when he said, "God will bless our diligence, not our laziness" (1977, 25). All the early Protestants made much of the fact that work was a creation ordinance that prevailed already in Adam and Eve's life in Paradise before the Fall. William Perkins thus comments that "Adam in his innocence had all things at his will, yet then God employed him in a calling" (cited in George 1961, 132).

But one can affirm work and scorn idleness without becoming a workaholic. Two things set a curb to excessive devotion to work in the original Protestant ethic. One was the ideal of moderation in work. The Puritan divine John Preston wrote, "Take heed of too much business or intending it too much, or inordinately" (ibid, 172). Richard Steele warned against moonlighting with the comment that a person ought not to "accumulate two or three callings merely to increase riches" (cited in Tawney 1926, 244). Philip Stubbes wrote, "So far from covetousness and from immoderate care would the Lord have us that we ought not this day to care for tomorrow, for (saith he) sufficient to the day is the travail of the same" (ibid, 216). Puritans like Steele and Stubbes were echoing Luther, who wrote a letter to Philip Melanchthon warning him not to overwork and then pretend you did it in obedience to God" (cited in Plass 1959, 787).

Secondly, the Puritans' religious practices took so much of their time that they could not possibly be compared to modern workaholics. For one thing, the Puritans were Sabbatarians who observed a nearly total prohibition of work on Sundays. Arthur Hildersham said that Sunday observance was especially necessary for hardworking people who were in danger of having their hearts "corrupted and glued to the world" (cited in Hill 1964, 175).

Then, too, the Puritans practiced some form of daily worship in the home. They also replaced Catholic holy days with celebrations of their own—Thanksgiving Day (which on its first occasion lasted three days), election days, days set aside for ordination of ministers, and wedding celebrations. A Puritan practice that endears them to me was their practice of celebrating private days of thanksgiving—occasions of worship and feasting to which they invited the minister, friends, and neighbors. The diary of one Puritan minister indicates that he attended anywhere from 47 to 64 such days of thanksgiving in a typical year (Davies 1948, 282).

Contrary to the claims of the Weber thesis, the Puritans did not make getting rich the goal of life. Thomas Watson said that "blessedness . . . does not lie in the acquisition of worldly things. Happiness cannot by any art of chemistry be extracted here" (1977, 25). Richard Baxter wrote that it brings glory to God "when we condemn the riches and honour of the world," adding that "when seeming Christians are worldly and ambitious as others, and make as great matter of the gain and wealth and honor, it showeth and they do but cover the base and sordid spirit of worldlings with the visor of the Christian name" (Kitch 1967, 156–157). This, incidentally, is the kind of quotation that gets left out of the picture in Weber's book. William Perkins claimed that "seeking of abundance is a hazard to the salvation of the soul" (ibid, 108), elsewhere commenting, "Let us consider what moved Judas to betray his master: namely, the desire of wealth" (George 1961, 172).

Nor did the Puritans regard wealth as a sign of God's favor, as Weber claimed. In fact, the Puritans saw an inverse relationship between wealth and godliness. Thomas Watson claimed that "true godliness is usually attended with persecution" (1977, 259). Baxter warned, "Remember that riches do make it harder for a man to be saved" (Hyma 1937, 224). Luther had likewise called "utterly nonsensical" the "delusion" that led people to conclude that if someone "has good fortune, wealth, and health . . . behold, God is dwelling here" (exposition on Genesis 19:2–3, excerpted in Plass 1959, 1436).

As for the claim of the Weber thesis that Puritans made work their religion, this seems to be a naive misunderstanding of the Protestant doctrine of calling. In brief, the Reformers spoke of a double calling. One is the general call that comes universally to all people and consists of the call to conversion and sanctification. In the words of William Perkins, "The general calling is the calling of Christianity, which is common to all that live in the church of God. [It] is that whereby a man is called out of the world to be a child of God" (Morgan 1969, 43–44).

Particular callings are the specific occupation and tasks that God places before us in the course of daily living. These include, but are not limited to, the job by which one earns his or her living. The concept of particular calling extends as well to being a parent or spouse, carrying out the garbage, being a good citizen, and a dozen other things. I do not, however, recall any of the Reformers or Puritans writing about leisure as a calling from God.

To sum up the first fallacy, almost from the start of my sojourns through Puritan ideas on work and leisure it became apparent to me that we cannot fault the Puritans for their work ethic (for extended discussion, see Ryken 1986, 1987). The Puritan work ethic was, in principle, a splendid combination of biblical doctrine and enlightened common sense.

II

This brings us to a second fallacy, which is the notion that if we want to establish an adequate leisure ethic today, we need to begin by abandoning the Puritan work ethic. Contemporary leisure theorists argue that the work ethic "no longer fits the needs of the hour" (Clarke 1982, 189), that we must "escape from the shackles of the work ethic" (Clemitson and Rodgers 1981, 174), and that we must "renounce the false notions of the dignity of work, the necessity of work, self-fulfillment through work, and . . . the duty to work" (Veal 1987, 26–27). "What we need is a non-work ethic," writes another (Ritchie-Calder 1982, 16). And yet another source tells us that "it appears . . . that society, both individually and collectively, would be happier, would be more harmonious and would have fewer problems if the work ethic were either destroyed or reconstructed" (Jenkins and Sherman 1981, 15).

Against such sentiments I would argue that we do not need to escape from the original Puritan work ethic but return to it. The original Puritan work ethic included as its basic principles that God calls people to work, that all legitimate types of work have dignity, that work can be a stewardship to God and a service to self and humanity, and that work should be pursued in moderation and in deference to spiritual concerns. These ideas are not inimical to leisure. On the contrary, leisure depends on our having an adequate work ethic.

In fact, the Puritans were right in granting priority to work—not because work is more noble or more worthy than leisure, but because it comes before leisure. Work is necessary to sustain physical life. We must work before we have the resources to play. As leisure theorists commonly note, the unemployed and poor do not lead rich leisure lives. This is not to say that leisure always requires money, but only that people without adequate financial resources for living lack the context and sense of psychological well-being that would enable them to pursue leisure in a meaningful way. Furthermore, work gives meaning to leisure. By itself, leisure quickly palls and loses its point. When seen as a contract to work and a reward for it, leisure takes on meaning.

The very identity of our leisure depends on the nature of our work. If our work wears us out physically, our leisure is likely to highlight relaxation. If our work is unrewarding, our leisure will be experienced as a sharp contrast to our work as we seek to compensate for what we find lacking in our work. If, by contrast, our work is delightful to us, we may extend its qualities and activities into our leisure life.

I have found much of the leisure theory lacking because it discusses leisure without relating it significantly to a work ethic. A certain unreality attaches to our talk about leisure if we do not sense its rootedness in work. Perhaps the distinctive contribution that Christianity can make to discussions of leisure is to assert that God created people to work, play, worship, and serve as part of a harmonious cycle.

To sum up, it is a fallacy to think that the Puritan work ethic is our enemy. The Puritan work ethic itself is good. The important question is whether one can have such a work ethic without having it produce an anemic leisure ethic.

III

The third fallacy is that the Puritans were opposed to recreation. Again this is a distortion of some things that are indeed true. It is true that the Puritans opposed some forms of recreation and passed laws prohibiting them. But the modern stereotype of Puritan opposition to recreation is based largely on a misreading of the evidence. The Puritans rejected all sports on Sundays and certain sports at all times. Their rejection of sports on Sunday was based on their view that the entire day was to be devoted to spiritual activities, chiefly worship and rest from the ordinary concerns of the week.

The Puritans rejected other sports on moral grounds. These included games of chance, gambling, bearbaiting, horse racing, May Day celebrations, and bowling in or around taverns. By modern standards, some of their prohibitions appear frivolous, such as their outlawing the game of shuffleboard.

It is also true that the Puritans rejected the system of holy days that had grown up around Catholicism. Under medieval Catholicism, such days had grown to as many as 115 days per year, not counting Sundays (Kelly 1982, 57). The Puritans rejected such days on religious grounds, and whatever leisure elements they contained went as well. But we should remember that social conditions were changing and that society was becoming less and less rural, so that the loss of church holidays would have occurred for economic reasons quite, apart from the Protestant movement. I have already noted, moreover, that the Puritans generated their own list of non-working days and festivals.

The more we learn about the Puritans, the more questionable older views of their hostility to recreation become. The best source of information is Hans-Peter Wagner's book-length study entitled *Puritan Attitudes Towards Recreation in Early Seventeenth Century America* (1982). It shows that the Puritans enjoyed such varied sports as hunting, fishing, bowling, reading, music, swimming, skating, and archery. Regarding recreations, a Puritan preacher said that Christians should "enjoy them as liberties, with thankfulness to God that allows us these liberties to refresh ourselves" (Foster 1971, 106). Another wrote that "God has . . . adjudged some diversion or recreation . . . to be both needful and expedient. . . . A wise and good man . . . is forced to . . . let religion choose such recreations as are healthful, short, recreative, and proper, to refresh both mind and body" (Wagner 1982, 46). The New England Puritan Cotton Mather preached a sermon in which he gave his parishioners advice about "how to employ the leisure of the winter for the glory of God" (14).

Most important of all, a parliamentary act of 1647, when the Puritans controlled the English Parliament, decreed that every second Tuesday of the month was to be a holiday when all shops, warehouses, and places of business were to be closed from eight in the morning until eight in the evening for the recreation of the workers (Scholes 1934, 110–111). In short, most of the modern charges against the Puritans on the subject of leisure are either untrue or exaggerated. They tend to be based on the Puritans' rejection of certain *manifestations* of leisure activities that were acceptable to the Puritans *in principle*.

IV

Having defended the Puritans as I have, I need to urge a caution, which I will elevate to the status of a fourth fallacy: it would be a fallacy to assert that because the Puritans endorsed the idea and practice of leisure they can therefore be credited with having had an adequate leisure ethic. I would note three main failings of the Puritans in regard to leisure.

One is what I regard as a legalistic attitude toward leisure activities. While affirming leisure in principle, the Puritans multiplied the rules used to determine whether a given leisure pursuit was legitimate. The number of such rules goes a long way toward undermining the Puritans' theoretic endorsement of leisure. Richard Baxter, for example, devised a list of eighteen qualifications that governed a Christian's choice of leisure (Wagner 1982, 48–49). According to these rules, leisure must be for the ends of serving God and helping us "in our ordinary callings and duty." Recreation must not be profane or obscene, and it must not harm others. Sports were deemed unlawful when they "occasion the multiplying of idle words about them." Furthermore, if a person chooses a "less fit and profitable" leisure pursuit "when a better might be chosen, it is . . . sin." For me, the net result of such stipulations is to instill an aura of suspicion about leisure, even though theoretically it is "lawful," to use one of the Puritans' favorite words.

The number of rules with which the Puritans circumscribed leisure suggests a related problem. The Puritans were simply too uneasy about leisure. They convey the impression of looking for trouble when they scrutinized the leisure activities that people pursued in their society. A New England law, for example, ordered constables to "search after all manner of gaming, singing and dancing" and to report "disordered meetings" even when they occurred in private homes (Dulles 1940, 6). In Boston, a request for an exhibition of tightropes walking was rejected "lest the said divertisement may tend to promote idleness in the town and great mispense of time" (ibid). This is similar in tone to a Connecticut law that prohibited "the game called shuffle board . . . whereby much precious time is spent unfruitfully" (ibid).

The general tenor of such Puritan pronouncements is a quickness to think the worst of leisure and to ban an activity that carried either the appearance of abuse or potential for it. In particular, the Puritans were too time-conscious and too utilitarian in outlook to produce a truly healthy play ethic.

This leads me to my third stricture of the Puritan view of leisure. The Puritans were not opposed to leisure in principle, but their defense of leisure was essentially a utilitarian defense. Leisure was good, in their view, because it makes work possible. Leisure was not valued for its own sake (that is, as self-rewarding), or as a celebration of life, or as an enlargement of the human spirit.

One Puritan wrote, for example, that "recreation belongs not to rest, but to labor; and it is used that men may by it be made more fit to labor" (Wagner 1982, 45). Recreation "serveth only to make us more able to continue in labor," wrote another (50). If work is the best use of time, then leisure becomes a frivolous use of time. Richard Baxter equated "pastimes" with "time wasting" and rejected the very word as "infamous" (Sasek 1961, 114). He therefore advised,

> Keep up a high esteem of time and be every day more careful that you lose none of your time . . . . And if vain recreation, dressings, feastings, idle talk, unprofitable company, or sleep be any of them temptations to rob you of any of your time, accordingly heighten your watchfulness. (Baxter as quoted in Weber 1930, 261)

If all of one's time is to be devoted to something useful, leisure will obviously fare poorly.

This is what often happened in the utilitarian ethic of the Puritans. Consider Luther's wording as he comments on work as a creation ordinance that prevailed in Paradise already before the Fall: "Man was created not for leisure but for work, even in the state of innocence" (exposition on Genesis 2:14, in Plass 1959, 14). It is one thing to claim that Adam was made for work, but why add the phrase "not for leisure"? I said earlier that leisure depends on work to give it purpose and identity, but this is not to say, as the Puritans often did, that leisure has value only because it makes work possible.

V

A final fallacy will provide a counterbalance to what I have said negatively about the Puritans on the subject of leisure. It is a fallacy to assume that because the Puritans had an inadequate view of leisure they have little to contribute to our own thinking about leisure. On the contrary, the original Puritans have much to contribute, partly by positive example, partly by negative example, and partly simply by allowing us to observe what happens when Christians attempt to combine faith, work, and leisure.

I have already praised the Puritans for refusing to theorize about leisure apart from work. Except for the independently wealthy, work will continue to absorb by far the most time in a person's waking hours. We need to remind ourselves that work extends far beyond our occupation or job. It also includes the tasks we perform beyond our hours on the job. Because most of a person's waking hours are devoted to work and tasks of necessity, not to have an adequate account of the worth of our work is to condemn most of life to something demeaning.

I have suggested that a lot of leisure theory is headed in the wrong direction because it begins with the assumption that work is bad or undesirable. But if we chalk one up for the Puritans for linking leisure to work, we can also see highlighted a perennial problem with which the human race has struggled, namely, the extreme difficulty people have in maintaining a balance between work and leisure. The social classes whom the Puritans vilified for sloth did, in fact, have an emaciated work ethic. But the Puritans had an impoverished play ethic.

Instead of pointing the finger of accusation at the Puritans as a way of escaping our own problems, we should acknowledge it as a problem that we, too, need to solve. We can view the Puritan dilemma as highlighting a question that we ourselves need to answer: Is it possible to have (simultaneously) a healthy Christian work ethic and a healthy Christian leisure ethic? Why do these two seem to be such inevitable rivals in our own lives?

The Puritans' failure to achieve a balance between work and leisure had a number of causes. One was an overvaluing of work at the expense of leisure. Another was a heightened sense of duty inadequately tempered by a sense of celebration. The Puritan aversion to all things Catholic led to a rejection of types of festivity associated with the older social order, including various recreations (Brailsford 1969, 122–157). The Puritans may have had a heightened sense of seriousness, and their strongly utilitarian preference for what was useful is well known. To the degree to which we see these negative tendencies highlighted in the Puritans, we can learn positive lessons from them.

I do not wish to leave this topic without posing another key question. The mid-twentieth century gave us the phrase "the leisure problem." The phrase still fits, but in a way opposite to its original meaning. Those who popularized the phrase thought that we were moving to shorter workweeks and that people would not know what to do with all their free time. The predictions were naively optimistic about the amount of leisure time that people would have. The chief problem with leisure today is that there is simply not enough of it (Schor 1991). A Harris survey found that the median number of American leisure hours dropped by ten hours per week between 1973 and 1987 (*New York Times*, 3 June 1990, 4E).

It has become common to speak of the time famine that prevails in Western societies today (Gibbs 1989). I do not see how we can avoid the conclusion that the leisure problem is more acute for Christians than for the population at large. The time famine is simply worse when we factor in the usual round of religious activities—church attendance, devotional activities, Bible studies, committee work, volunteer work, and service to those in need. Time and money that might otherwise have been spent on ordinary leisure pursuits instead go to Christian causes.

Furthermore, there are qualities of the Christian life that resist the very idea; they include a sense of duty and "oughtness," seriousness, service, and self-denial. One point on which Max Weber was on target was in his identification of what he calls asceticism as an essential ingredient of the Protestant ethic and one of the things resistant to the idea of leisure.

Asceticism is the wrong word to use, but the idea is accurate. Leisure presupposes such ideas as legitimate self-indulgence, self-satisfaction, and self-fulfillment. It does not thrive in an ethic of self-denial. Yet Christ calls us to deny ourselves. We therefore need to ask, Are there ingredients of the Christian life that are intransigent to leisure? Are there, in fact, ways in which the Christian life is a hindrance to leisure? The Puritan experience highlighted the tensions I have noted. But it also contained within itself a partial solution that can be instructive to us today. I doubt that the Puritans would have regarded religious worship as leisure, but there is a sense in which the Puritans put religious activities in the place where others put ordinary recreations. After all, one of the standard ways to define leisure is on terms of its ability to refresh, to provide a break from everyday routine, to draw a boundary around the acquisitive aspects of life. Although the Puritans failed to grant sufficient credence at a theoretical level to the non-utilitarian side of life, in practice they valued their non-working hours more than we (or they) might think if we listened only to their pronouncements.

Many of the Puritans' religious activities and exercises infused an element of godly leisure into their lives. I think, for example, of their prizing of "Christian conference," by which they meant conversations with Christians of like mind that left the conversers refreshed. John Winthrop recorded in his diary a conference with a Christian friend or two," adding that "God blessed it unto us, as we were all much quickened and refreshed by it" (McGee 1976, 196). An extension of this desire for social interaction was the Puritans' love of dinners and social meals.

The Puritan Sabbath also had a dimension of leisure to it. It set a limit to the acquisitive urge. In fact, William Ames used this to distinguish between proper and improper Sunday activities. Inappropriate activities were "those which concern our wealth and profit" (1968, 299). Nicholas Bownde similarly argues that "we cannot attend to God's business if we are encumbered with worldly business on Sunday" (Dennison 1983, 39). The Puritan Sabbath was time off for the timeless and a way of thanking God for what had been freely given instead of produced by human work.

It is customary for leisure theorists to divide the slice of life into three pieces, with work and leisure at the poles and a middle category called semi-leisure. Activities that fall into the middle category can be regarded as either work or leisure, depending on the attitude with which we pursue them. A leading goal should be to nudge as many activities as possible into the leisure category. I will have to speak personally when I say that for me religious services, private and public, tend to fall into the realm of duty. This is not to say that I do not enjoy them but that the motivation for them is a sense of their being a requirement of the Christian life. I have found that the spectacle of Puritan delight in religious activities buttressed my awareness of that middle section of the time continuum called semi-leisure that I need more of in my life. Another point at which we can learn positively from the Puritans was their insistence on relating leisure to moral standards. The Puritans have been much maligned for this, but I think the Puritans were right to refuse to exempt leisure from morality. The discussion and practice of leisure in our own century are conducted by most people in an amoral atmosphere in which religious implications are considered irrelevant. This secular spirit has invaded the practice of leisure by many Christians as well.

The Puritans stand as a corrective. They expected leisure pursuits to measure up to the criterion of being "lawful." William Perkins, for example, listed four religious and moral principles by which to judge leisure: (1) recreations must be "of the best report"; (2) they "must be profitable to ourselves and others, and they must tend to the glory of God"; (3) their purpose "must be to refresh our bodies and minds"; (4) their use "must be moderate and sparing" of time and "affections" (Sasek 1969, 114). There is something potentially legalistic about such a list, but its virtue is that it applies moral standards to leisure pursuits.

The same concern for morality in leisure underlies some of the Puritan prohibitions of selected recreations. Dennis Brailsford's history of sport in England correctly ascribes Puritan strictures to moral reasons, noting Puritan "attacks on dancing, for its carnality; on football, for its violence; on maypoles for their paganism; and on sports in general for their despoliation of the Sabbath" (1969, 130). The Puritans objected to bear-baiting and cockfighting as being cruel to animals and violent for people. They disliked sports at taverns because of the drunkenness and low moral standards that usually prevailed at such places. They objected to plays and fictional romances because of the immoral behavior portrayed in some of them. Even when I disagree with where the Puritans drew the line, I admire them for applying Christian moral standards to leisure activities.

Another way in which the Puritans can serve as a model is their ideal of Christian culture as a leisure pursuit. The bad reputation of the Puritans in regard to culture and the arts is largely, though not wholly, based on a misreading of the evidence. It is well known that the Puritans removed art and organs from the churches, but this was an objection to Catholic worship and ceremony, not to music and art in themselves. In fact, after removing organs and paintings from churches, the Puritans often bought them for private use in their homes (Scholes 1934, 6). Oliver Cromwell moved an organ from an Oxford chapel to his own residence at Hampton Court, where he employed a private organist; and when one of his daughters was married, Cromwell engaged an orchestra of 48 to accompany the dancing (ibid, 5).

The stereotype of the Puritans as uneducated is wrong. They were highly educated. Their education, moreover, gave them an acquaintance with classical culture, and the earliest translators of classical texts into English were Puritans (Conley 1927). At their best, the Puritans valued what I will call Christian culture, by which I mean culture that by God's common grace expresses truth and beauty even when produced by non-Christians (Ryken 1986, 157–171, 189, 261).

There is evidence that the Puritans favored intellectual and cultural leisure pursuits over physical recreation. They were great readers, for example. Music was also valued. My impression is that people interested in leisure theory today conceive of leisure almost exclusively in terms of physical recreation. I fear that in our sports-oriented society leisure excludes the arts, the mind, and the imagination. In a media-oriented society and in a day of quick gratification, moreover, leisure is often mindless and passive. A Gallup poll found that 58 percent of Americans have never finished reading a book (Schlesinger 1971, 77), while another survey revealed that nearly half of Americans never read a book of any type (Mitgan 1978, 13). An international study of time usage confirmed that Americans read far less that Europeans (Godbey 1980, 85). The Puritans show that leisure need not be viewed as the occasion for us to take a holiday from the mind, or be conceived only in physical terms.

It will come as no surprise that the Puritans, devotees of moderation as they were, urged moderation in the amount of time and money that a person spends on leisure. Mather noted, for example, that "for a Christian to use recreations is very lawful, and in some cases a great duty," yet "to waste so much time in any recreation . . . as gamesters usually do at cards and dice . . . is heinously sinful" (Wagner 1982, 62). Cotton Mather similarly warned that although "moderate recreations. . . are more than a little healthful and useful," nonetheless

> the most harmless recreations may become very culpable and hurtful for want of observing proper rules with regard to time, place, company, manner.. . God expects that in everything you . . . act under the governance of reason and virtue, and accordingly that you . . . be always sparing of [diversions], that you time them well, regulate them prudently, make them give place to business, make them subserve religion. (61)

I can imagine someone feeling uneasy about the somewhat utilitarian spirit of that statement, but the comment about leisure subserving religion brings into my mind the extent to which sports have become the dominant American religious ritual on Sundays. The church to which I belong had to change the night of its annual congregational meeting because it regularly fell on Super Bowl Sunday. When I was growing up in the Christian Reformed milieu of rural Iowa, my interest in sports did not "subserve religion," to use Cotton Mather's phrase, but instead was my religion.

Although the chief leisure problem in our culture is its scarcity, for a minority of people the opposite is true. These people live for leisure. The amount of money they spend on leisure is immoderate. In how many offices or factories does not one encounter the syndrome of the endless weekend—not only living for the weekend but talking about it all week long? How early in the week does your checkout clerk tell you to have a good weekend? Nor could we overlook the extent to which the young are today's leisure class. The capacity and expectation for being entertained is more insatiable with each recent generation of young people, as any parent of teenagers or any teacher of young people can attest.

A final area in which we can learn from the Puritans on the subject of leisure is the way in which they took leisure seriously and approached it thoughtfully. I have paid my disrespects to the eighteen rules with which

Richard Baxter surrounded the choice of leisure pursuits. But let's look at this a second time. At least Baxter dignified leisure with conscious choice. Even though Brailsford's survey paints a largely negative picture of the Puritans' influence on physical sports in English society, Brailsford nonetheless concludes regarding Puritanism that "one of its great strengths was that it did ask questions about [recreation's] role and purpose. . . . Just to ask 'what is physical fitness *for?*' was a decisive contribution to the history of physical education" (1969, 157).

In today's evangelical subculture, most people pretend that leisure is unworthy of the Christian's life. So they neglect to think about it as they think about work. When I did the research for my book on work and leisure I found a flourishing literature on the subject of work, but except for Robert Johnston's book on leisure (1983), I felt as if I was working in a vacuum when I did the chapters on leisure.

Leisure is the subject of neglect in the contemporary church. When did you last hear a sermon on the subject of leisure? The result is the syndrome of mediocrity by default. By this I mean that people act as though leisure is not important in their lives and therefore drift into whatever leisure activity pushes itself into their path. The first steps toward excellence in leisure will come when we decide to give the subject of leisure our best thinking, when we make our leisure our best thinking, when we make our leisure pursuits a conscious choice, when we choose leisure pursuits that enhance our personal identity and meet the goals that we set for our leisure, and when we regard leisure as part of the stewardship of life. On some of these points, at least, the Puritans can serve as a model to emulate.

References

Ames, W. 1968. In *The marrow of theology*, edited by J. D. Eusden. Boston: Pilgrim.

Brailsford, D. 1969. *Sport and society: Elizabeth to Anne*. London: Routledge and Kegan Paul.

Clarke, R. 1982. *Work in Crisis*. Edinburgh: St. Andrews Press.

Clemitson, I. and Rodgers, G. 1981. *A life to live*. London: Junction Books.

Conley, C. H. 1927. *The first English translators of the classics*. New Haven: Yale University Press.

Dennison, J.T. 1983. *The market day of the soul: The Puritan doctrine of the Sabbath in England, 1532–1700*. Lanham, NY: University Press of America.

Dulles, F. R. 1940. *America learns to play: A history of popular recreation, 1607–1940.* New York: Appleton Century.

Foster, S. 1971. *Their solitary way: The Puritan social ethic in the first century of settlement in New England.* New Haven: Yale University Press.

George, C.H. and George, K. 1961. *The Protestant mind of the English Reformation, 1570–1640.* Princeton: Princeton University Press.

Gibbs, N. 1989. How America has run out of time. *Time,* April 24, 58–67.

Godbey, G. 1980. *Leisure in your life: An exploration.* Philadelphia: Saunders College.

Hill, C. 1964. *Society and Puritanism in pre-Revolutionary England.* New York: Schocken.

Hyma, A. 1937. *Christianity, capitalism, and communism: A historical analysis.* Ann Arbor: George Wahr.

Jenkins, C. and Sherman, B. 1981. *The leisure shock.* London: Eyre, Methuen.

Johnston, R.K. 1983. *The Christian at play.* Grand Rapids: Eerdmans.

Kelly, J.R. 1982. *Leisure.* Englewood Cliffs, NJ: Prentice Hall.

Kitch, M.J., ed. 1967. *Capitalism and the Reformation.* London: Longmans, Green.

McGee, J.S. 1976. *The Godly man in Stuart England: Anglicans, Puritans, and the two tables, 1620–1670.* New Haven: Yale University Press.

Mitgan, H. 1978. Study finds nearly half of U.S. do not read books. *The New York Times,* November 14, 13.

Morgan, E. 1969. "The Puritan ethic and the American Revolution." In *Puritanism and the American experience,* edited by M. McGiffert, 183–197. Reading, MA: Addison-Wesley.

Phillips, R. 1986. The new Calvinists. *The Chicago Tribune,* November 5, section 7, 5–8.

Plass, E.M., ed. 1959. *What Luther says: An anthology.* St. Louis: Concordia.

Ritchie-Calder, L. 1982. Education for the post-industrial society. In *Continuing education for the post-industrial society,* edited by N. Costello and M. Richardson, 11–22. Milton Keynes: Open University Press.

Ryken, L. 1986. *Worldly saints: The Puritans as they really were.* Grand Rapids: Zondervan.

Ryken, L. 1987. *Work and leisure in Christian perspective.* Portland: Multnomah.

Sasek, L.A. 1977. *The literary temper of the English Puritans.* New York: Greenwood.

Scholes, P. 1934. *The Puritans and music in England and New England.* London: Oxford University Press.

Schlesinger, A.J. 1971. Implications of leisure for government. In *Technology, human values, and leisure,* edited by M. Kaplan and P. Bosserman, 68–91. Nashville: Abingdon.

Schor, J.B. 1991. *An overworked America: The unexpected decline of leisure.* New York: Basic Books.

Tawney, R. H. 1926. *Religion and the rise of capitalism.* New York: Harcourt, Brace.

Veal, A. J. 1987. *Leisure and the future.* London: Allen and Unwin.

Wagner, H. 1982. *Puritan attitudes towards recreation in early seventeenth-century New England.* Frankfurt: Peter Lang.

Watson, T. 1977. *The Beatitudes.* Edinburgh: Banner of Truth Trust.

Weber, M. 1930. *The Protestant ethic and the spirit of capitalism.* New York: Routledge and Kegan Paul.

SECTION TWO

Methodological Issues

Much time is spent in leisure sciences and leisure studies trying to define leisure. Theorists puzzle over the meaning of leisure, but no clear conceptualization emerges for it or for the related terms of recreation and play. Definitions of leisure abound. James Murphy (1974) has identified at least six possible definitions of leisure: (1) leisure as free time, (2) leisure as a function of social class, (3) leisure as anti-utilitarian activity, (4) leisure as non-work activity, (5) the classical view of leisure as a condition of mind or state of being, and (6) the holistic view of leisure. Within this context, the search for meaning becomes a daunting task as Sylvester so vividly portrays:

> Imagine . . . the bewilderment a naive researcher suffers when discovering that leisure may be free time, freedom, an activity, a state of mind, or a license of some sort. Grasping the meaning of leisure is sufficiently frustrating that our innocent colleague might prudently move on to a seemingly simpler concept, like play. But the conceptual labyrinth of leisure is mild compared to the misty meanings of play. In fact, only one conceptual matter is crystal clear. The critical task of meaning is fraught with difficulties, and few researchers handle it satisfactorily. Consequently, leisure studies is plagued by conceptual confusion. (1990, 292)

A crucial question to be asked is: Where do we start in our philosophical discussion of leisure? Francis Bregha (1980b), who believes leisure is "inviting us to a philosophical discussion of its destination," believes this question is "the basic difficulty in the formulation of leisure's philosophy" (1980a, 18, 15). He goes on to write: "We are facing the initial philosophical difficulty . . . . When the task is to explain it (leisure) philosophically, we must call in an outside principle, such as God, reason, historical determinism or nature" (18). In another essay, Bregha explains how a divorce has taken place and leisure is no longer linked to God. He concludes, "Who is to guide us through the maze of good and evil now that God is absent and freedom is perceived in many ways?" (1980a, 37).

For a Christian, any philosophical discussion of leisure must naturally be carried out within the context of the divine. While society has divorced leisure from God, the Christian asserts that the ultimate purpose of leisure can only be found when it is again linked to the divine, for God is the Creator and Lord of our lives. If He is not therefore acknowledged as the Lord of leisure, then we cannot develop an adequate and meaningful understanding of leisure. Therefore, it is essential for Christians to begin any consideration of the meaning of leisure with the recognition that leisure must be God-centered and God-directed.

How do we proceed from this starting point of a God-centered understanding of leisure? Within Christendom there have been, and are, numerous approaches of how to relate Christianity to the world and culture in which it finds itself. Richard Niebuhr (1951) in his classic book, *Christ and Culture*, identifies five approaches: (1) Christ Against Culture, (2) The Christ of Culture, (3) Christ Above Culture, (4) Christ and Culture in Paradox, and (5) Christ the Transformer of Culture.

In the first paper in this section Gordon Spykman applies Niebuhr's fifth approach, the transformational approach to formulating a Christian perspective in the leisure sciences. In this approach, Christ is seen as the transformer of culture, one aspect of which is leisure.

Spykman's article is primarily a theological and philosophical study. Such works have not been predominant in the leisure sciences within the last few decades. Until very recently leisure scientists have held the belief that leisure science, similar to the various social sciences, ought to be deductive, objective, and value-free. The empirical and positivist method was considered to be the best way to understand leisure. However, there is some evidence that leisure science may be entering a period of post-positivism characterized by a pluralism of ethical, historical, interpretive, and critical methods of study. In the second article in this section, Paul Heintzman summarizes and discusses the transitions taking place in leisure sciences. He concludes that the transitions taking place present Christians with a tremendous opportunity and challenge to openly understand and explain leisure phenomena from a Christian perspective.

Paul Heintzman

References

Bregha, F. 1980a. Leisure and freedom re-examined. In *Recreation and leisure: Issues in an era of change*, edited by T. L. Goodale and P. A. Witt. State College, PA: Venture.

Bregha, F. 1980b. Philosophy of leisure: Unanswered questions. *Recreation Research Review* 8 (July): 15–19.

Murphy, J. 1974. *Concepts of leisure: Philosophical implications*. Englewood Cliffs: Prentice Hall.

Niebuhr, H.R. 1951. *Christ and culture*. New York: Harper.

Sylvester, C. 1990. Interpretation and leisure science: A hermeneutical example of past and present oracles. *Journal of Leisure Research* 22 (4): 290–295.

Chapter Four

Toward a Christian Perspective in the Leisure Sciences

GORDON SPYKMAN

The scientific study of leisure time is moving strongly to the fore. A major in recreation and leisure sciences is not only thinkable, but realizable. How is this possible? This development is probably due to the pressures of history, the influence of affluence, and the availability of more discretionary time than our parents and grandparents ever dreamed of. What shall we do with the rest of the week after 35 or 40 hours of work? How shall we handle early retirement? The forces of history are compelling us to face up to these questions of leisure time and recreation and, as Christians, to do so in a Christian way. Are there biblical norms for dealing with leisure time? How are we to engage in leisure without becoming sluggardly, thus bringing it under biblical judgment?

I shall now submit a rationale for the legitimacy of a Christian address to the question of leisure time and recreation. Such a case should have been there all along, but wasn't. I shall assume that leisure is one valid God-given aspect of life among others. Like every other aspect of life (such as worship, work, governing, marriage, buying and selling, feeling, and social relations), it is open to theoretical reflection. Just as we reflect on feelings in psychology, social relations in sociology, and political involvement in political theory, it is also legitimate to reflect theoretically on the nature and structure of this thing called leisure time. Some of my colleagues have trouble swallowing this approach. As I see it, they live with the false notion of what they choose to call pure science based on a dubious distinction between theory and praxis. This view would question the legitimacy, for example, of doing art over against studying the philosophy of art. So also it would advocate a study of the history and philosophy of leisure, but reject a "hands on" approach to it. Such a mind-set is more Greek than Hebrew or Christian.

Praxis and Theory

A more helpful approach is the model of serviceable insight. This involves gaining insight into all the various aspects of life, including leisure, and making such disciplined insight serviceable in fulfilling our callings in life to be all that we are called to be. In pursuing this approach, a right view of the relation between theory and praxis is important. Praxis is prior to theory. Praxis is first-order knowledge, while theory is second-order knowledge. You can get along without theory, but you can't get along without praxis. For example, in some fashion we all have to know how to handle money, make change, buy a loaf of bread, and pay the rent. We need to know something about how money works in order to engage in the theory of economics. If a person has no practical understanding of money, he or she cannot undertake a theoretical study of economics. Take another example. A person must know that if you cut all the way around the trunk of a tree, it will die. One must know this in a practical way as a basis for understanding the theory of capillary action. Down to earth experience also teaches us that flowers turn toward the light; in botany we call it phototropism. Again, one must know something about bodily movements as a way into studying physiology. As illustrated by these examples, praxis is always prior to theory.

The same is true in studying leisure. One must have some ordinary sense of taking time out from work, of sitting back and relaxing, of engaging in recreational activity—some practical knowledge of, insight into, or feel for such things before one can seriously engage in what we call the leisure sciences. Not only such practical experience, but also theoretical reflection upon it is a legitimate way of knowing things. Accordingly, academic inquiry into what is going on during leisure time is both legitimate and important. It can be helpful in deepening, enriching, and broadening our critical insight into recreational practices. It can help to account for leisure time habits. In so doing, it can also help in correcting and reforming this dimension of life.

At the foundational level, therefore, there is nothing quite as practical as good theory. Good theory enhances our understanding of daily praxis. Perhaps most importantly, it helps to avoid "ad hocism." An "ad hocish" lifestyle leads to making decisions today which are wholly unrelated to what was decided yesterday and perhaps also totally unrelated to decisions to be faced tomorrow. In the end there is no consistency, no pattern to such a life. Without a worldviewish framework, without a measure of theoretical reflection as context for dealing with the practical issues of life as they come up one after another, the biblical idea of "singlemindedness" remains an elusive goal.

A Christian Perspective on the Leisure Sciences

What is the place of leisure in life? What role is it designed to play? I shall look at these questions in terms of a biblical worldview. The last couple of decades have witnessed a strong resurgence in worldview studies. Traditionally, philosophical reflection was oriented largely to worldviews, looking at life in terms of the big picture. Thinkers such as Thomas Aquinas and Immanuel Kant set out to sketch totality pictures describing how life holds together in holistic ways. The analytical philosophy of our times, however, tends to break life down into bits and pieces. The focus is on "word-chopping" and reducing reality to manageable pieces.

But now the tide is turning once again. Out of the current resurgence of worldview studies has come the publication of a spate of excellent worldviewish books, such as Arthur Holmes's *Contours of a World View* (1983), James Sire's *The Universe Next Door* (1978), *The Transforming Vision* (1984) by Richard Middleton and Brian Walsh, and Albert Wolters' *Creation Regained* (1985). Behind these studies lies H. Richard Niebuhr's well-known book *Christ and Culture* (1951), which explores five classic perspectives on life as they have arisen in various western Christian communities over the past two millenia.

Drawing upon such resources, I shall retrace some of the major contours of a Christian worldview and seek to locate some of its major confessional reference points. This reformational outlook will serve then to shape a Christian view of leisure. In following this line of reasoning I shall be emphasizing Niebuhr's fifth type, "Christ the Transformer of Culture"; Robert Webber's third model, "The Transformational Model," in *The Secular Saint* (1979); and the central theme in Wolters' book as reflected in its sub-title, "Biblical Basics for a Reformational Worldview."

A reformational worldview involves a principled, structured, and normatively directed view of life. "Principled" refers to certain fundamental starting-points or presuppositions (from *pre-sub-ponere*, "to put something underneath all else in advance"). Certain basic principles or pre-suppositions always undergird one's worldview. In addition, a worldview must have a certain structure and direction. As I explore a reformational worldview, I assume that what holds for one aspect of life also holds in its own unique way for others. What holds, for example, for marriage as marriage, for work as work, for worship as worship, also holds for leisure as leisure—each area of life in its own unique way.

There are certain ground-rules for the game of life given by God the Creator for each sphere—such as the spheres of marriage, work, government, and worship. Certain norms hold for each of these aspects of life, including leisure. As a relative outsider to your discipline, I am not well acquainted with the norms that hold for leisure. I shall simply draw out a few implications taken from other areas of life, which come as givens of a reformational worldview.

It is clear, first of all, that some people make too much of leisure. Leisure has been sold out to commercial interests. It is also possible, however, to make too little of leisure. Perhaps we were guilty of this in the past. But nowadays, with a hedonistic spirit abroad, many people make too much of it. They work for the sake of a leisurely weekend. Instead of enjoying a leisurely weekend to equip them for going back to work, leisure becomes the goal toward which everything else is directed. So, like other things in life, one can make too much of leisure—but too little as well. To cheat on leisure time is to short-change the creation order. For there is a time and a place for leisure that is given in, with, and for the creation.

Gordon Dahl writes that "most Americans tend to worship their work, to work at their play, and to play at their worship" (1972, 12). What a vicious cycle! How are we to break out of it? How shall we allow leisure to come to its own in the Christian life? What Dahl is saying, it seems to me, is this: leisure is the key to the meaning of life as a whole. He defines leisure as the free spirit. We are to work leisurely, to play leisurely, and to worship leisurely. Leisure is an attitude that ought to pervade everything that we do. In this respect, it is like the biblical idea of holiness. It is wrong, for example, I think, to sing "Take time to be holy." Holiness isn't the type of thing we take time out to do. Holiness, that is "dedication to the Lord," should characterize all that we do. Dahl seems to be saying something like that about leisure. Leisure ought to characterize everything that we do. Again, it is similar to freedom. If the Lord has made us free, we are free indeed—free in marriage, free in work, free in leisure. For Dahl leisure turns out to be something like holiness, like freedom, like confessing "trust and obey for there is no other way." Live leisurely, for there is no other way to live the Christian life. To paraphrase the apostle Paul, "Whether you eat or drink, or whatsoever you do, do it leisurely." Paul said, of course, "do it all to the glory of God." But Dahl would say,

do it in a leisurely fashion, which is also a total religious orientation. Leisure is meant to shape life as a whole.

A Dimension of Life

In contrast to Dahl's viewpoint, I understand leisure in a more traditional sense. I see leisure not so much as an attitude that shapes all of life,
but as one aspect of life along with other aspects. Not as a direction-giv-
ing force in life, but as a societal structure. Think of it this way: if I were
to say that all of life is worship, what then is the particular meaning of
that which happens on Sunday? How shall I distinguish what happens
in church on Sunday from the events of the other days, if all of life is
worship? So also, if I were to say that all of life is leisure, what happens
then during a coffee break which differs from tacking bluebooks? What
is then distinctive about vacations? What is different about recreation? If
everything is leisure, the problem arises: what can we then say in a focused
way about leisure itself'? I shall therefore discuss leisure as one aspect or
dimension of life among others. And I shall approach it from the point
of view of three basic ideas.

Leisure Along the Biblical Story-Line.

Within a biblically reformed Christian perspective on leisure, three
points call for a bit of emphasis. First of all there is the biblical story-line,
which runs through the pages of Scripture as they shed light on our life
together in God's world. This story-line basically follows the pattern of
creation, fall, and redemption, on the way to the consummation of all
things. Within this unfolding drama of salvation, the Bible captures the
entire history of our world.

Starting with the creation narratives in Genesis 1 and 2, let us try to
read between the lines. There we discover that God has given humankind
different tasks, different callings, different vocations. In his book, *Ethics*
(1955), Dietrich Bonhoeffer describes four such mandates. He lists only
four; however, I think of these as cross-cut samples of many others. As
society becomes increasingly more complex, more and more tasks tend
to emerge. But what holds for these four, holds as well for all the others.
Bonhoeffer mentions work, worship, marriage, and government. He does
not include leisure, assuming, its seems, that these four exhaust all our
God-given callings. I think he is mistaken on this point. But he is right
in recognizing that there are mandates that are given in, with, and for the
creation. We are to "till the soil"—there is thus a place for work. Another

task is to marry and raise a family. We are also to govern creation on behalf of its Maker. The creation order also includes a learning task—education. God marches the animals past Adam, who is to give each of them
a name. In a dim and distant way, this prefigures what we do in taxonomy,
identifying and classifying things.

Leisure is present too. Adam and Eve are called to walk with God in
the cool of the day. God creates a place for little sabbaths, not just one
day in seven, but repeatedly day after day. We should think of every coffee
break as a little sabbath—a time for rest, relaxation, reflection, and recreation. Later in Scripture we are introduced to the epitome of all those
sabbaths—the Year of Jubilee. Even the land was to have a little leisure.
Slaves were to be set free, so they could also be at ease again. Family re-
unions were to take place. Farms lost to greedy land barons were to be
returned. So Jubilee, the weekly Sabbath, and the little sabbaths along the
way, taken together, reflect the fact that given in, with, and for the creation
is also a time for leisure.

Near the dawn of human history, however, the creation fell. Like all
else, leisure time too came under the power of sin. It too is burdened by
the curse. As a result, all kinds of destructive things take place. People
make too much of leisure, or too little. We become workaholics or we
become hedonists.

That is where the exodus from Egypt comes in. Exodus means redemption, salvation, liberation from slavery. In Egypt the Israelites were
made into workaholics. Leaving "the house of bondage" meant they no
longer had to work all the time. Sabbath became reality—time out. Life
is meant to offer a place for rest, for peace, for recreation. Now for us
as Christians, in Christ, proleptically through the Old Testament and in a
fulfilled way through the New Testament, leisure has been restored to a.
rightful place in life. We are now called to explore what that rightful place
is. For just as Christ has restored marriage, work, worship, as well as the
norms for public justice, so Christ has also restored our calling to engage
Christianly in leisure and recreation.

Now we look forward to the *eschaton*, the consummation of all things
in the end. The Bible, in its full extent and in all its parts, is the story of
how a garden is becoming a city. It all begins with a garden. Only God can
plant such a garden. The city, however, involves human activity. People
take trees that God has planted, cut them down, strip them into lumber,
build houses, push them close together, and so make cities. Accordingly,
the first picture that greets us as we open the Bible is that of a garden.

The last picture we are left with at the close of the Bible is that of a city. Our pilgrimage is not a return to the garden, but a movement onward toward a city. World history matters, because it is kingdom history. It is therefore all the more important. The treasures of the nations will go into the new Jerusalem. Among those treasures, I believe, is good, sound, healthy leisure.

The new heavens and the new earth will reappear as this earth renewed under renewed heavens. I don't think God is going to start all over again. He does not create junk and he does not junk what he has created. He will take this world, though fallen, but now in the process of being redeemed, and restore it not to what it originally was, but to what it was and still is meant to become. The dross will be consumed, the gold refined. Nothing good will go to waste, no beneficial leisure activities either. I like to speculate therefore that there wilt be tennis-courts there and probably folk dancing too. There will most likely be time for choir singing and listening to Mozart. But also a place for tiddly-winks, flying kites, and other forms of simple recreation. This then is how I see leisure unfolding along the biblical story-line.

The Holistic Character of Leisure

A second distinctive feature of a reformational worldview is its holistic character. As Niebuhr (1951) and Webber (1979) point out, most Christian traditions are dualistic. They break life into counter-parts: they hold, for example, that human beings are partly body and partly soul. Or perhaps also partly spirit. As a case in point, the theologian Louis Berkhof (1941) holds that humans are made up of two constitutive parts, one called body and the other soul. Often this dualism goes hand in hand with a worldview which divides reality into sacred and secular realms. This is utterly misleading. For actually life is 100 percent sacred and 100 percent secular—secular in the sense that there is only one place to live it, in this *saeculum,* and sacred in the sense that it is lived always and everywhere before the face of God. Life therefore has both horizontal and vertical dimensions. But it is in both senses holistic. All the major realities of life, all the major concepts in Scripture are holistic. Take the idea of covenant: it embraces everything. God covenanted his entire creation into existence. All of life is therefore covenantal. We live within covenantal bonds. Similarly with the biblical idea of the kingdom: every good cause is a kingdom cause. For the kingdom embraces all of life. The same is true of love: the central love command embraces every life-relationship.

Wolters puts it this way:

One way of seeing the uniqueness of a reformational worldview is to use the basic definition, of the Christian faith given by Herman Bavinck: "God the Father has reconciled His created but fallen world through the death of His Son, and renews it into a Kingdom of God by His Spirit." The reformational worldview takes all the key terms in this ecumenical trinitarian confession in a universal, all-encompassing sense. The terms "reconciled," "created," "fallen," "world," "renews," and "Kingdom of God" are held to be cosmic in scope. (1985, 10)

All these are comprehensive concepts. We cannot say of the covenant or of the kingdom of God: it is here, but not there. Leisure too is a holistic term not in the sense that it covers life as a whole, but in the sense that it involves the whole person. It is mistaken therefore to say that leisure is spiritual, but not physical. Or to say it is partly of the body and partly of the spirit. For we do not exist as souls that have bodies. We are 100 percent bodily creatures and also 100 percent spiritual. Soul points to the whole person looked at from the inside out, while body refers to the whole person looked at from the outside in. Romans 12 speaks in this vein about the "renewing of our mind" and the "presenting of our bodies." The whole person experiences spiritual transformation from the inside out and this inner transformation bears fruit outwardly in the presentation of all our bodily acts in service to the Lord and our fellow human beings. This is true to the biblical meaning of "holiness"—dedication of life as a whole. The biblical idea of "freedom" is also holistic. It reopens the doors to God's world. Sin closed the world down. Christ re-opens it. The whole world is now open to us. We are free to move about in our Father's world. Freedom means reopenedness—which includes reopening the windows of our lives to times of leisure.

A Basic Distinction: Structure and Direction as it Applies to Leisure

My third point relates to structure and direction. In the case of Dahl, leisure is viewed directionally, as a total orientation of life. It raises the question: which way is one's life moving—for Christ or against Him? Viewed as a directing force, leisure is like freedom and holiness: it is holistic on this view: leisure is direction-setting for life as a whole. But one then makes too much of it. For there is more to life than leisure, just as there is more to life than labor or worship. Structurally leisure is one activity alongside of others. Functionally the basic question is therefore this: are the structures and functions of our leisure/recreation activities shaped by Holy Spirited dedication or dedication to some other spirit? John Calvin employs the following concepts in describing the varying directions in life along the biblical story-line of creation, fall, and redemption: God arranged things, sin de-arranged things, Christ is re-arranging things. Herman Bavinck uses the following terms: God formed, sin deformed, and Christ reforms. I prefer the terms: direction, misdirection, and redirection. In all of these formulations the structures remain intact. But there is a change in direction. There is a certain structural and functional continuity to leisure, but its direction undergoes radical and sweeping changes. In the measure that the Christian community now lives by the life-renewing work of Christ, it can enjoy the blessings of re-directed participation in leisure and recreation.

References

Berkhof, L. 1941. *Systematic theology*. Grand Rapids: Eerdmans.

Bonhoeffer, D. 1955. *Ethics*. London: SCM.

Dahl, G. 1972. *Work, play, and worship in a leisure-oriented society*. Minneapolis: Augsberg.

Holmes, A. 1983. *Contours of a world view*. Grand Rapids: Eerdmans.

Middleton, R. and Walsh, B. 1984. *The transforming vision*. Grand Rapids: Eerdmans.

Niebuhr, H. R. 1951. *Christ and culture*. New York: Harper and Row.

Sire, J. C. 1978. *The universe next door*. Downers Grove: InterVarsity.

Webber, R. 1979. *The secular saint: A case for evangelical social responsibility*. Grand Rapids: Zondervan.

Wolters, A. 1985. *Creation regained: Biblical basics for a reformational worldview*. Grand Rapids: Eerdmans.

Chapter Five

Leisure Science, Dominant Paradigms, and Philosophy: The Expansion of Leisure Science's Horizon

PAUL HEINTZMAN

Until very recently leisure scientists have held the belief that leisure science, like other social sciences, ought to be deductive, objective, and value free. The empirical and positivist method was considered the best way to understand leisure. Presently, there is evidence that leisure science may be entering a period of post-positivism characterized by a pluralism of ethical, historical, interpretative, and critical methods of study.

The transitions taking place in leisure science are reflected in five articles in a special issue of the *Journal of Leisure Research* (JLR), Volume 22, 1990. The articles were adapted from papers presented during the opening session of the 1989 Leisure Research Symposium entitled, "Leisure Science, Dominant Paradigms, and Philosophy: Critical Reflections and Responses."

In the last recommendation of the last paper in the JLR special issue, Ellen Weissinger writes:

> It seems imperative that we should continue the conversation that has begun with these papers . . . we should expect in this translation process to encounter confusion. We should not expect to understand immediately. But we should begin the struggle. . . . The pointing, the asking of questions, the struggle to understand divergent ways of knowing can only lead to greater insight into the phenomenon about which we are so curious. (1990, 315, 316)

In this paper I would like to respond to this challenge. I want to continue the conversation. I want to continue the struggle. And I want to do that from a Christian perspective.

Methodologically, I will summarize, discuss, and interact with specific issues addressed in this special issue. I will organize my presentation around the following headings: Philosophical and Historical Background, Interpretation and Hermeneutics, Values, and Paradigm Shifts. The latter part of the paper will be devoted to a Christian response to the paradigm shifts in leisure science as identified by this special issue of JLR.

Philosophical and Historical Background

The introductory article by Karla Henderson (1990), entitled "Leisure Science, Dominant Paradigms, and Philosophy: An Introduction" provides a framework for the following four papers. Henderson observes, correctly I believe, that leisure researchers have avoided the philosophy of leisure science. However, philosophy of science provides the framework which underlies informed inquiry. It is concerned with the assumptions involved in producing knowledge.

Henderson (1990) provides useful historical background related to the philosophy of science and leisure research. She relies heavily upon an article by Kamphorst, Tibori and Giljam (1984) entitled "Quantitative and Qualitative Research: Shall the Twain Ever Meet?" It is important to review this historical material as questions underlying leisure research are rarely asked.

From ancient time the goals of science had been wisdom, understanding the natural order, and living in harmony with it. People saw the world as a "divine order" and science was pursued for the glory of God. During the Renaissance period this view of the world began to be questioned and a new view of reality was developed. It was thought that people could influence what happened in the world. Scientists started to discover, or we could say rediscover, the laws of nature.

Kamphorst et al summarize how the natural sciences, utilizing the cause and effect model, developed the logical expression: A influences or leads to B. At first, A and B were both aspects of nature and it was the natural world that was explored. Initially social relations were not included in this new view of the world. However, this limitation also changed during the Enlightenment period which was characterized by a strong belief in the human possibility to create one's own world (including the social order) and by a strong belief in human goodness. It is within this framework that the early sociologists worked. They focused on the explanations of human behavior within the social reality that A leads to B.

Kamphorst and colleagues describe how, in later decades, the interior world of humans was recognized as a factor that deeply influenced human behavior. A new set of variables was brought into the A leads to B model for the explanation of human behavior. During the 20th century more and more variables were examined in the logical scheme of causes and effects. Scientists developed statistical techniques to express the correlations in the A leads to B model. Methods for the measurement of the variables in this cause-and-effect model were developed and the inter-relatedness of the numerous variables of the A and B types were studied. Highly complex explanatory models were developed. Rules for the scientific process were developed to improve the reliability-and validity of scientific work. Kamphorst et al summarize the process that was developed:

- look around in the world; see what others have written about the subject under study and the variables that influence the subject.

- develop a theory regarding the explanation of the subject in terms of A leads to B model,

- test the theory by researching reality,

- and as long as it can't be falsified it can be regarded as true. (1984, 26)

In brief, this has been the traditional position of social science, including leisure science. The tendency of the leisure scientist to follow this biological and physical model has often meant that research questions are broken down into little pieces and then dissected as if no connection existed.

Additional historical background is provided in the JLR special issue by Thomas Goodale in an article entitled, "Perceived Freedom as Leisure's Antithesis." Goodale (1990) places leisure studies within the context of social scientific research. He traces how the study of leisure over the past century has shifted toward positivist, operationalist, analytic, and reductionist research.

Goodale suggests that the modem study of the use of free time began in the late 1800s with the "scientific charity" movement. Information was gathered to support the causes of reformers. Information-gathering was openly political, economic and social, and conducted by community activists. Goodale claims that this type of study "was not scientific in any modem sense, and not even research except in the broadest sense" (1990, 296).

Goodale describes how in the late 1920s the study of leisure moved from community activists to academics and was most prevalent in sociology, especially community studies as it related to the arrangement of community life and institutions. "This was not adversarial but descriptive, not in a quantitative sense but as portraits in words . . ." (1990, 296). After the second World War, emphasis was on descriptive studies, predominately sociological, which related sociodemographic variables to the use of free-time. Attention shifted from communities to sub-groups delineated by education, income, occupation, and similar variables. These descriptions were by numbers: descriptive, quantitative, and empirical, but primarily atheoretical. In the 1960s the study of leisure became increasingly sophis-ticated, with the use of multivariate statistics, and with rigorous attention to the elements of design such as variables, theories, and hypotheses.

According to Goodale, in the 1970s and 1980s social-psychology be-came the major disciplinary foundation for leisure research. Increasing emphasis was placed on the individual rather than the group, as well as on the subjective dimensions of leisure, such as the role of perception, counseling, and barriers. Therefore, research shifted from the political, economic, and social to individual perception. The setting moved from the community to the lab. Research became more positivist, operational-ist, and analytical. According to Goodale (1990), this may be the domi-nant paradigm at present. There is some evidence that leisure science may be entering an era of post-positivism. Journals in the leisure field have re-cently begun to include ethical, historical, interpretive, and critical articles. Pluralism rather than a dominating positivism has become characteristic of research in the leisure field. Legitimacy of other than positivist ways of knowing is grudgingly acknowledged.

Interpretation and Hermeneutics in Leisure Science

In his article "Interpretation and Leisure Science: A Hermeneutical Example of Past and Present Oracles" Charles Sylvester (1990) presents some thoughts on interpretation and leisure science using text hermeneu-tics. He presents seven conclusions and recommendations, five of which I will review under the headings: The Written Word, Hermeneutics, and Implications for Leisure. The remaining two will be discussed under the section Paradigm Shifts.

The Written Word

1. The written word is the permanent expression of knowledge. It provides the "preknowledge" needed for all subsequent understanding. (Sylvester 1990, 294)

Sylvester states, "The account of the pursuit of knowledge is mainly re-corded in print" (290). Thus anyone who pursues knowledge becomes enmeshed in a long series of intellectual traditions characterized by discovery, discourse, and disagreement. Sylvester believes we are linked to such diverse figures as Plato, Aristotle, Bacon, Descartes, Hegel, Comte, Hume, Locke, Kant, Marx, Weber, Dewey, and Wittgenstein. In the field of leisure research we have been guided by such people as de Grazia, Kaplan, Driver, Neulinger, Czikszentmahalyi, Iso-Ahola, Mannell, and Shaw. Each of us is shaped by the intellectual practices of the past.

I may be reading too much into Sylvester's article, but I am encouraged by his emphasis on the written word, and not just the empirical method, as a source of knowledge. After all, the written word is important to us as Christians. We believe in a God who has spoken in history and supremely in Christ, "the Word made flesh." The speech of our God in history is recorded in the written word, the Bible. This recognition of the importance of the written word and of intellectual traditions provides a place for the written word of Scripture and the JudeoChristian tradition to be heard in the pursuit of the understanding of leisure. The understanding of leisure is not limited to empirical and scientific studies. However, as Sylvester points out, most researchers have accepted the convention that empiricism is the most positive and progressive way to understand leisure.

What I find discouraging about Sylvester's list of diverse figures is the absence of persons linked to the Judeo-Christian tradition. No mention of Christ. Where is Augustine, Calvin, Luther, or closer to home Josef Pieper? Unfortunately, many contemporary leisure scholars turn to Aristotle for guidance in their thinking about leisure; they completely ignore Christ, the biblical record, and twenty centuries of Christian tradition. Or is it that Christians have been slow to draw upon the richness of their tradition as it relates to leisure? I would suspect that both are true.

At the same time Christian scholars do not always do justice to the intellectual traditions (written word) that have shaped leisure. For example, Robert Johnston (1983), in *The Christian at Play*, although acknowledging that the theological task involves the consideration of traditional sources, quickly dismisses the classical view of play (leisure)—and also the Protestant model—after only a brief one-page discussion of it, in favor of the Hebraic Model. Similarly, Leland Ryken (1987), in his book *Work and Leisure in Christian Perspective*, devotes only one page to the description of the Greek ideal of leisure which he believes "remains a standard for excellence in leisure." To fully understand leisure we need to take a more comprehensive look at the intellectual traditions which have shaped it.

Hermeneutics

Sylvester writes:

> 2. Hermeneutics is the method and theory of understanding the meaning and significance of texts.

> 3. The subject of hermeneutics is the understanding of language. Language, in turn, must be understood in its historical context. . . .

> 6. We have listened poorly to our intellectual traditions, leading to misappropriation, misunderstanding, and misdirection. (1990, 294, 295)

Sylvester describes hermeneutics as "the philosophical inquiry that tries to understand the meaning and significance of written works for the study of leisure" (291). He believes that hermeneutics involves two interrelated tasks. One task is dependent on language skills. This task is very important in leisure studies, for as we all know, the study of leisure is fraught with conceptual confusion. Second, historical background, sympathy, and imagination is necessary in hermeneutics. Ideas, including ideas about leisure, are deeply embedded in the flow of history. Classical and modern views of leisure arise out of two totally different worlds, making historical consciousness necessary when discussing leisure concepts.

For example, Sylvester notes that many modern writers turn to Aristotle and classical leisure as their starting point for a discussion of leisure. However, they embrace Aristotle's thought with their own specific purposes in mind and thus refer to leisure in ways that have little if any relation to Aristotle and classical leisure. Often their appropriations have been illegitimate, leading to mistakes and misdirections in our understanding of leisure. Thus, Sylvester argues, correctly I believe, for the use of good language and hermeneutical skills in the study of leisure.

Christians have the experience of hermeneutical inquiry in biblical studies and theology to draw upon as an aid in understanding leisure. Hermeneutics provides us with the language and historical skills to understand texts. Any Christian who takes their faith seriously will develop the language skills and historical appreciation necessary to understand scripture. These same skills are helpful in studying the intellectual traditions which have shaped leisure.

But have Christians utilized these skills in their study of leisure, let alone their study of scripture? Ryken notes that many books claim to present a Christian theology of leisure, but most of them are "notably vague and insubstantial, with almost no attempt to root an author's personal (and sometimes fanciful) opinions in the Bible" (1987, 182). Even

Ryken, whose starting point is always the Bible, at times could have been more exhaustive and systematic in the hermeneutical and exegetical task of appropriating the meaning of the biblical message for a contemporary theology of leisure. An example is his brief discussion of rest, based on the rest of God, the fourth commandment, and the example of Jesus resting. From this he suggests that the "biblical principle of rest provides a space within which leisure can occur" (187). While this is a starting point, a more detailed examination of the biblical theme of rest from creation to the sabbath-rest of Hebrews has much to offer a theology of leisure today.

Implications for Leisure

Sylvester states:

> 4. Hermeneutics possess ethical, political, epistemological, and ontological implications for leisure research. (1990, 294)

Sylvester gives an example from Aristotle who he believes did not consider leisure as a theoretical subject. He believes the topic Aristotle was investigating in the *Nicomachean Ethics* was not the nature of leisure but how to use it. Aristotle was concerned with how to live the good life, not the theoretical question of the nature of goodness. He writes that practical knowledge, the type of knowledge required for moral conduct, is different from theoretical knowledge. He recommends phronesis (practical knowledge), otherwise known as prudence, the virtue of moral judgment, over episteme (theoretical knowledge).

Yet, Sylvester (1990) notes that leisure studies has embraced the rationality of empiricism to the near exclusion of moral understanding. Indeed he observes that it is imperative in today's science to keep fact and value strictly separate. Yet, Aristotle's approach to science, moral, and theoretical knowledge, though different, is complementary. Sylvester notes the irony of the leisure studies field which has devoted so much attention to Aristotle yet has failed to hear his message.

The point Sylvester is making is, I believe, consistent with the biblical notion of truth, knowledge, and wisdom. Arthur Holmes's *All Truth is God's Truth* (1977) is helpful here. Holmes notes that an implication of the claim that all truth is God's truth is that truth is intrinsically personal, not autonomous, not abstract, and not to be approached with detachment and objectivity. A look at Scripture helps us understand the personal nature of truth, knowledge, and wisdom.

Truth (*emeth*) in the Old Testament is primarily an ethical and not an epistemological term. It denotes reliability and fidelity and is used of behavior (Genesis 24:49), of promises (2 Samuel 7:28), and of just laws (Nehemiah 9:13). Truth is primarily a matter of inner character which is only derivately issued to describe a quality of words and deeds. Propositional truth in Scripture relies on the personal truthfulness of God.

For the Greek philosophers knowledge was generally abstract, objective, and conclusive which suggests a theoretical or a spectator attitude to life. Biblical writers used verbs which suggest epistemological subjectivity:

> They emphasize less the static qualities of objects and more the human act of knowing. . . . The verb is even used in the Septuagint of marital intercourse: plainly a man does not "know" his wife in a detached, theoretical way, nor is our knowledge of God and his grace detached and theoretical either. To know is to know for oneself, to interiorize what is learned, to act on it, to make it one's own. Such knowledge is life-related. . . . Knowledge, being personal and not detached, brings responsibility: a person must measure up to the truth he knows and behave accordingly. (Holmes 1977, 36)

Thus, knowledge is not an impersonal accumulation of lifeless facts, but a very personal involvement.

The Biblical term for wisdom follows the same pattern. It is a God-given understanding of life that is personally edifying. Wisdom is always personal and is personified in Proverbs 8 as having been with God from the beginning of eternity and is seen as the divine source of all human wisdom. Thus, from the biblical perspective human knowledge is not detached and purely theoretical but intensely personal. Such knowledge needs to be considered in leisure science.

Values in Leisure Sciences

Goodale suggests three modest proposals in response to reservations, in particular the value-free claim, of positivist, reductionist social science. His first proposal is as follows:

> 1. We could be more sensitive to our biases and communicate them openly. If values are unavoidable, as they appear to be since they are the human content of our lives, let us talk about what we are committed to and what not. We need not be apologetic about having values. (1990, 301)

Goodale discusses the inevitable intrusion of values in leisure research. He notes that there tends to be widespread agreement that leisure researchers should keep their biases under control. But at the same time he concludes that values are unavoidable in leisure research for at least three reasons.

First, leisure researchers value leisure, and therefore, are inclined to certain subjects and certain results. Goodale writes: "There seems little doubt that our interest in barriers is to reduce them, our interest in satisfactions is to increase it, our interest in feeling states is to help people feel good and so on" (1990, 297). From this perspective leisure researchers are not value free.

Second, it is difficult to turn subjective impressions into objective social science. The question arises as to whether objectivity is an attainable ideal in the social sciences where it is impossible to be totally free from subjective judgments. Every step in the research process is value laden, including the choices of subject, problem, data, and methodology.

Third, leisure research is not guided by pure, intrinsic curiosity. Our environment introduces a variety of biases such as fund and grant sources, money and time constraints, and publication pressures. Goodale concludes that "values seem bound up in our work in several ways." Goodale's conclusion is congruent with that of Alan Storkey's graphic description of social research in *A Christian Social Perspective*:

> The *neutrality* of social facts is . . . suspect when we recognize that what actually happens in a survey is as follows: the sociologist *chooses* a certain area of study, *selects* certain issues that he considers to be important, *defines* the groups that he is to study, *decides* what kind of questions to ask and how to ask them. The data is then analyzed according to certain criteria that is *considered* to be important. Often answers are precoded to bring out what is *significant*. Clearly the framework of interpretation is already present, and the evidence is assessed within a perspective. Neutralism is impossible and any claim that the facts are "objective" is severely compromised. (1979, 97)

Goodale also writes that we must recognize that values are not without meaning. We act on our values and the resultant actions have consequences such as the preservation of life, being healthy, safe, literate, decently fed, clothed and housed. The recognition of values and their meanings in leisure science, as advocated by Goodale, should be an encouragement for Christians to openly articulate their values when studying and understanding leisure.

Paradigm Shift in Leisure Science

All five papers in this special issue are fundamentally concerned with the dominant leisure research paradigms and a possible shift from an empiricist paradigm to an interpretationist paradigm. Figure 1 provides information about these dominant paradigms.

For Henderson the discussion of dominant paradigms is not an "either/or" situation, but rather:

> The goal is to make leisure science more inclusive. . . . The important aspect is not the positivists or the experimental methodology versus hermeneutical ap-

---

FIGURE I: TYPES OF SOCIAL SCIENCE

EMPIRICIST	INTERPRETATIONIST
OTHER NAMES	
Positivism Scientific Method Deduction Rationality Quantitative Methods	Post-Positivism Hermeneutics Inductive Phenomenology Qualitative Methods Depth Interpretation Symbolic-Interactionism
TASK	
Explains: Addresses the observable facts and causes of social phenomena apart from subjective states.	**Interprets:** Attempts to make sense of an object of study.
COMPARISON WITH NATURAL SCIENCE	
Differs in the techniques used for the discovering of facts, not in the way facts are explained or hypotheses are tested.	Primary difference is that "interior" (subjective) aspects of human behavior are integral to social science. One must interpret as well as observe behavior.
THE NATURE OF SCIENCE	
Stresses objectivity and observable sensory data. Ignores beliefs, attitudes, intuitions, etc. which are thought to prevent accurate scientific work.	Science is a general method that can be applied to a variety of areas. A science in which subjective states are possible.
PURPOSE OF SOCIAL SCIENCE	
Borrows from natural sciences. Argues that verified by prediction are the only valid explanations and should be the goal of the social sciences.	Explanation may have a broader meaning than in the empiricist model; understanding is the appropriate goal of the social sciences.
BASIC DIFFERENCE	
Social scientific knowledge may be constructed without reference to the human meanings, intentions, and understandings of the participant involved.	Consideration must be given to human meanings and intentions, since in social science, human behavior, not inanimate objects, are being observed.

proaches, but how we can understand the phenomenon of leisure and inquiry. . . . Leisure can be better understood from an inclusive rather than a bounded perspective. . . [from] the possibility of multiple options. (1990, 284–285)

She sees the weaknesses of the scientific method and the need for pluralistic approaches:

> The use of reason and rationality found in the physical and natural sciences has not been always productive for leisure scholars. . . . While much can be learned from the application of the scientific method emanating from the physical and natural sciences, social science and the study of leisure behavior can and should be examined based on interpretative assumptions and pluralistic methods. (287)

As noted earlier, both Sylvester (1990) and Goodale (1990) recommend moving beyond empirical methodologies to pluralistic methods. Sylvester, who believes that leisure studies have embraced the rationality of empiricism to the near exclusion of hermeneutical inquiry and moral understanding, claims that leisure science requires both hermeneutical inquiry and empirical inquiry.

> 5. Hermeneutical inquiry and empirical inquiry are different, yet complementary. Both are demanded for knowledge. Yet leisure studies has largely eschewed hermeneutics. . . .
> 7. Along with empirical methods, hermeneutics should be included in graduate education. (Goodale, 295)

Goodale writes, "Given the many reservations with positivist, reductionist, etc. social science . . . perhaps it is time to entertain some modest proposals those reservations invite" (1990, 301). These proposals include the following:

> We could incorporate in our work more efforts to define and describe the real world and take it into account. . . . We might want . . . to view ourselves as a bridge between the "hard sciences" and the humanities. (301)

The fourth author in this special issue, J. L. Hemingway, in "Opening Windows on Interpretative Leisure Studies," suggests that the present understanding of leisure is too shallow. Hemingway argues for intersubjectivity and depth interpretation in the study of leisure. He claims, "The dominance within leisure studies of a single research framework, namely, a combination of empiricism and social psychology, has led to shortcomings in both our investigation and understanding of leisure" (1990, 303). In empirical social research there is some irreducible world of which humans may have experience, but which exists independently of human activity. For Hemingway, the fatal flaw in empirical social research is that the social world is treated the same as the natural world, when in fact it is not. He argues that the natural world is not self-referential while human interpretations of the social world influence the world in which people act.

Hemingway believes that the process of interpretation provides the necessary basis to make physical and psychological concepts humanly meaningful, a dimension which is lacking in the empirical method. In the empirical model we miss an awareness of how intersubjective practices influence and are influenced by the interpretations of the participants. We give up attempting to delve beneath the surface. In empiricism, meaning is reduced to measurement; what cannot be measured has no meaning. But that which is intersubjective resists measurement.

Furthermore, Hemingway points out that empiricist analysis is unable to comment on the meanings of different leisure patterns:

> It can say neither that one leisure pattern is good, and the other bad, nor that one is more desirable than the other. It cannot say that a society in which one or the other pattern prevails is healthier, or richer, or more humane, than another society in which a contrasting pattern holds. (1990, 307)

Depth interpretation, according to Hemingway, goes beyond the limitations of empiricism by being open to experience, rather than forcing experience to adapt to the demands of method. He concludes that through depth interpretation "we will find the web of leisure's connections to society expanding: we will enlarge and enrich the horizon against which our inquiry takes place" (308).

In the final article, "Of Revolutions and Resistance: A Response to Philosophical Criticisms of Social Scientific Leisure Research," Weissinger, writing from a social scientific view, cautions against the tossing out of empiricism. She points out that adopting different ways of understanding has the advantage of overcoming the biases of a single paradigm. She writes:

> Pluralistic methodologies . . . have much to offer. Interpretive, phenomenological or qualitative methods differ from science not only procedurally, but also epistemologically. In other words, they are based on vastly different sets of assumptions. . . . I don't think it is necessary to throw aside our chosen method, nor do I believe that every researcher should be obligated to incorporate multiple methodologies in their professional repertoire. . . . It may be important for social scientists to actively facilitate the work of researchers who utilize different methods. (1990, 313)

The point is clearly made by these five authors that leisure science must be empirical as well as interpretive and critical, with each mode of inquiry informing the other.

A Christian Response

How do we as Christians respond to this paradigm shift and the use of multiple methodologies? I would like to step back for a moment and see how we have responded to the empirical model. Timothy Sheratt writes:

> The question why is as innocent a question as can be asked in the world today but its past is murky. There was a time when it was not asked because the man and woman walked with God. Then it was asked and sin and guilt became part of the world. Empirical verification became a possibility too. This meant there were two ways to answer the question why. There was the eternal way of God's revelation and the new way of empirical research and verification. . . . The eternal way . . . retained its innocence for centuries, well into the Christian era. The eternal way is now ignored in "serious" research. The temporal, empirical way has now become dominant and innocent. (1982, 77)

Is the empirical way innocent? Is the empirical way compatible with the eternal way? Are the two ways diametrically opposed? Ronald Burwell (1981) has identified three approaches to integration for Christianity and sociology, which are applicable to all, the social sciences, including leisure science.

Unrelated

The first approach, which assumes that the empirical way is innocent, is that Christianity and social science are categorically different and unrelated. Essentially this is a denial of the possibility or necessity of integration. Christianity and science are seen as having different and unrelated languages or logics so that confusion results if you try to integrate them. If any relationship between the two exists, it is limited to how a Christian manifests certain personal characteristics or values (e.g., honesty) while engaged in social science. Science is the realm of fact while beyond is the realm of value. This position is reflected by the following statements of John Scanzoni:

> We must insist on a distinction between Christianity and various disciplines. . . . Any science is a set of generalizations induced from observations about the empirical phenomenon. Christianity . . . is a set of deductive propositions, many of which are beyond the ken of empirical verification. (1972, 123ff.)

The problem of this approach is that it puts Christians in a paradoxical position: on the one hand they are conscious of the importance of values in daily life, but on the other hand they accept the common view that values have no place within social science. As a result compartmentalization of life ensues. Yet not only do Christians desire consistency, wholeness, and integrity in their beliefs and commitments, but they are to bring all of life under the Lordship of Christ.

Separate but Related

A second approach is that Christianity and social science are separate entities which have a complementary or hierarchical relationship. Thus, the empirical way and the eternal way are seen as being compatible. The two ways separately provide partial knowledge but when combined lead to enhanced understanding and a total picture.

The complementary view is reflected by Russell Heddendorf who believes that social reality exists on two levels (spiritual and secular):

> The proper study of social reality must run on two tracks. Study of the current social situation must proceed with a parallel study of the eternal universal situation. One track would describe man's construction of reality. The other would give some understanding of God's creation of reality . . . . Science focuses at the historical moment while Christianity scans the eternal horizons. . . . Together they form a more complete picture of the complexity of social reality. (1978, 13, 15)

The problem of the complementary approach is how supposedly mutually complementary explanations are to be handled when conflicts arise. The hierarchical approach, as reflected by Milton Reimer, appears to solve this problem:

> The discipline of sociology, is in itself neutral and descriptive, not normative. . . . [What is required is] the subordination of the discipline to the authority of the Scriptures . . . . When it speaks on topics that have implications for sociology, it takes precedence over secular authority. (1982, 20)

Although this position recognized that the eternal way sometimes takes precedence over the empirical way it seems to see the empirical way as innocent. Reimer writes: "Valid sociological data (or raw facts) are not inherently hostile to a biblical perspective . . . . The Christian must assume the ultimate coherence of sociological data with biblical truth" (1982, 11).

Interpenetration

The third approach is an interpenetration of social science by the Christian worldview. In this approach the empirical way is not necessarily innocent and thus is not necessarily compatible with the eternal way, although at the same time it is also not diametrically opposed to it. Thus, a dialectic is set forth whereby Christianity informs one's social science and one's social science introduces revisions into one's Christian worldview. As Nicholas Wolterstorff in *Reason Within the Bounds of Religion* puts it:

> The religious beliefs of the Christian scholar ought to function as control beliefs within his devising and weighing of theories .... [However] sometimes he should allow scientific developments to induce his revisions in what he views as his authentic Christian commitment. (1976, 66, 90)

Only this approach, which is truly dialectical, is worthy of the name "integration." However, very few social scientists who are Christians have been known for their attempts at dialectic integration.

At this point it should be noted that the above categories are rather simplistic and that it is more likely that approaches range along a continuum. Along this continuum,

> It is indeed true that commitment to a new positivistic (empirical) view of social science diminishes the likelihood that one will expand efforts to integrate one's science with Christian faith; even as it increases the probability of indulging in some form of compartmentalization. (Moberg 1981, 210–211)

Nevertheless, there has been a traditional willingness among many Christians, as reflected by the statements of Scanzoni, Reimer, and Heddendorf cited above, to hold to the empiricist paradigm in order to protect the purity of social science from ideological and religious contamination. There has been a strong belief that empiricism is the only acceptable source of knowledge and that alternative techniques are problematic or will destroy the truth-seeking potential of social science. Thus, in the past many Christian social scientists have uncritically accepted the empirical way as being innocent.

Recently, challenges to empiricism in the social sciences have emerged from several sources (Kuhn 1962, Habermas 1971, Gouldner 1970, Hesse 1980), and as pointed out by Goodale (1990), there is growing awareness of the nonscientific dimension (e.g., valuing) of the social sciences. These challenges have been around for a few years; however, as Weissinger (1990) notes, social scientific leisure researchers have been slow to recognize the importance of joining the dialogue.

These challenges to empiricism have implications for the way Christians integrate their faith with leisure science. If the traditional objectivity ideal of the empirical model is impossible in social science theorizing, and valuing is necessary, the proposal of a social theory, according to Mary Hesse, should seek for and respect the facts to be had, but it must also appeal explicitly to value judgments. A consequence of Hesse's argument is that the criteria of acceptability for social theories is pluralist:

> If we wish to talk of *choice* of values it also follows that we presuppose a certain area of freedom in the activity of theorizing—we are not wholly constrained to adopt particular theories either by facts, or by adoption of particular value goals, or by social and economic environments. (1980, 202)

Such theoretical pluralism gives the Christian leisure scientist a basis on which to develop theories which are characterized by their Christian perspective on society and people. If theoretical pluralism is possible, an epistemological break with empiricism is set up in which the relevance of Christian commitment and beliefs to leisure science could then be articulated in a more direct and integrated manner. If one sets aside empiricism and adopts the interpretationist model, the way is open for the dialectical integration of one's Christian worldview with leisure science. The Christian who acknowledges the subjectivity of the knower need not feel threatened by the. idea that one's worldview affects the data-of social science. Rather, as David Lyon (1983) proposes, a whole spectrum of biblical insights on humanness, including values such as neighborliness, justice, obligation, rights, and authority, can be allowed to penetrate leisure science.

Not all Christians advocate a break with empiricism. Donald Mackay views the attack on the ideal of objective, value-free knowledge as "symptomatic of the practical atheism of our day" (1980, 202) and seems to retain the empiricist model of natural science as his standard for all science. David Moberg (1980) takes a more moderate stance. He believes that both the empiricist and interpretationist models recognize the subjectivity of knowers and actors, but the approach of their analysis differs. He claims that many empiricists have sought concise generalizations to cover vast ranges of human behavior which tend to be oversimplified, abtruse, even "demanding to human nature" while the failure of many interpretationists, even to try to generalize, raises questions about the scope and utility of their work. Therefore, he believes that both the empiricist and interpretationist models are limited in and of themselves, but each can be used to complement each other in research and theoretical work. The authors of the JLR special issue have come to a similar conclusion. For example, Weissinger writes, "Adopting diverse ways of knowing has the critical advantage of overcoming the potential barriers of a single paradigm by enriching our ability to conceptualize, investigate and understand leisure" (1990, 313).

It might be possible to adopt both paradigms alternatively. Hesse writes:

> There are areas in the social science where the methods and criteria of the natural sciences are both workable and desirable. There are general laws of human behavior . . . there are models and ideal types whose consequences can be explored deductively and tested and there are limited predictions which are sometimes successful. (1980, 200)

However, Hesse goes on to say that "much social science which is currently acceptable is not and probably never can be of this kind" (200). Therefore, it is necessary to develop criteria that specify the situations under which a social scientist might operate as an empiricist or an interpretationist.

An acknowledgment that both the empiricist and interpretationist models are appropriate in certain situations would be helpful in avoiding the fallacy of reductionism, as noted by Hemingway (1990), where one analysis is taken to be the definitive view of reality. Since the analysis of both empiricism and interpretationism abstract from the full complex of reality, they result in the reduction or simplification of the complexities of reality. Malcolm Jeeves asserts that one must avoid identifying "the model with the reality which it expresses" (1969, 79). Moberg warns that anyone who sells out to empiricism or interpretationism is in danger of falling into "a form of idolatrous exclusivism, for human reality is far too complex to be covered by any one approach" (1981, 213). The appropriate approach is to use many different images and models so as to increase our understanding of social reality.

Conclusion

Christianity is not tied or linked exclusively to one paradigm or philosophy of science. Rather, Christians are concerned with truth and recognize that humans are created in the image of an infinite God. To understand the complexity of human behavior and human experience, including leisure, a variety of methods are required. Therefore, Christians should welcome the adoption of different ways of studying and understanding leisure as advocated by the authors of this special issue of JLR.

Theoretical pluralism should make it easier for the Christian to dialectically integrate one's faith with leisure science. Weissinger writes that we are at "a new place of opportunity and challenge. The key is to seize the opportunity and move forward in our ability to explain and understand leisure phenomena" (1990, 310). Christians are at a strategic place in leisure studies. The transitions taking place in leisure science present Christians with a tremendous opportunity and challenge to understand and openly explain leisure phenomena from a Christian perspective.

Finally, the integration of leisure science with one's faith is not easy; it involves struggle. Adoption of one methodology or model in leisure science is not a guaranteed route to truth. Rather, in the words of Moberg, "dialectical integration essentially goes back to a personal, lifelong, lifegiving trust in the One whom to know is to have life eternal" (1981, 213).

References

Burwell, R. 1981. Sleeping with an elephant: The uneasy alliance between Christian faith and sociology. *Christian Scholars' Review* 10 (3): 195–208.

Goodale, T. 1990. Perceived freedom as leisure's antithesis. *Journal of Leisure Research* 22 (4): 296–302.

Gouldner, A. 1970. *The coming crisis of western sociology.* New York: Basic Books.

Habermas, J. 1971. *Knowledge and human interests.* Boston: Beacon.

Heddendorf, R. 1978. Studying social reality: The case of the calling. *Christian Scholars' Review* 8 (1): 10–24.

Hemingway, J. L. 1990. Opening windows on interpretative leisure studies. *Journal of Leisure Research* 22 (4): 303–308.

Henderson, K. 1990. Leisure science, dominant paradigms, and philosophy: An introduction. *Journal of Leisure Research* 22 (4): 283–289.

Hesse, M. 1980. *Revolutions and reconstructions in the philosophy of science.* Bloomington: Indiana University Press.

Holmes, A. 1977. *All truth is God's truth.* Grand Rapids: Eerdmans.

Jeeves, M. 1969. *The scientific enterprise and Christian faith.* Downers Grove: InterVarsity.

Johnston, R. 1983. *The Christian at play.* Grand Rapids: Eerdmans.

Kamphorst, T. J., Tibori, T. T., and Giljam, M. J. 1984. Quantitative and qualitative research: Shall the twain ever meet? *World Leisure and Recreation* 26 (6): 25–27.

Kuhn, T. 1962. *The structure of scientific revolutions.* Chicago: University of Chicago Press.

McKay, D. 1980. Value-free knowledge: Myth or norm? *Faith and Thought,* 107:202.

Moberg, D. 1981. Response to Burwell. *Christian Scholar's Review* 10 (3): 209–214.

Reimer, M. 1982. The study of sociology: An introduction. In *Christian Perspectives on Sociology,* edited by S. Grunlan and M. Reimer. Grand Rapids: Zondervan.

Ryken, L. 1987. *Work and leisure in Christian perspective*. Portland, OR: Multnomah.

Scanzoni, J. 1972. Sociology. In *Christ and the modern mind*, edited by W. Smith. Downers Grove: InterVarsity.

Sheratt, T. 1982. By what authority: Verification of theories in the social sciences. *Journal of the American Scientific Affiliation* 34 (2): 77–83.

Storkey, A. 1979. *A Christian social perspective*. Leicester, England: InterVarsity.

Sylvester, C. 1990. Interpretation and leisure science: A hermeneutical example of past and present oracles. *Journal of Leisure Research* 22 (4): 290–295.

Weissinger, E. 1990. Of revolutions and resistance: A response to philosophical criticisms of social scientific leisure research. *Journal of Leisure Research* 22 (4): 309–316.

Wolterstorff, N. 1976. *Reason within the bounds of religion*. Grand Rapids: Eerdmans.

SECTION THREE

Present Practices and Challenges in Leisure

While the conceptual discussion of leisure is unresolved and ongoing, we cannot let this task hinder us from addressing the leisure practices, issues, and challenges of our day. Thus with this section we move from the theoretical and the methodological to the practical. Gordon Dahl's article (Chapter Six) is a bridge from the theoretical to the challenges of today. We cannot help but remember the predictions of the 1960s and 1970s about an "emerging leisure-ethic" and the "coming leisure society." The work-week was to be shorter, vacations were to be longer, and technological advancement would save us from much of the drudgery of work. But, as we enter the 1990s, these predictions have not come true. In fact there is some evidence that we are working longer and that we are busier than ever. Dahl documents the myth of free time and the rise of the worth-ethic before concluding that theology has failed to address the issue of leisure adequately. Theologically and practically the church has failed. Thus we are brought back to definitional issues again, and Dahl introduces the concept of "worcreation."

While Dahl is critical of the church's failure to address the leisure issues, he notes that the New Age movement reflects a profound search for spiritual meaning and values which it is providing answers to. While he recognizes that much of the New Age is not of value, he sees the need to follow it critically. Thus, in the next chapter (seven), Glen Van Andel examines the challenges, positive and negative, that arise in the leisure field due to the influence of the New Age Movement.

The New Age Movement is a profoundly spiritual movement, albeit a very eclectic one. But Christianity too has a spiritual tradition that is very relevant to leisure. Joe Teaff, in Chapter Eight, draws connections between Christian spirituality and leisure. He concludes that true Christian spirituality can flourish only in a climate of leisure.

In Chapter Nine, Cathy O'Keefe documents how leisure and Christian spirituality are linked in L'Arche to create a loving community where those with developmental disabilities are both accepted and provided with the opportunity to manifest God's presence. O'Keefe concludes that leisure is the glue that binds these loving communities together.

In the final chapter of this section (ten), the concept of community and its importance for leisure is extended to include the earth. Don De-Graaf notes how dwindling natural resources create conflicts between many different kinds of recreation user groups. However, the earth is increasingly recognized as part of our community. DeGraaf advocates a "humans with nature" or stewardship model of our relationship with the earth. He believes that park and recreation educators must personally and professionally change their behavior in order to protect the earth.

Paul Heintzman

Chapter Six

Whatever Happened to the Leisure Revolution?

GORDON DAHL

About 25 or 30 years ago, some leading American scholars and commentators were discerning elements of a social revolution—a revolution which would affect the fundamental values of American culture and eventually reshape the life styles of most American citizens. Although its elements were both complex and diverse, it was often called a "leisure revolution" because one of its most significant features was the promise, or threat, of increased leisure for nearly everyone.

Most Americans, of course, welcomed the promise of more leisure as relief from the demands and drudgery of their jobs and household chores. Technology was almost universally seen as a humane and liberating force, progressively lifting the burdens of work from the shoulders of men and women—leaving them free to pursue more pleasurable interests.

Some, however, saw a darker side. Participating in a panel discussing the major problems confronting Americans during the second-half of the twentieth century—problems which included the nuclear arms race, the war in Southeast Asia, and rising rates of crime and drug abuse—Eric Sevareid, one of the most widely read and respected journalists of these times, claimed that "the most dangerous threat to American society is the rise of leisure and the fact that those who have the most leisure are the least equipped to make use of it" (Lee 1964, 17).

Those for whom a leisure revolution became a focus for serious research and commentary identified several post-World War II social and economic trends as its major components. These trends included:

1. The shortening and re-shaping of the standard work-week for employed persons.
2. More paid holidays and vacation time.
3. Increasing lengths of non-working periods in the human life-span (that is, more years spent in education and retirement).

4. Steadily rising levels of personal and family income.
5. Proliferation and growth of leisure-related industries.
6. Expanding systems of transportation and electronic communication.
7. Expanding programs of public health and human services.
8. Increasing role of governments (local, state, federal) in providing leisure facilities and services.
9. Human liberation movements and generally increasing emphasis upon the
   value of personal freedom.
10. Mounting skepticism of traditional values, especially as they are related to
    work and family (Dahl 1972, 25–40).

Most of these trends have continued, more or less, to the present, but
few people today are associating them with a "leisure revolution." In fact,
a growing complaint among contemporary Americans is that there is not
enough leisure! Ironically, the very people whose lifestyles and values have
been most dramatically influenced by leisure trends (that is, the young,
healthy, educated, middle-class Americans) are now worrying that they
will have less, rather than more, leisure than preceding generations!

Actually, as the studies of John Robinson (1989) at the University of
Maryland (and various other scholars) clearly show, most Americans today have more leisure than ever before, but their perception—and perhaps their day-to day experience—is telling them otherwise. In a Harris
Survey (Gibbs 1989), the typical American reported that he or she had 37
percent less leisure in 1988 than in 1973. Their average vacation shrunk
to a little more than three days, instead of the five to seven days common a decade ago. And, these respondents complained, more and more
weekends and holidays are consumed in necessary household tasks, family
obligations, and shopping.

What happened? Who stole the leisure from the leisure revolution?
Twenty-five years ago, social scientists were asking, "What are people going to do with their abundance of free time?" Today they might well ask,
"Where will people find the free time to do all the things they feel they
have to do?"

So what happened to the so-called "leisure revolution"? This paper
will attempt to answer that question by offering three perspectives drawn
from my own experience as a monitor of leisure trends and as a prac-
titioner in various leisure-related fields. The first is an analysis of what
I consider to be the myth of free time which has distorted perceptions
of the leisure revolution for both the general public and for many of
the leisure-related professions—including those of recreation and reli-

gion. The second perspective is what I discern as the emergence of a new "worth-ethic" which is turning upside-down the work-leisure juxtapositions which social scientists were describing at the onset of the leisure revolution. Finally, I will offer some explanation, although not a defense, of American religion's failure to address the meanings and values of leisure as a source of spiritual and social development—thereby permitting its secular subversion into permissiveness and perversity.

"The Myth of Free Time"

The long-term cultural promises of a leisure revolution have been consistently subverted by widespread acceptance of definitions and values pertaining to leisure which were derived from industrial capitalism of the nineteenth and early twentieth century. Instead of defining and valuing leisure in terms of its own multifaceted and open-ended possibilities, Americans have generally settled for a narrow economic and sociological meaning: Leisure is time which is not spent at work. Hence, it becomes something that can be quantified in terms of hours or days or weeks or months—and it is almost always referenced in relationship to work. For most Americans, including many who do not usually settle for simple definitions and cheap meanings, leisure became associated with blocks of time that were not committed to gainful or obligatory work.

It is understandable that economists and sociologists adopted meanings for leisure which defined it as periods of time and juxtaposed it with work, but it is unfortunate that so many others—including most professionals in recreation and religion—have done so, also. I realize that professionals today, in both fields, no longer settle for such simple-minded meanings, but I think we need to be reminded of how powerfully they influenced those who established the recreation profession and shaped its role in American colleges, communities, and churches. One needs only to refer to the early textbooks and treatises on recreation to see how notions of "free time" and "non-work" pervaded the meanings and values of recreation.

I will cite just two examples: The first from Martin and Esther Neumeyer, authors of one of the earliest and most widely-used textbooks in recreation:

> Definitions of leisure vary a great deal, but the chief emphasis is upon the time element. . . . Leisure is the free time after the practical necessities of life have been attended to. (1958, 14)

The second is from Charles Brightbill, one of the foremost advocates for recreation as both an academic discipline and a community service:

> Leisure is essentially a block of time. . . . (1961, 20)

> Leisure is best identified with time—time beyond that required . . . . for existence and subsistence. . . . (1966, 13)

> Work, of course, precedes leisure, which, in turn, may be our reward for having fulfilled a useful role. . . . (1966, 24)

From this narrow and derivative conception of leisure came the meaning and. purpose of recreation. According to the Neumeyers:

> Recreation . . . is the chief way most people spend their leisure. However, the emphasis in leisure is on the time element, whereas recreation refers to the way leisure is spent. (1958, 17)

Or, as Brightbill summarized it, the primary purpose of recreation is to constructively fill our leisure time (1961, 9).

Other conceptualizations of leisure and recreation were offered, to be sure, from the classical definitions of Sebastian de Grazia (1962) and Joseph Pieper (1952) or the more elaborate sociological constructs of Joffre Dumazedier (1962) and Max Kaplan (1975) and the psychological interpretations of John Neulinger (1981) and Robert Neale (1969), to mention only a few of many who have provided us with definitions of leisure.

In fact, defining leisure and justifying recreation became a popular pastime in itself among many of those who were preparing us for the leisure revolution. Nevertheless, it was the "free time" and "non-work" notions that prevailed—even in most academic departments of leisure studies and in most programs of community and church recreation.

The leisure "problem," therefore, became that of an abundance of free-time, a problem faced heretofore only by the incapacitated and the incarcerated. And the mission of leisure studies and recreation became that of helping individuals, families, communities, and congregations fill that "free time" with constructive activity.

The contemporary complaint about not enough free time is the direct result of society's acceptance of an inadequate conception of leisure—and, to some degree at least, the acquiescence of leaders in both recreation and religion to society's narrow expectations. Instead of turning to programs of recreation and religion for leisure experience, more and more Americans today are turning away from these programs in order to protect what they call their "leisure time." In many communities, the schools, churches, and community recreation programs are competing with each other for the loyalty and "free time" of their constituencies, often adding to; rather than relieving, frustration and stress. If there is a leisure "problem" among middle-class Americans today, it is certainly not "what are we going to do with all this free time' but rather "how do we choose between all the things we can do with such limited time."

The notions of "free time" and "non-work" subverted a "leisure revolution" at another crucial point, as well, by failing to account for time required for the development and enjoyment of leisure interests and the work of maintaining leisure implements. In other words, a "leisure revolution" has not only involved changes in the economics and sociology of production; it has inaugurated an era marked by the increasing importance of consumption—including the time and effort which must be expended in consumption. Since the early sixties, or roughly concurrent with the leisure revolution, it has been the consumption of goods and services, rather than their production, which has provided the driving force of the American economy. (American consumption has also been driving the economies of Japan and several Third-World Nations.)

For many Americans, leisure has become almost synonymous with consumption. Yet the operative conceptualizations of leisure, that is "free time" and "nonwork," fall far short of defining or describing either the economics or sociology of consumption. The paradox of the present situation is that many Americans are so preoccupied with the demands of their leisure activities, their leisure implements, and their leisure lifestyles that they are convinced that they have a shortage of leisure time.

There is a "leisure problem," to be sure, and it originates in a faulty definition of leisure—a definition which appeared to offer great opportunities for both religion and recreation. If a leisure revolution means simply that more and more people will have more and more "free time' what greater mandate, what higher mission, can there be than that of spending that free time in religious and recreational activity? But if the deeper meaning of a leisure revolution is that time is always precious—indeed, that time is life itself—will anyone really want to waste it in activities that merely distract them from what they deem to be the more important aspects of their lives?

The New "Worth-Ethic"

The emphasis upon "free time" definitions of leisure was greatly encouraged by an increasing disenchantment with work and mounting criticism of the traditional work ethic in many sectors of American society. Social scientists, for example, provided us with libraries of literature about the alienation, depersonalization, and other hazards of the industrial workplace. Popular literature and opinion polls indicated that more and more Americans were becoming more and more unhappy with their jobs.

But there was good news ahead! More and more work was being taken over by machines. The time and energy spent in working was steadily shrinking. By 1965, the standard work-week was calculated at between 35 and 37 hours—and by 1985 it would be down to 20 or perhaps even 15 hours! And many Americans would be able to retire at age 40 or 45 (O'Toole 1972).

In other words, there was widespread belief that work had lost most of its traditional human values—its role as a source of self-development, personal identity, and social organization—and was steadily yielding to technological advances. The human values which were once associated with work will henceforth be found in leisure. This transfer, of course, meant that leisure and recreation could no longer be just fun and games: they had to provide dignity and discipline for individuals, keep families happy and intact, and become the basis for community identity and spirit. A tall order for something seen as flimsy as "free time" or as fragile as "non-work"!

But instead of disappearing with advances in technology, work in America has steadily increased! More Americans are working than ever before and many of them are working more hours, days, and years than a decade ago. Furthermore, the "leisure revolution" has itself become a major generator of jobs. According to one study, for example, nearly 40 percent of all the new jobs which were created between 1965 and 1975 were related to leisure trends. Nearly 60 percent of new jobs filled by women and minorities were leisure-related (U.S. Department of Commerce 1977). In other words, instead of ushering in a period when Americans would be working less and less, the "leisure revolution" has Americans working more and more.

Numbers of jobs and workers, however, tell only part of the story. For our purposes, at least, the more significant changes have been in the quality of the work experience and the meanings and values for work which seem to be gaining among Americans.

There are several significant trends which are enhancing the work experience for many Americans. These include:

a. More flexible working schedules. More than 35 percent of all employed workers now have some sort of "flex-time" arrangement, allowing them some choice as to when they begin and finish their day's work. About one-fourth enjoy some variation of the traditional five-day week, enabling them to schedule larger blocks of time for other interests. About 8 percent are involved in job-sharing arrangements.

b. Perhaps the two most dramatic work trends of the past decade, however, are those of working at home and becoming an entrepreneur. Nearly three and a half million corporate workers perform most of their job functions right in their own homes, through the use of computers and other electronic equipment. Nearly five million have successfully launched their own businesses, and another five million or so are presently struggling with this option.

Not all workers would agree that these trends are positive—especially those who have been laid-off from high-wage manufacturing jobs or dislodged from comfortable corporate positions. Indeed, there is great anguish and uncertainty within the American work-force, but the overall trend represents a "revaluing" of work as a positive and liberating experience. The fact that much of this "re-valuing" has been involuntary, that is, brought on by massive dislocations in the work-force, does not nullify its long-term positive benefits to a post-industrial society.

c. Studies of workers 20 and 25 years ago reveal that most workers valued their jobs primarily for their material rewards—their rate of pay, their job security, their fringe benefits, and the retirement plan. The work itself was usually boring and meaningless. Often it was dangerous to the human body and deadening to the human spirit. Having a "good" job meant having one that paid well, not necessarily one that was important or enjoyable. Today, a "good" job is one in which a worker experiences his or her worth as a person.

Thanks to the trends that have been associated with a leisure revolution, Americans are exchanging the traditional work-ethic for a new and promising "worthethic."

Americans still expect to be paid well for their work, but other values have steadily gained in importance. Today's workers expect their jobs to offer self-esteem and opportunities for self-expression. For many, it is the sense of freedom and fulfillment, rather than just the paycheck that makes working worth the time and effort invested. In fact, more and more people are seeking careers into which they can pour as much of

themselves as possible—their time, their energy, their skills, their imagination—in expectation that there will be abundant payoffs beyond material
rewards.

According to Daniel Yankelovich (as cited in Harris and Trotter, 1989),
who has been monitoring American social trends for decades,

> the job is now the center of excitement in American lives. . . . Younger and
> better educated job-holders bring to the work place a new value system that
> emphasizes the expressive side. (33)

Ironically, the same generation that showed such disdain for the American work-ethic and work systems in its youth (and even sought to establish a "counterculture") are in its maturity, re-investing in work values with
an almost fanatic intensity. They value their leisure—perhaps more than
ever before—but the old notions about leisure as respite or escape from
working have become irrelevant. More often than not, leisure has become
an extension of work, part of a larger pattern of self-development and
fulfillment rather than an opportunity to pursue alternative pastimes.

There will be those who will claim that this re-investment in work values is merely a resurgence of the traditional work-ethic which has been a
powerful force in American character and culture for centuries. Certainly,
there is much continuity with that tradition—especially if there is some
recognition that the so-called "work-ethic" has had a variety of meanings
and shades of value throughout history.

In the context of a "leisure revolution," however, the new worth-ethic
represents a profound shifting of values. Instead of being considered in
juxtaposition, work and leisure must now be seen as complementary avenues to self-realization. No longer can it be said that work oppresses and
leisure liberates, or work rewards extrinsically while leisure rewards intrinsically, or work is what must be done for others while leisure is that which
we do for ourselves, or any of the other distinctions by which leisure was
often validated (especially by professionals in leisure services). In fact, no
longer can recreation be valued and marketed chiefly as an alternative, as
an antidote, to work! It must either find its meaning in support of the new
worth-ethic or risk being dismissed as irrelevant to careers of satisfaction
and success.

According to a Gallup Survey (Harris and Trotter 1989), 43 percent of
those who exercise regularly report that one of the chief reasons they do
so is to be more creative and energetic at work.

Twenty-five years ago, Americans were working in order to enjoy higher levels of leisure; today they are using their leisure to attain higher levels

of performance in their jobs.

In many ways, the worth-ethic is a culmination of the leisure trends identified earlier in this paper—especially the trend towards human liberation and increasing emphasis upon the value of personal freedom. A worth-ethic inspires men and women to offer themselves as whole persons to a prospective employer or contractor, instead of merely selling their time, labor, and skills. It also inspires them to expect more than just a position and a paycheck.

As T. George Harris and Robert Trotter put it, "the rising work ethic—the drive to perform at our best—is part of our rising expectations about ourselves. We've entered the age of the enhanced self" (1989, 33). Above all, the worth-ethic brings back into the workplace and the work systems many of the human factors, especially the creativity and serendipity of persons freely expressing themselves and fully relating to one another, that were systematically eliminated by automation, specialization and other forces of industrial progress. In other words, leisure no longer comes after, outside, and apart from work; it is in, with, and under the work itself.

The Failure of Theology and Ministry to Address Leisure

Both the institutional church and theology have failed to address leisure. Churches, by and large, at least mainline Protestant churches, have backed away from departments, programs, and models of leisure ministry and leisure service. The exceptions are the Southern Baptists and the Latter Day Saints which are the only major denominations that have concentrated efforts at the national and regional levels to promote recreation and leisure as parts of their ministry. The churches who were at the forefront of responding to the New Leisure in the 1950s and 1960s have all but abandoned the scene as far as leisure ministry is concerned. They are still providing camps, but the mainline denominations have become most competitive with schools and recreation departments for people in terms of recreation.

Christians and others have also, instead of doing the hard work of translating religious, theological, biblical, and other categories into spiritual experience, bought into pop psychology. Spiritual and religious life is often defined in terms of psychological categories of adjustment and self-fulfillment. Or we've divided the body of Christ into sociological categories: singles, elderly, couples, men, and women. Such categorization has only devastated the family. Sociological categories have become the way we have come to handle people. But I am not sure this is the best way as it makes family ministry as well as talking about the wholeness of the body of Christ much more difficult.

In terms of theology, we still equate the concept of calling with career and the concept of career with job even though we know better theologically and experientially. Calling is more than calling to a career, an occupation, or a job. It has not been the church, but the disruption and dislocation in the work scene that has helped us understand this. A person can't count on a single career, such as a doctor, plumber, minister, or teacher, anymore. A person must have a multiple career today. We need a calling which enables us to shift from one occupational field to another and still have a sense of wholeness, accountability, and calling in the Christian sense. But where are we providing ministry to those who are in transition—those who are losing their jobs or are in the midst of career shifts or abrupt change?

When discussing stewardship, we are still talking in terms of subduing the earth—the production of material wealth and the exploitative use of nature instead of living in harmony with nature; it's an exploitative ethic which operates unchallenged. Yet, we are seeing in what is happening to people, the environment, and the third world, the perils of this approach. One of these days we will pay the price for this. Before that day we need to re-orientate our theological approach to many of these things. Some re-orientation is taking place. But the churches are not in the forefront. It is happening out there in the secular society and through some of the New Age movement.

Protestantism is still afraid of the four S's: Sexuality, Sensuality, Silence, and Solitude. If we look at society and where people really are, we would realize that an enlightened understanding of leisure can provide ministry and meaning. The church hasn't yet learned to address the four S's in an effective way. We're uncomfortable with addressing the issues of sexuality such as the big issues of the ordination of women and homosexuality. We are nervous about sensuality which involves sexuality, enjoyment, and pleasure. If it feels good, we think it must be sinful. Silence and solitude are hard to come by. The four S's are rich territory for leisure and leisure understanding. They are waiting there for us to address theologically and programmatically.

We are also still defending the traditional family. We admit that the nuclear family is not there anymore; but in terms of the church's priorities, ideas, and wishes, the church wants to put us all back together again in the nuclear family if it could. We idealize the nuclear family as the model from the Garden of Eden, but the story of the Garden of Eden suggests it wasn't such a good family.

We are still impoverished aesthetically: our architecture is functional; our art is representational, moral art. We haven't developed an aesthetic appreciation.

We are still caught up in the chronic American religious phenomenon of primitivism. We would really like to go back to the Bible. We would really like somehow to extract those universal principles, those few simple truths from the Bible and apply them to today, to put them on and live by them, despite the differences between the prevailing worldview of the biblical period in comparison to our own. We are all doing it; we attempt to extract those truths from scripture and attempt to relate them to life today. There is nothing wrong with it. I don't mean to discount it. It is a valid way to do theology, but it is not the only way. We haven't developed, explored those other ways. We need to do that.

Work and leisure are not distinct; they lie on a continuum. The concept that I am working with now and trying to develop is "Worcreation." I'm trying to fill this concept with three components. I define leisure today as worcreation, which is a combination of work, worship, and recreation. Leisure is being able to combine work, worship, and recreation in a free and loving, holistic way which integrates these three elements as much as possible. Although a person goes to different places to perform different functions, leisure lies in integrating these three aspects in order to experience wholeness in one's life, family, and community.

We shouldn't concentrate on analyzing the differences between work, worship, and recreation, but on affirming the continuum. Working, recreating, and worshipping are all different aspects of the same thing. The same person is doing the same thing in an ideal and optimal state. When I can experience wholeness, the integration, the interrelationships, the continuum between my work (the things I have to do), recreation (the things I do because I don't have to) and worship (the things I do because of my relationship with God), then I am at leisure and I can experience the freedom I have as a Christian. I am allowed to experience, to express, to contribute, to receive from the life, the world, and the gifts God has given me. When we define recreation in this setting, it is not so much an alternative to work and labor, but rather my appropriate response to God. We have to transcend the dichotomy between work and recreation. If we define or juxtapose recreation with work we are in trouble.

My appropriate response to God involves, first, a profound sense of gratefulness and, second, self-transcendence. A profound sense of gratefulness involves gratitude for creation, redemption, life, health, skill, and opportunity. It is a response of Thank-You. Expressions of gratitude include Celebration (exuberance, joy); Reverence (relationships with others, loved ones, neighbors, and the environment); and Remembrance (a sense of direction and being part of history, culture, and art, as opposed to just being an atom).

Self-transcendence, first, involves going one step past Maslow's self-actualization. It involves going beyond one's individual needs, quirks, and complaints in order to establish harmony with others and the natural world. In this process one does not lose one's individuality, but one's individuality is transcended for the sake of meeting and integrating with those around so that the whole becomes more than the sum of the parts as in an orchestra or choir. Second, self-transcendence involves hospitality which is sharing with those in need, as well as sharing in the life of the cosmos and the world. It involves giving back to nature through nurture and affirmation, as well as taking from nature. Through service an individual is relating everything one is, wants to be, and is able to be with everything in the world.

In conclusion, leisure is freedom, opportunity, and possibility. In Calvinist terms, it is the mandate to extend the Lordship, in terms of freedom in Christ, to everything I'm doing in creation and what creation is doing in me. Christians, including church leaders and theologians, need to do the hard work of helping people apply the spiritual values of both creation and freedom in Christ to their leisure experiences.

References

Brightbill, C. 1961. *Man and leisure: A philosophy of recreation.* Englewood Cliff, NJ: Prentice Hall.

Brightbill, C. 1966. *Educating for leisure-centered living.* Harrisburg, PA: Stackpole Books.

Dahl, G. 1972. *Work, play and worship in a leisure-oriented society.* Minneapolis: Augsburg Publishing House.

de Grazia, S. 1962. *Of time, work and leisure.* Garden City, NY: Doubleday.

Dumazedier, J. 1962. *Toward a society of leisure.* New York: Free Press.

Gibbs, N. 1989. How America has run out of time, *Time* (April) 58–67.

Harris, T.G., and Trotter, R. 1989. Work smarter, not harder. *Psychology Today* 23 (2): 33.

Kaplan, M. 1975. *Leisure: Theory and policy.* New York: John Wiley and Sons.

Lee, R. 1964. *Religion and leisure in America.* New York: Abingdon Press.

Neale, R. 1969. *In praise of play.* New York: Harper and Row.

Neumeyer, M., and Neumeyer, E. 1958. *Leisure and recreation.* New York: Ronald Press.

Neulinger, J. 1981. *To leisure: An introduction.* Boston: Allyn and Bacon.

O'Toole, J. 1972. *Work in America.* Cambridge: MIT Press.

Pieper, J. 1952. *Leisure: The basis of culture.* New York: New American Library.

Robinson, J. 1989. University of Maryland Time Use Study Project cited by *Minneapolis Star-Tribune.* July 7.

U.S. Department of Commerce. 1977. *Summary Reports.*

Yankelovich, D. 1989. *Psychology Today* (March) 33.

Chapter Seven

Leisure and the New Age Movement: New Challenges for Christians

GLEN VAN ANDEL

"What's gone wrong with the children?" asks Dr. Carolyn Vash, a senior research associate at the Human Interaction Research Institute, during a keynote address at the National Recreation and Park Association Congress in San Antonio. "Our children are killing themselves and others; they use drugs and act out sexually and defy authority." Why? "Because our society has lost the sense of meaning and purpose," is Dr. Vash's response. Adolescents, she reports, no longer embrace a value system that was once right but has gone wrong and "is getting wronger by the minute." Our contemporary values are inadequate because they are based on erroneous working assumptions of science which hold that truth can only be discovered through observations of the material world. Thus, contemporary science has focused our attention on the "how" of life and has virtually ignored the metaphysical questions of "why." She adds that many religious doctrines on cosmology have been shown to conflict with scientific knowledge about the material world which has caused an increased interest in the Eastern religions which emphasize a nonmaterialistic or mystical view of the universe. Materialist science is ending, Vash predicts, because the spiritual questions that seek meaning and purpose from life cannot be answered by the mechanistic, deterministic, and reductionistic methods of modem science. By implication, contemporary religions that have been influenced and shaped by Western thinking are also inadequate to address these basic problems. Given this scenario, she proceeds to outline a worldview which suggests that everything in the universe can be explained by the phenomenon of "conscious energy" or "energetic consciousness." The post-modem working assumption of this philosophy is the primacy of consciousness.

Dr. Vash's pronouncement of this new worldview is only one of several voices in the field of recreation and leisure studies. An article published in

National Recreation and Park Association monograph, *Philosophy of Therapeutic Recreation: Ideas and Issues*, suggests that the New Age consciousness movement allows us to create a new structure for society that is flexible and interactive at all levels of the universe (Howe-Murphy and Murphy 1987). The authors claim that this new paradigm allows the leisure field to address problematic nonmaterialistic issues such as explaining the nature of a recreation experience and its effect on the individual.

Likewise, articles in *Therapeutic Recreation Journal* (McDowell 1986; Halberg and Howe-Murphy 1985) have called for modifications in the therapeutic recreation profession to accommodate the "restructuring of American society." Of particular interest is the profession's relationship to the holistic health service delivery model that emphasizes the integration of the mind, body, and spirit. Modem reductionistic medicine tends to separate the body into parts and views disease as a mechanistic malfunction that is treated as an isolated component. In contrast, holistic health care promotes the "treatment of the whole person, helping the person bring mental, emotional, physical, social, and spiritual dimensions of his/her being into greater harmony" (Otto and Knight 1979, 3).

From these examples and others (see also Howe-Murphy and Charboneau 1987; McDowell 1983), it becomes clear that proponents of the New Age movement are seeking to bring their view of the world to the recreation and leisure field. The intent of this paper is to identify the key characteristics of the movement, critique its philosophy and practices, and determine what we can learn from New Agers. The paper will also identify major New Age themes articulated in the recreation and leisure literature and provide an alternative response from a Christian worldview.

The Nature and Scope of the New Age Movement

With best-selling books like *Dancing in the Light* (MacLame, 1985) and *The Aquarian Conspiracy* (Ferguson, 1980) leading the way, the New Age movement has thrust itself on contemporary society. According to Ferguson, one of the primary cheerleaders for the movement, the impact has been significant.

> Broader than reform, deeper than revolution, this benign conspiracy for a new human agenda has triggered the most rapid cultural realignment in history. The great shuddering, irrevocable shift overtaking us is not a new political, religious, or philosophical system. It is a new mind—the ascendance of a startling worldview that gathers into its framework breakthrough science and insights from earliest recorded thought. (23)

Fueled by the latest discoveries of quantum physics in modern science and the writings of ancient mystics of Eastern religions, the movement has emerged from a coalition of like-minded people, groups, and organizations who embrace similar spiritual and social changes that they allege will ultimately result in self-actualized individuals who share a global and cosmic unity with all reality.

Claiming the failure of contemporary Western philosophies, including traditional Christianity and Secular Humanism, New Agers seek to provide new answers to contemporary problems. Moralism and materialism are bankrupt and must be replaced with a system of beliefs that promises greater understanding of the deep truths we all seek, truth and meaning that cannot be found through what they perceive to be philosophies steeped in religious dogmatism and determinism or scientific rationalism and reductionism.

At the core of much of this reaction is their disenchantment with Platonic dualism, the belief that all reality is separated into two kinds of being, physical and spiritual. Human beings, according to Plato, serve to connect these two spheres through our physical bodies and our spiritually-based souls. New Agers rightly conclude that conceptualizing the world in this way has contributed to distortions and in many cases the disintegration of human interactions, ecological systems, and religious teachings. Further, Platonic dualism has distorted how we view our work, our play, and our worship. Dahl confirms this perspective when he concludes, "We've become a people who worship our work, work at our play, and play at our worship" (1972, 12). Dualistic thinking effectively separates rather than integrates all forms of material and nonmaterial matter and thus contributes to social, political, ecological, psychological, and spiritual dysfunction. Since so much of our culture is predicated on dualistic systems of thought, New Age advocates are calling for a new way of conceptualizing the universe.

Basic Tenets of the New Age

Although the disenchantment with contemporary systems of thought is a common theme among New Age adherents, there is great diversity in their views of how these problems might be resolved. This makes it difficult to identify specific principles that could be embraced by all. However, Douglas Groothuis (1988; 1986), an evangelical Christian author of two books and numerous articles on the New Age, has suggested that there are at least eight basic tenets that are commonly held by New Agers.

1. Probably the most widely held belief and the one that addresses the dualism problem is that all reality is interrelated and interdependent. There is no perceived difference between persons and matter, good and evil, light and darkness—all is one. As physicist and philosopher Fritjof Capra claims, "The ultimate state of consciousness is one "in which all boundaries and dualisms have been transcended and all individuality dissolves into universal, undifferentiated oneness" (1982, 371). Using the work of general systems theory, which views the whole as greater than the sum of its parts, Capra attributes consciousness to everything in the universe, thus linking it all together.

2. A closely related belief is that all is God. All things become part of a divine reality and as such assume perfection. This pantheistic notion is nicely summarized by Shirley MacLaine who says, "I *know* that I exist, therefore I AM. I know the god-source exists. Therefore IT IS. Since I am part of that force, then I AM that I AM" (MacLaine 1985, 420). The god of Shirley MacLaine and of the New Age is an amoral, impersonal energy force that exists in all things.

3. If God exists in all things then it follows that we are all gods. If we have a limitation it is due to our own ignorance. Our primary goal is "to awaken to the god who sleeps at the root of the human being" (Roszak 1977, 225).

4. If we are to achieve this goal and thus realize the "Higher Self," we must be enlightened by new insights and understanding that will reshape how we perceive ourselves and the world around us. We need to achieve a new level of consciousness that will allow us to truly experience the spiritual power and energy we need to realize our unlimited potential. Groothuis notes that New Agers believe, "Western Culture has shaped our consciousness, trimming our experience and taming our metaphysics. We remain content with the everyday illusions of human limitation and finitude" (1986, 22). A variety of consciousness-raising techniques and strategies such as meditation, yoga, self-hypnosis, and biofeedback are used to free and transform consciousness to attain "at-one-ment" or "self-realization."

5. Since the essence of all religion is to be found within each person, there are many ways to discover truth. Christ is one of many sages who may lead us to the divinity in us all. Cosmic unity requires that all uniqueness of doctrine or the "externals of religion" be ignored and integrated into one common truth. Thus all religions become one (syncretism).

6. Many years ago Julian Huxley established another important tenet that has been adopted by New Agers when he asserted that "man is that part of reality in which and through which the cosmic process has become conscious and has begun to comprehend itself. His supreme task is to increase that conscious comprehension and to apply it as fully as possible to guide the course of events" (1959, 236). Such evolutionary optimism, New Agers declare, cannot be expected to arise out of a contemporary Western worldview that has in fact contributed to the global problems we are experiencing. Rather, they call for a change in consciousness that will result in "spiritual futurism" (Hubbard 1982, 157). That is, as we recognize that we have the "Messiah within" we can be empowered to create a new view of reality that will radically transform every aspect of the universe. Cosmic evolutionary optimism is the great hope for the New Age.

7. Since we are all gods and "all reality is one," we do not live under any objective moral law. There can be no good or bad and therefore no sin in a world that is a unified conscious whole. Rather, "every vile and wretched thing you do broadens your understanding . . . . If you want to do any one thing regardless of what it is, it would not be wise to go against that feeling; for there is an experience awaiting you and a grand adventure that will make your life sweeter" (Gardner 1987, 18). Evil to the New Ager is only that which keeps us from achieving cosmic unity.

8. There is widespread acceptance among New Agers toward the practice of contact with other spirits through mediums or "channelers." Getting in touch with our collective consciousness allows the person to achieve a "higher" level of spirituality and oneness with the One.

Although these tenets are generally accepted by New Agers, they are seldom explicitly stated in the professional literature. Therefore, it is not always clear to the reader what underlying assumptions the writer is using in his or her presentation. Discernment of the New Age worldview influence on a particular area of life, such as a professional discipline, requires some understanding of the key principles and a recognition of how these principles might be applied to a field of study.

But we in the Christian community need to do more than simply increase our awareness and understanding of this movement. We also need to consider how we should respond to this new worldview that seems bent on transforming all of our traditional values and beliefs and establishing a virtual utopia on earth. John Cooper, professor at Calvin Seminary, states,

> From a Christian point of view, it would be easy to critique and quickly reject a worldview that seems so unbiblical. It relativizes Jesus Christ, promotes self-salvation, denies the personal nature of God, erases the Creator-creature distinction, denies a stable creation order, removes the difference between good and evil, lacks abiding moral order and in a hundred other ways directly contradicts truths essential to biblical Christianity. (1987, 302)

But before we reject this philosophy out of hand it may be useful to analyze what makes the New Age worldview so attractive to our contemporaries. Richard Mouw, in his book *Distorted Truth*, makes the point that assessing non-Christian thought with a rather single-minded focus on truth is at times counter-productive. "Paradoxically, this fixation on the truth often leads to many untruths. By issuing a dogmatic pronouncement about a specific 'ism' Christian people regularly miss much of what is going on in the pattern of thought and action that the 'ism' represents" (1989, 7).

Similarly, Donald Cronkite suggests that there is much for us to learn from New Agers. He relates an experience he and his family had at Chaco Canyon the day after some fifteen hundred people had gathered to celebrate the Harmonic Convergence and usher in the beginning of new age. He observed that

> any fair person . . . would have had to say about those devotees of the New Age, "See how they love one another!". . . I wonder what the church is going to do with the New Age movement in the years to come. Will we listen at all and try to learn? They have something to teach us about being open, and we probably have something to teach them about being too open. They have something to teach us about emotion, and we have something to teach them about careful thinking. We have a common concern for love and justice and peace and harmony, and surely, if we aren't too defensive about competing for adherents, we can help each other.

> If nothing else we need to look long and hard at ourselves and wonder why so many bright and eager seekers are going elsewhere. (1987, 7)

Mouw suggests that one way to understand these seekers is to examine their hopes and fears and trustings. He describes hopes and fears as the driving forces of the human spirit while trustings are the steering mechanism that guide our choices. If we analyze the tenants of the New Age Movement from this perspective, we gain valuable insight into the seekers of the "One."

The Hopes and Fears of New Agers

What are the hopes and fears that might lead to endorsing the undifferentiated unity of all reality? First, this perspective is really a slightly distorted version of what God really wants for us and thus what we want for ourselves. God's original intent in creation was a world centered in Him where harmony and love were the norm. Christ also prayed that we might be united as one even as the Godhead is one (See John 17). The message of the Gospel to which we subscribe is toward redeeming and reclaiming the broken world for God and restoring wholeness to all of creation. The New Age movement has the right idea but has subscribed to a counterfeit version of how this unity is to come about.

The movement may also be attractive to some because it addresses the fallacies of reductionist thinking of scientific humanism. All reality for the humanist can be fully described and interpreted as a natural process, the core of which is the atom. In a world where people have been encouraged to narcissistically "find yourself' or to "do your own thing," many feel alienated and lonely. The "new physics" (Capra) seeks to connect rather than separate, to bring people and the cosmos together into a unified whole, as in a "cosmic dance." The obvious hope is to create, through a higher level of consciousness, a new order of reality that joins all things together into an integrated and synchronized whole: a cosmic order where there is peace and harmony, love for one another, and the integration of the ecological system in which we live. If we think about it, it's really a hope not unlike our own in which we long for a new unified heaven and earth.

Another fear is that such a new world order will not happen unless we all become involved in the process of creating and designing it, thus becoming creators of a new universe. Such a task cannot be left to a distant and rigid God but must be actively pursued by all creatures. The secular humanists chose to eliminate God and replace him with science; the New Agers choose to promote all of creation to become gods. "Rather than secularizing the divine, the New Age movement would 'divinize' the secular" (Mouw 1989, 78).

The inclusion of the occult in the New Age movement has been a source of enchantment for some in an otherwise bland and boring world, a world that has been meticulously described and explained by scientists in a technological culture that leaves nothing to the imagination. The occult also provides for a unique form of trusting in a secularized culture that "no longer fears God [but paradoxically] fears everything in the world"

(Mouw 1989, 106). By adopting a spiritual leader as a "guide" we are no longer alone, left to fend for ourselves in an unpredictable world. Thus the occult provides the source of faith and hope for a spiritless, secularized society.

Thus, we must realize that advocates of the New Age paradigm, including leisure professionals, are honestly seeking to understand basic questions about human nature and the world in which we live. Of particular interest is the attempt to explain the nature of a leisure experience.

The New Age and the Leisure Profession

The Nature of the Leisure Experience

As might be expected, New Age-oriented leisure professionals promote the awareness, acceptance, and understanding of the spiritual or existential dimension of the leisure experience. They argue that the metaphysical nature of the New Age paradigm appears to be more conducive to explaining the illusive nature of the leisure experience. The ultimate leisure experiences are often characterized as having mystical or spiritual qualities often described as "peak" or "flow" experiences. New Agers suggest that a genuine leisure experience emanates a feeling of oneness with the universe, a feeling of being connected to all else, a sense of being connected with oneself and a sense of "waking up" out of the usual slumber to see a glimmer of what is true. Unfortunately, according to New Age proponents Howe-Murphy and Murphy, the Newtonian paradigm tends to focus attention on the external, material world and therefore leisure researchers fail to recognize inter-relationships with the spiritual domain. Conversely, the New Age paradigm recognizes that the inner world and spirituality are central in determining the nature, direction, and meaning of our individual lives. They add, "Spirituality connects us with the essence of ourselves and with the power of the universe. For those who accept and nurture their spirituality, it is the key to having a fulfilling life" (Howe-Murphy and Murphy 1987, 45).

McDowell, well-known for his work in leisure counseling, develops a similar comparison between leisure viewed from a traditional dualist perspective and that of the New Age.

> I strongly believe there is a difference between a worldly style of leisure and one filled with a deep sense of spirit (and I'm not talking religion here!). We risk leisure pathology in our clients and ourselves if we believe leisure can

only be bought, planned, scheduled, earned, put into a timeframe, consumed, experienced on the physical or mental plane of our ego. Leisure wellness must include the awareness and expression of one's sense of spirit. . . . The greatest challenge of the leisure profession as a whole, and therapeutic recreators specifically, is to know this spirit well. Plan to touch this spirit at will, embracing it within your bodymind. Do anything you can to discover it deeply within yourself and your clients and to arouse its energy. What you will discover is that this spirit is the life force energy behind the hope and will that heals and keeps one well. It is what makes leisure Leisure, not as something you do, but as something you feel deeply inside. (1986, 37)

To their credit these authors recognize the superficial and utterly futile state of a "worldly style of leisure." Their solution is to engage a new source of energy that will enable us to achieve ultimate leisure satisfaction, wholeness, and freedom. In fact, McDowell suggests that as helping professionals, we must first begin to mend our clients' broken spirit before we can hope to mend their broken body or mind. The "spirit" being referred to is the divine within us or what Roszak (1977) called, "the god who sleeps at the root of the human being" and is the source of all power.

As a Christian leisure professional, I share the assessment of my New Age friends as they denounce the bankruptcy of the leisure experience in a godless, narcissistic, materialistic culture. I also agree that much of our professional literature has not recognized or considered the spiritual dimension of the human being and its implications for understanding the potential impact of a leisure experience on the whole person—body, mind, and spirit. This omission has been the result of a pervasive secular humanistic philosophy in the leisure field that has ignored or denied the spiritual component in all aspects of life. The New Age movement is attempting to recover this essential element of our nature, distorted as this effort may be.

Although there has not been much recognition of spirituality in the professional literature, the Christian community has continued to develop this theme from a number of different perspectives. Many of these works were reviewed by Sylvester, who documents how, throughout the twentieth century, the element of free choice in play, leisure, and recreation has been associated with the ultimate purpose or end in life, both as a means to achieve that purpose or as a significant element of the ultimate end (1987, 177–188).

More specifically, Christian authors such as Joseph Pieper, Arthur Holmes, and Gordon Dahl have called us to strengthen our commitment to live life meaningfully, every minute; reevaluating the existential dimension of our play and leisure attitudes. In his classic book, *Leisure: The Basis of Culture,* Pieper states,

> Leisure... is a mental and spiritual attitude. ... It is, in the first place, an attitude of mind, a condition of the soul. ... Leisure is a form of silence, of that silence which is the prerequisite of the apprehension of reality; only the silent hear and those who do not remain silent do not hear. ... For leisure is a receptive attitude of mind, a contemplative attitude, and it is not only the occasion but also the capacity for steeping oneself in the whole of creation. (1964, 40–41)

Arthur Holmes and Gordon Dahl speak of the attitude of play as a product of a harmonious and right relationship with God. It is in this relationship that we find true freedom, the basis for our ultimate rest and leisure. It is this relationship that empowers us to live fulfilling and satisfying lives.

Holistic Health

As noted earlier in this paper, New Agers have also emphasized the construct of holistic health and wellness which includes nutritional awareness, physical fitness, stress management, environmental sensitivity, and self-responsibility (Ardell 1981). Wellness is a measure of how we are taking care of ourselves in an attempt to integrate our lifestyle needs/conditions with the environment we face (McDowell, 30).

Central to the holistic health movement is the concept of wellness, defined as the "optimal functioning, balance and integration among the physical, mental, emotional, and spiritual aspects of the individual within a supportive personal, social, and physical environment" (Howe-Murphy 1986, 24). Although the holistic health movement is an eclectic combination of concepts and techniques, at its root is the consciousness paradigm that seeks to bring cosmic unity and wholeness through personal empowerment. Individuals are taught to integrate these determinants of wellness into their lifestyle in order to achieve optimum health and function. Health in this context is more than the absence of disease. Leonard (1987) notes,

> The conventional physician considers a person well if he has no symptoms and falls within the normal range in a series of diagnostic tests. Yet, this "well" person might smoke heavily, take no exercise, eat a bland, sweet, starch diet, and impress all who meet him as glum, anti-social, and emotionally repressed. To a New Age practitioner, such a person is quite sick, the carrier of what biologist Rene' Dubos calls "submerged potential illness." In the New Medicine, the absence of overt disease is only the starting point, beyond which a whole world

of good health beckons. (Reisser, Reisser, and Weldon 1987, 16, 81)

Leisure professionals have promoted wellness and holistic health through leisure counseling and therapeutic/rehabilitation programs. Clients are challenged to care for themselves and take responsibility for actions and choices that will move them toward complete integration of consciousness of the body-mind and spirit and ultimately high level wellness. Allowing individuals opportunities for becoming aware of their physical, emotional, mental, and spiritual selves through involvement in recreation activities is a key role for therapeutic recreators in the New Age paradigm. It is through this process that clients are encouraged to learn to accept and love themselves which is central to the New Age concept of living a balanced lifestyle. According to some New Agers, the role of the therapist may become that of a "therapeutic spiritual guide." In such a capacity the therapist calls upon intuition and is concerned primarily with the discovery of the inner self.

Healing and ultimate wellness is understood to evolve from the client's mind/body/spirit interaction within a supportive, interactive, and expansive environment. The guide assists in reducing stress, guiding in assessing and discovering personal capabilities, encouraging the development of self-confidence, self-esteem, and a positive mental attitude, and generally creating an environment conducive to well-being and personal expression. Of special interest to the therapeutic recreator is the balance between work and leisure and how that might contribute to healing.

For the Christian, wellness involves the integration of life around the principles of God's Word and opening ourselves to the Lordship and presence of Jesus Christ. Much of what is promoted as New Age medicine has a counterpart in God's plan for our lives. Anxiety and worry are addressed by Christ in the beatitudes (Matthew 6:25–27). Living under the control of the Spirit brings such gifts as love, joy, and peace. Other moral, social, and economic guidelines are similar to those found in New Age literature urging followers to practice compassion and empathy, to serve and love others, and to care for the earth.

Wellness, to the Christian, does not promise perfect harmony and health and wholeness indefinitely. We recognize that we live in a fallen world where all of creation "groans" under the weight and circumstance of sin. We are called to bring light, to restore, to reclaim the world from the ravages of sin and bring it back into a harmonious relationship with God as we join with Jesus Christ and become his hands, his feet, his eyes, his ears, and his mouth in a needy world. As Christian helpers, we show compassion; endorse each person as an image bearer of God having worth and value irrespective of status, health, sex, or any other condition; and recognize that the ultimate and most important need shared by all humans is that of the spiritual relationship with the Creator of the universe. When our sins are forgiven through the death of Christ on the cross, we are truly made well and are once again whole.

An Environmental Ethic

A final New Age theme that we will discuss is the need to promote an environmental ethic. Since New Agers view all the cosmos as being part of a whole and having divine status (panthesim), their concern for the environment is strong to say the least. At the same time, their perception of Christian stewardship is associated with the view that the Christian religion is shaped in large part by Platonic dualism and Newtonian reductionism which has caused the present ecological crisis. The mechanistic separation of human beings from their environment has contributed to impoverishing, exploiting, polluting, and destroying the environment (Howe-Murphy and Murphy, 50).

As Christians we must applaud the efforts of our "enlightened" New Age friends to reclaim and restore the earth for its intended purpose. However, such actions should stimulate us to develop, interpret and promote a biblically based environmental ethic that will provide a foundation for the Christian community to take a leadership role. Unfortunately, as Wilkinson noted, the environmental issue was one of those many issues that has been initiated in large part by those outside the Christian community. This underscores the fact that we have done little to place the message of the Gospel in terms of our own culture (1987, 27).

Conclusion

The Christian community has much to offer seekers and proponents of the New Age. But if we are to be effective, we must rethink previous assumptions and in some cases break new ground to discover the relevancy of Scripture to contemporary cultural and professional issues. Wilkinson suggests that when we come to the living Word of God with new questions,

> we may find in it new answers—a process that causes us to reflect not only on the nature of interpretation and of knowledge itself, but also on Christian teaching about the illuminating and comforting Spirit of God, which, Jesus promises, will guide the church into all truth. Nevertheless, clarity and honesty

alike demand that we acknowledge the cultural framework of this current re-questioning—which in many ways is a reinterpretation—of Scripture. (Wilkinson 1987, 28)

Only then can we begin to provide answers that will satisfy the hopes and fears of those who seek to fill the void in their lives with the "One." And only then will we be able to respond appropriately to those who ask, "What's gone wrong with the children?"

References

Ardell, D. B. 1986. *High level wellness.* Berkeley, CA: Ten Speed Press.

Capra, F. 1982. *The turning point.* New York: Simon and Schuster.

Cooper, J. 1987. Testing the spirit of the Age of Aquarius: The New Age Movement. *Calvin Theological Journal,* 295–305.

Cronkite, D. 1987. Love among ruins. *The Reformed Journal.* September 7, 6–7.

Dahl, G. 1972. *Work, play and worship in a leisure oriented society.* Minneapolis: Augsburg Press.

Ferguson, M. 1980. *The Aquarian conspiracy.* Boston: J.P. Tarcher.

Gardner, M. 1987. Issness is her business. *New York Review.* April 19.

Groothuis, D. 1988. *Confronting the New Age.* Downers Grove: InterVarsity.

Groothuis, D. 1986. *Unmasking the New Age.* Downers Grove: InterVarsity.

Halberg, K., and Howe-Murphy, R. 1985. The dilemma of an unresolved philosophy in the therapeutic recreation. *Therapeutic Recreation Journal* 19 (3): 7–15.

Hansel, T. 1979. *When I relax I feel guilty.* Elgin, IL: D. C. Cook.

Howe-Murphy, R. and Murphy, J. 1987. An exploration of the New Age consciousness paradigm in therapeutic recreation. In *Philosophy of therapeutic recreation* edited by C. Sylvester, 41–54. Alexandria, VA: National Recreation and Park Association.

Howe-Murphy, R., 1986. Guest editor's note. *Therapeutic Recreation Journal* 20 (2): 24–38.

Hubbard, B.M. 1982. *The evolutionary journey.* San Francisco: Evolutionary Press.

Huxley, J. 1959. *Religion without revelation.* London: Max Parrish.

MacLaine, S. 1985. *Dancing in the light.* New York: Bantom.

McDowell, C.F. 1983. *Leisure wellness: Concepts and helping strategies.* Eugene, OR: Sun Moon Press.

McDowell, C.F. 1986. Wellness and therapeutic recreation: Challenges for service. *Therapeutic Recreation Journal* 20(2): 27–38.

Mouw, R. 1989. *Distorted truth: What every Christian needs to know about the battle for the mind.* New York: Harper and Row.

Otto, H., and Knight, J., eds. 1979. *Dimensions on wholistic healing: New frontiers in the treatment of the whole person.* Chicago: Nelson-Hall.

Pieper, J. 1964. *Leisure: The basis of culture.* New York: Random House, Pantheon Books.

Reisser, P.C., Reisser, T.K., and Weldon, J. 1987. *New Age medicine: A Christian perspective on holistic health.* Downers Grove: InterVarsity.

Roszak, T. 1977. *Unfinished animal.* New York: Harper and Row.

Sylvester, C. 1987. The ethics of play, leisure, and recreation in the twentieth century, 1900–1983. *Leisure Sciences* 9, 173–188.

Wilkinson, L. 1987. New Age, new consciousness, and the new creation. In *Tending the garden: Essays on the Gospel and the Earth,* edited by W. Granberg-Michaelson, 6–29. Grand Rapids: Eerdmans.

Chapter Eight

Contemplative Leisure Within Christian Spirituality

JOSEPH D. TEAFF

The Western and Christian conception of the contemplative life is closely linked to the Aristotelian notion of leisure. Leisure in Greek is "skole," and in Latin "schola," the English word "school." The word used to designate the place where we learn is derived from a word which means leisure. The Septuagint version of Psalm 46:10, "Have leisure and know that I am God," begins with the Greek "skolasate." What, then, is the mode and manner of the mind's spiritual knowledge that allows humans through leisure to know God?

The process of knowing, according to Greeks such as Aristotle and Plato, as well as medieval thinkers, is the action of *ratio* and *intellectus* working together. Ratio is the power of discursive, logical thought that involves searching, examining, abstracting, defining, and drawing conclusions. On the other hand, intellectus is spiritual knowledge that includes elements of receptive contemplation, effortless awareness, and purely receptive vision.

Discursive thought (*ratio*) and intellectual contemplation (*intellectus*) are related not only as activity to receptivity, or tense effort to passive acceptance, but also as toil and trouble to effortless possession. Antisthenes the Cynic, one of Plato's companions, viewed Hercules as the human ideal because he performed superhuman labors. Kant, who spoke of philosophizing as "herculean labor," viewed "intellectual contemplation" as costing nothing and as such is questionable. Thomas Aquinas, in the *Summa Theologica*, states that "the essence of virtue consists in the good rather than the difficult" and "not everything that is more difficult is necessarily more meritorious." Aquinas contended that the highest form of knowledge comes to humans effortlessly and without trouble like a gift (that is, sudden illumination, a stroke of genius, true contemplation).

The value placed upon intellectual work can be traced to two prin-cipal themes: 1) The view that regards human knowledge as attributed exclusively to discursive thought, and 2) the notion that the effort which knowledge requires is a criterion of its truth. The exaggerated value placed upon hard work appears to be based upon humanity's mistrust of everything that is effortless since a human can only enjoy, with good con-science, what has been acquired with toil and trouble; and human refusal to accept anything as a gift. If to know is to work, then *our knowledge is the fruit of our unaided activity and effort, so it would follow that knowledge includes nothing which is not due to human effort, and there is nothing gratuitous* about it, nothing inspired, nothing given about it.

The Christian understanding of God's relationship to humanity de-pends upon the existence of gift, that is, "Grace." The Holy Spirit is Him-self called a "gift" in a special sense. God is not only just but is loving, and everything claimed follows upon something given graciously and un-earned to humanity. In the beginning there is always a gift.

Leisure and Christian Spirituality

A fundamental theme of Christian spirituality involves the tension be-tween an active doing and a passive experience of being for its own sake. For the Type-A personality, who is accustomed to self-definition based on an incessant stream of accomplishments, a vague or undefined sense of non-goal-directed being can offer a different kind of challenge. For the person who has experienced religion primarily as a series of rituals or exercises, the passive experience of transcendence can offer a new and different form of religious experience. This notion of the receptive experience of a Transcendent Other has sometimes led to accusations of laziness or quietism associated with contemplation, when in fact the au-thentic experience of a creative, inspired passivity allows a person to meet the demands of the Christian life more fully.

How is the Christian to understand leisure? For some, leisure is an-other word for laziness, idleness, and sloth (*acedia*). In the Middle Ages, however, it was understood that *acedia* meant that a human did not give the consent of one's own being. Idleness, in the medieval view, meant renouncing the claim implicit in one's human dignity, that is, the divine goodness immanent in oneself: a person does not want to be as God wishes one to be and does not wish to be what one fundamentally is. Leisure is only possible when a human is at one with oneself, when one accepts one's own being as a gift from a loving God, and one's acceptance of the world as gift.

True Christian spirituality can flourish only in a climate of leisure. If our whole life is occupied with working, competing, earning and similar activities, there will be little time to welcome the new, the unexpected, the strange, the surprising. What then is leisure? According to Pieper, leisure "is a mental and spiritual attitude"; it is "an attitude of mind, a condition of the soul" (1963, 40). Leisure "is a form of silence, of that silence which is the prerequisite of the apprehension of reality. . . it means more nearly that the soul's power to 'answer' to the reality of the world is left undisturbed" (41).

Pieper notes that leisure affords opportunities for being steeped in creation. Nature itself is one of the best teachers of silence and stillness. Thomas Merton expresses this when he writes of the "virgin point" between darkness and dawn when "creation in its innocence asks permission to 'be' once again, as it did the first morning that ever was" (1966, 131). How different, Merton remarks, is human wisdom, for

> we know the time and dictate the terms. We are in a position to dictate the terms, we suppose: we have a clock that proves we are right from the very start. We are in touch with the hidden inner laws. We will say in advance what kind of day it has to be. Then if necessary we will take the steps to make it meet our requirements. (20)

Much of the imagery in Scripture and worship comes alive as we develop an awareness of nature. To witness how soil and rain and weeds affect the growth of a garden is to grasp more concretely the parable of the sower (Matthew 13:1–23) or to learn about the fruitfulness of God's word (Isaiah 55:1–11). To observe the growth of plants and animals is to better understand the requirements of time and nurturing care in our personal growth. To notice the cycle of the seasons is to give ourselves an opportunity to reflect on God's activity in our lives over the course of the liturgical year and on the religious experience of new life, growth, maturity, and death in Christ.

We need to create spaces of silence and solitude in which to get acquainted with our true selves. The secrets of the personality unfold most readily when our faculties can rest from continuous activity. Discovering the true self, the image of God within, cannot happen apart from entering into the mystery of Christ through worship and the individual prayer that prepares for and continues the saving act of Christ in our personal lives. But the symbols and rituals of our corporate worship will be much more intelligible to the person who is discovering and dealing with his or her personal symbols through day-to-day awareness of thoughts and emotions.

Christian spirituality must also create a welcoming space and time for the word of God in Scripture. In opening our lives to the word of God, we relive the experience of the disciples on the road to Emmaus—our meager efforts to entertain the Lord result in an awareness of God as host offering love and mercy, pardon and life beyond the fathom of the human heart. Because the purpose of this holy reading is to promote union with God, not to peruse a certain number of chapters or pages, the practice of Scripture reading is impossible without leisure, silence, and solitude in which we can listen to the Spirit of God speaking through his word to our own spirit.

A welcoming, compassionate attitude towards people is the surest sign of authentic growth in self-awareness and attentiveness to the word of God. Freedom to be an individual paradoxically flows from experience within community, and community is the result of individuals freely responding to Christ's invitation to share the task of building up his Body through loving service in His name. The experience of community provides ample opportunities to learn tolerance and forgiveness of ourselves and others, sensitivity to the needs of individual members, the strengths and gifts each can contribute to the group, and the value of communal support in our personal lives.

Conclusion

Christian spirituality thrives best in a leisure atmosphere where time and space are allotted for "being" as well as "doing." By seeking and honoring the mystery present in nature, our inner life, Scripture, and community, we become more fully aware of God's continual presence everywhere.

References

Aquinas, T. 1964. *Summa theologica.* New York: McGraw-Hill.

Merton, T. 1966. *Conjectures of a guilty bystander.* New York: Doubleday.

Pieper, J. 1963. *Leisure: The basis of culture.* New York: New American Library.

Chapter Nine

Leisure at L'arche: Communities of Faith for Persons with Developmental Disabilities

CATHY O'KEEFE

I have been intrigued by the topic of sports and Christianity because, whether my husband and I or our five children are involved in team and individual sports or not, we live in a sports culture, one that has increasingly developed a mystique that parallels religion with it own rituals, language of worship, and cult-like following. At my house there is almost nothing more sacred for my four sons and husband than pro-basketball playoffs, especially when the Lakers are involved. My children are involved in team sports and I am hanging on every word of the talks presented here this weekend for a framework in which I can blend their interests with the Christian values that I so want for our whole family.

My talk focuses on something that I would expect each of you has in your community also—adults living in group homes for the mentally ill and/or retarded. While our focus on them is miniscule compared to our social preoccupation with sports, I wanted to talk to you today about leisure in one particular system of homes because I would like you to return to your own communities sensitized to the wonderful gifts available to you and your families in sharing leisure with people who have special needs due to developmental disabilities.

I was not able to be here last year, but I listened to all the tapes and heard Joe Teaff mention Henri Nouwen, a high-powered theologian who taught at both Harvard and Yale, and who discovered in a community called L'Arche a way of "being" that deeply affected his own spirituality. Joe talked about Henri's decision to live at L'Arche and care for one man there. In doing the simple tasks of daily living with this man, he came to appreciate a slower, more leisurely pace and discovered God in the simple activities that assistants and residents participated in together. Henri Nouwen (1988) describes his experiences beautifully in his book *The Road to Daybreak*, the name of the community in Toronto where he lives.

Transitions in Care for Persons with Developmental Disabilities

Back in 1970, as a student at Spring Hill College, a Jesuit institution in Mobile, Alabama, I visited Searcy State Hospital, a typical large institution for the mentally ill situated, like many state hospitals of that time, in a rural area away from the city. I had volunteered to do art with the men on the toughest unit—the unit for the criminally insane. This unit made the environment in *One Flew Over the Cuckoo's Nest* look like the Hilton. The hospital was terribly overcrowded and it was common to find men crouched in shower stalls reading their Bibles just to get some space and silence amid the insanity.

In therapeutic recreation courses we review litigation that significantly affected the rights of special populations to community integration and recreation. Most of our texts mention the Wyatt vs. Stickney lawsuit in 1974 that blew open the entire issue of treatment for the mentally ill. The State of Alabama, that is, Governor George Wallace, controlled the mental health system at that time. Conditions had become so bad at Bryce Hospital in Tuscaloosa that staff members were quitting in droves and the remaining ones were threatening action. A fourteen-year-old boy named Ricky Wyatt was admitted to Bryce, but had no access to a psychiatrist, or any physician for that matter, for a two-month period. His aunt, at the encouragement of Dr. Stonewall Stickney, Mental Health Commissioner at that time, filed a lawsuit on her nephew's behalf over lack of treatment. It was Dr. Stickney's hope that the court could force the state's hand in improving care for the mentally ill.

Providentially, Judge Frank Johnson, classmate and nemesis of George Wallace, received the case and promptly turned it into a class action suit. The result was that the control of the entire mental health system was taken from Governor Wallace and put into receivership under the court. Thus began a movement in this country to deinstitutionalize the mentally ill and retarded, a movement that some claim has contributed significantly to the number of homeless people on the street who are incompetent and need to be under someone's supervision. However, one only has to see homeless people choosing to huddle over a grate rather than return to the institution to appreciate the brutal conditions that must have existed all over this country in the decades before the seventies.

Like many people in the mid-seventies I believed that normalization and the creation of community-centered group homes and residential facilities for the mentally ill and retarded would really turn the tide in the care of these people. In those early years many wonderful programs were begun and, under court order, staffing was improved incredibly. Institutions were compelled to hire one master's level Therapeutic Recreation Specialist and ten activity specialists per 250 patients. Life in the community for the mentally ill and retarded seemed, at that time, full of promise.

L'Arche

I brought with me a video about L'Arche called *The Heart Has Its Reasons* to introduce you to what I believe is an incredible sign to the world of how Christianity can be lived in community with persons who have developmental disabilities. In it you will meet Jean Vanier, the founder of L'Arche who gave up prominent social status as the son of the Governor General of Canada and a career as a university professor to live with "mentally handicapped" adults in a village in France. After this film I want to explain how leisure is uniquely used to nurture community and how, ironically, all who are associated with L'Arche come away nurtured in their spirituality by the people who live there. My hope is that you will take insights from this session back with you to your own town and make an effort to bring your own Christian values to developmentally disabled people who live there.

The L'Arche philosophy is based entirely on the beatitudes and Christ's last public address in Matthew's Gospel on salvation through loving relationship with "the least of our brothers and sisters."

Listen to the words of Henri Nouwen about his experience with L'Arche:

> It was important for me to be reminded again of this gift of the handicapped. They see through a facade of smiles and friendly words and sense the resentful heart before we ourselves notice it. Often they are capable of unmasking our impatience, irritation, jealousy, and lack of interest and can make us honest with ourselves. For them, what really counts is a true relationship, a real friendship, a faithful presence. Many mentally handicapped people experience themselves as a disappointment to their parents, a burden for their families, a nuisance to their friends. To believe that anyone really cares and really loves them is difficult. Their heart registers with extreme sensitivity what is real care and what is false, what is true affection and what is just empty words. Thus, they often reveal to us our own hypocrisies and invite us always to greater sincerity and purer love. Being at L'Arche means many things, but one of them is a call to greater purity of heart. Indeed, Jesus speaks through the broken hearts of the

handicapped who are considered marginal and useless. But God has chosen them to be the poor through whom he makes His presence known. This is hard to accept in a success and production-oriented society. (1988, 19)

In 1975 I met Jan Risse, a Trinitarian nun who, like Mother Theresa of Calcutta, left her order to answer a "call within a call." She had received her master's degree from Harvard School of Divinity and later met Jean Vanier. In the sixteen years since first meeting Jan, I have been a "friend of L'Arche," that is, someone who voluntarily associates with their community in order to live in friendship with the residents and their assistants.

Leisure at L'Arche

I have visited and talked with Jan Risse several times in preparation for this talk. I asked her about life and leisure in L'Arche and what she would want you to know about its charisma. She said, "You must tell them how much we dance at L'Arche, for it is the language of sheer joy without words and since many of our people cannot speak, it is a great avenue for community expression."

I have danced with the people of L'Arche and been amazed at how their uninhibitedness affected me. It matters not to them whether you are in sync with the music or are dancing alone or with a partner. Their dance is permeated with laughter, spontaneous and unusual moves, and frequent clapping in support of one another's efforts.

Jan also reminded me that the simplicity of leisure in L'Arche is so because leisure is centered not on the activity itself but on the joy of being together no matter what the activity is. Oddly, I am reading more and more articles in the secular press about simpler living. These articles describe a shift in focus from the sensory excitement that we in first-world countries have needed in our leisure, to an awareness of the joy of any activity when it revolves around relationships or our own sense of inner peace.

I must tell you that because L'Arche is a worldwide community of homes, there is available to its members a network of hospitality for travelers. Outer appearances might lead one to assume that mentally handicapped people rarely travel, and certainly L'Arche is not a wealthy community. So I was bowled over in the early seventies when I learned that Jean Vanier planned and executed what I can only describe as the "field trip of the century." L'Arche arranged for four thousand people to go on a trip to France. They chose Lourdes not only because of its pilgrim significance but because it is a town that welcomes people who are disabled and had accommodations for wheelchairs and the like. It was a coming together and celebration of life for handicapped people and their families with much singing and dancing, exchange of conversation and stories. This first trip was documented in a film called *Pilgrimage* that I like to show my students because the central message was so profound: everyone needs something to look forward to, to experience, and to reflect on as a memory. How glibly we accept this truism for ourselves yet deny its truth for the disabled!

L'Arche is also enriched by the culture brought to it by the assistants. It is common to find people from many countries living together at L'Arche. In Mobile we have assistants from India, Germany, and Great Britain, and from places in the U.S. like Iowa, Chicago, Louisiana, Wisconsin, and Massachusetts.

L'Arche also centers leisure around mealtime, a truly eucharistic reflection. Meals are times of great sharing and joy. Even the preparation of the meal is an opportunity for pleasure, as assistants and residents work together making homemade breads and desserts. Every evening ends with community prayer around a candle, songs, and the recitation of the L'Arche prayer. Every weekend finds the community taking advantage of invitations of local friends to swim in backyard pools or join in baptisms, weddings, and the like. The residents of L'Arche are also involved in leisure activities at a variety of local churches. Some communities are also connected to academic institutions and their residents take classes through continuing education.

Earlier I told you that I naively anticipated normalization and deinstitutionalization to be an answer to the meaninglessness and hurt that so many disabled people had experienced in earlier years. We have many state-sponsored group homes now in Mobile, and in the last decade since their establishment I have seen some very serious signs that the old ways are still very much in place. Many group homes have "parents" who have little or no training in knowledge of handicapping conditions or techniques for treating them. Many are poorly paid and, hence, do not stay with the home for any length of time. What I am seeing are "mini-institutions" in which disabled people are housed, but not nurtured, where there is no celebration of life, but only a routine of daily living activities basic to work, eating, and sleep. Many have little or no recreational opportunities outside of TV and an occasional trip to the mall. Staff interact with residents in their daily care, but often with little sense of sharing life, receiving as well as giving, or enjoying leisure together.

I have seen staff of these homes take residents to an activity and then stand off to themselves until the residents are finished and their "work" as staff resumes. Sadly, I have seen many signs that the same old hurts and rejections are there, but concealed in small homes in the community rather than in the large hospitals of the past. I am distressed that many of the residents of our group homes are herded to community activities with little preparation, guidance, or help in processing the meaning of the activity. Most have little to look forward to, experience, and reflect on as memory. My guess is that as long as staff consider themselves surrogate "parents" to adult "children," as long as pay is the primary motivation for their presence in these homes, and as long as little training is required of the caregivers, we will have what I believe is merely a shifting of location of the institution.

It seems to me that what L'Arche shows the world is that when the love of Christ through love for the poor is the context in which care is given, both caregiver and receiver of care are nurtured. Jean Vanier reminds us that we are all handicapped to some extent. The Christian focus of love in L'Arche is to announce the ridiculous—that we NEED them to teach us to trust, laugh easily, live more in the moment, enjoy the presence of others, and accept one another unconditionally. Wasn't it St. Exupery in *The Little Prince* who said, "It is only with the heart that one can see clearly."

The Good News is truly paradoxical to the world. What the world would consider tragic biological mistakes, Christians at L'Arche look upon as a gift. What the world sees as unworthy of our attention, Christians at L'Arche view as an important opportunity for an experience of God's presence.

Leisure in L'Arche is the glue that binds the community. It is a state of being completely at home and comfortable with one's own woundedness and the woundedness of others. It is a slower pace in which moments are savored and recalled over and over again as reminders that play done lovingly in community is surely the Kingdom of God here and now.

First, I invite all of you, to learn more about L'Arche and its unique Christian sign to the world community about the gifts available to us from having people with developmental disabilities living in our communities. Second, I urge all of you to apply the Gospel in your own communities by seeking out people like those who live at L'Arche and becoming friends with them. My own children were at first frightened by the severity of problems that the L'Arche residents in Mobile have. But, over time, they have become at ease with disabilities and have really enjoyed the parties we have shared with them. I have learned to play with my own children more spontaneously because of L'Arche.

Every Christmas the L'Arche community invites friends and benefactors from Mobile to a big dinner party. One favorite activity after dinner is drawing the name of a manger figure from a box and then rendering it in clay. To see the local bishop, lawyers, professional people and the like struggling to make a sheep look like a sheep is an essay in images. For it is in this playful art that you can hardly tell the figures made by the "handicapped" people from those made by the university professors or the doctors.

Because of what I have learned at L'Arche, I really understand Paul's prayer in Ephesians 3 for myself: "Lord, give me the power of your Spirit for my hidden self to grow strong so that you may live in my heart through faith." My hidden self is that which is most divine, most purely loving, most incredibly joyous. It is the vulnerable me, the child-like me—it is the me revealed by my friends at L'Arche.

I tell you most solemnly (as the scripture says), that when you too can love like one of these, you will begin to understand "the breadth and length, the height and depth, until knowing the love of Christ which is beyond all knowledge, you are filled with the utter fullness of God" (Ephesians 3:18–19).

FIGURE I: LEISURE ACTIVITIES POPULAR WITH THE L'ARCHE COMMUNITIES

PHYSICAL
  Walking
  YMCA memberships (swimming and exercise classes)
  Softball
  Bowling
  Horseback riding
  Jogging
  Tennis
  Yard work

SOCIAL
  Community Theater Dancing
  Community night
  Church-related activities (many denominations are represented)
  Neighborhood events
  Activities for peace and justice
  Faith and Light Activities (a social support group for families)

Visits to biological families
"Friend to friend" program with local college students
Inviting friends of L'Arche to dinner
Parties for almost any imaginable occasion
Mardi Gras celebrations
Making and sending homemade cards and newsletters
Pen pals
Concerts
Giving presentations about L'Arche in local communities
Open house
"Relief Night"—friends of L'Arche substitute for assistants and participate in an evening with the residents
Picnics
Caroling at Christmas time
Cooking
Rocking on the porch
Fishing

INTELLECTUAL
Watching the news together and talking about topics of interest
Reading the newspaper together.
Visits to the library
Cultural lessons from assistants who come from other countries
Life skills classes
Writing and sending L'Arche newsletters and receiving them from other homes
Reading aloud
Attending special classes through the local college's continuing education program
Attending local lectures on peace and justice issues
Attending Sunday school at the church of each resident's choice
Tutors once each week

SPIRITUAL/EMOTIONAL
Daily prayer in community
Daily time set aside for individual prayer
"Faith and Sharing" retreats
Monthly day of prayer
Weekly worship in churches of each resident's choice
"Friend to Friend" program with college students
Accompaniment/Companioning arrangements with friends of L'Arche
Community meals
Dances
Group singing
Pet care
Birthday parties (each resident is asked to describe the ways in which the birthday honoree has been a gift to him or her)
Spiritual direction from within or outside the L'Arche house
Individual therapy for handicapped residents who need it

SPECIAL TRIPS TAKEN BY RESIDENTS OF THREE L'ARCHE COMMUNITIES IN THE PAST FEW YEARS (KANSAS, IOWA, AND MOBILE)
Camping in the Colorado Rockies
Camping at the Lake of the Ozarks
Regional L'Arche gathering in Bardstown, Kentucky
Ministry to Handicapped Convention in Washington, D.C.

State and National Special Olympics events

The L'Arche community in Kansas traveled to Chicago, Calgary and Winnipeg for visits to communities there.

The Mobile community has traveled to Marysville, Tennessee; New Orleans, Louisiana; Bardstown, Kentucky; St. Louis, Missouri; and gone camping at the Gulf of Mexico many times. They have made retreats with other L'Arche communities in Canada and Iowa.

References

Nouwen, H.J. 1988. *The Road to Daybreak*. Garden City, NY: Doubleday Publishers.

Chapter Ten

Unless Someone Like You Cares a Whole Awful Lot

DON DEGRAAF

One of the key issues in the 1992 presidential race was the value crisis in America. Many people think that a number of the problems we face as a nation can be traced back to the breakdown of the family and the resulting loss of traditional values by our society. Proponents of these thoughts feel that Americans have been caught up in a culture where the allure of excess has led to a society where buying is more important than giving, having is more important than being a part of.

> It often seems that the sterile ceremonies of consumerism are the most profound rituals Americans share as a people. These value questions—about how we have chosen to live our lives and how that's affected our children, about how the nagging sense of personal freedom and rampaging materialism yield only greater hunger and lonelier nights—have been quiet American obsessions for some time now, the source of a deep, vexing national anxiety. (Klein 1992, 18)

Despite the interest in values education by the American people, there is still little consensus on what values to teach and who should teach them. Schools are attempting to step into the "value void" and are developing curriculums which address a core set of values like tolerance, honesty, respect, especially in the formative years while sidestepping more "hot" issues like abortion, birth control, capital punishment, and racism (Salholz 1992).

Educators in park and recreation have not escaped this values debate. Although there is often talk that recreation is a matter of personal preference and that park and recreation professionals are supposed to accommodate such preferences, some professionals now want to start making judgments about what kind of activities to encourage. This debate of whether park and recreation professionals are obliged to serve popular tastes for recreation or try to elevate them seems to be most intense in the area of outdoor recreation where dwindling natural resources create conflicts between many different kinds of special user groups. The growing environmental crisis has elevated this debate even further as is evident by the report of the President's Commission on Americans Outdoors.

In 1987, the President's Commission on Americans Outdoors released its report on the state of outdoor recreation in America. The commission was charged by the President with reviewing public and private outdoor recreation opportunities, recommendations for future action to accomplish this goal. An integral part of making these recommendations work is creating an outdoor ethic in Americans, an ethic that goes beyond practicing techniques such as minimum impact camping to a philosophy that pervades life itself.

The report concludes that for the past 25 years we have emphasized the role of government in conservation and environmental problems, and have given little attention regarding the role of the individual. A land ethic has not been created in the minds of individuals. Today, no attempt to protect the environment will be successful unless ordinary people are willing to adjust their lifestyles and develop a personalized environmental ethic. Many experts agree that education is a key component in developing an environmental ethic which emphasizes the ability to make conscious moral decisions and to understand how and why those decisions are being made and how certain behaviors are affecting the earth and other people. Developing such an ethic in students demands that values must enter into the teaching process.

This need to bring values into the classroom offers Christian educators in the park and recreation field a unique opportunity and a difficult challenge. The opportunity magnifies itself in the fact that many philosophers have pointed out how science and religion are intertwined in solving the environmental crisis. As Leopold has noted:

> No important change in ethics was ever accomplished without an internal change in our intellectual emphasis, loyalties, affections, and convictions. The proof that conservation has not yet touched these foundations of conduct lies in the fact that philosophy and religion have not yet heard of it. In our attempt to make conservation easy we have made it trivial. (1966, 220)

Lynn White, who in the late 1960s postulated that Christianity was responsible for the environmental crisis, made an even stronger connection between religion and the environment, when he wrote, "More science and more technology are not going to get us out of the present ecological crisis until we find a new religion, or rethink our old one" (1967, 1206). Leopold's quote and the work of White and others who have expanded on his work challenge Christians to develop an environmental ethic with others wherever and whenever we can.

Yet the challenge of integrating Christian values into courses taught at secular colleges and universities still remains. Thus the purpose of this paper is twofold. First, this paper strives to identify a Christian environmental ethic. Second, it attempts to identify how Christian educators can teach and promote such an environmental ethic in the midst of a secular world.

What is an Outdoor Ethic?

According to the United Nations, a positive environmental ethic, comprised of a set of values and behaviors that help to preserve the ecological integrity of the earth, must be seen as a part of each person's total being. Implicit in developing a personal outdoor ethic is the concept of responsibility to each other and for the earth itself. In the words of Leopold such a land ethic

> simply enlarges the boundary of the community to include soils, water, plants, and animals or collectively the land. It demands that each question of human's relationship to his environment be studied in such terms of what is ethically and essentially right as well as what is economically expedient . . . . A thing is right when it tends to preserve the integrity, stability and beauty of the biotic community. It is wrong when it tends to do otherwise. (1971, 204)

Developing such a land ethic means re-thinking our relationship with the earth. In his book, *The Steward: A Biblical Symbol Come of Age* (1990), Hall has identified three models which define our relationship to the earth historically. These models include the following: *Humans over nature, Humans in nature,* and *Humans with nature.* Using these three models Hall explains the historic progression of man's relationship to the earth and gives Christians a powerful metaphor to deal with the present-day environmental crisis.

The *Humans over nature* model has been the dominant model of our age and is the basis for White's argument that Judeo-Christian beliefs are the root of society's environmental problems. This model's basic premise is that an omnipotent God created the world and directed humankind to "be fruitful and multiply, and replenish the earth and subdue it: and have dominion . . . over every living thing that moveth upon the earth" (Genesis 1:28). Within this context wilderness became an adversary of humans as they tried to create a paradise on earth which ordered and served the needs of mankind. This attempt is reflected in the early experiences of the Israelites. According to Nash (1982) wilderness was seen as an arid wasteland cursed by God. This view led to a conviction that the environment was an evil kind of hell, a testing ground where a chosen people went to be humbled and made ready for the land of promise. Nash further points out that in the New Testament, Christ was led up by the Spirit into the wilderness to be tempted by the devil (Matthew 4:1). "This experience, complete with forty days of fasting, alluded to the testing of Israel during the Exodus, and wilderness retained its significance as the environment of evil and hardship where spiritual catharsis took place" (Nash, 17). Through such experiences the wilderness was seen positively as a place to draw close to God. Despite this view, wilderness never lost its harsh and forbidding character. It was always seen as an environment to wrestle with in an attempt to bring order to this world. Overall there was no fondness in the Hebraic tradition for wilderness itself (Nash 1982).

This aversion to wilderness was carried on into the Middle Ages when people began to look to science and technology to help win the battle against nature. Before this time science was traditionally seen as aristocratic, speculative, and intellectual in intent, while technology was seen as lower class, empirical, and action-oriented. When these two processes were combined, humankind greatly increased in its ability to transform nature.

These beliefs crossed the Atlantic to the New World with the early settlers as they began the process of subduing the wilderness and using it for the public good. By the 1800s the ability to apply knowledge to the task of making nature serve man became known as "Yankee ingenuity." This attitude has continued into the twentieth century as our modern society views nature as a commodity to be exploited and turned into profit. White made note of this attitude when he wrote, "We are superior to nature, contemptuous of it, willing to use it for our slightest whim. . . . To a Christian a tree can be no more than a physical fact. The whole concept of a sacred grove is alien to Christianity and the ethos of the West" (1967, 1206).

As society collectively began to respond to the environmental crisis, many turned to a different ancient paradigm of simply seeing humans as a part of nature or actually seeing nature as god (pantheism). In this view God can be found in everything including plants, animals, and human beings. Human beings are simply a part of the environment. This approach can be seen in the words of Chief Seattle's famous response to the U.S.

government in the 1850s when he stated, "All things are connected, whatever befalls the Earth." On one hand, this approach is very appealing in that it encourages people to treat the earth and its inhabitants with more respect because we are all part of the same web of life. We are dependent on each other for our collective survival. However, on closer examination the *Humans in nature* approach seems to negate the uniqueness of humans, that humans are different from the rest of the animal world. People are the only species that can think and make conscious decisions. Specifically humankind is the only species that can be held accountable for its actions. Thus, we are not simply part of the creation; we are in some ways unique.

The *Humans with nature* approach presents a paradigm which builds on the uniqueness of humans to call Christians to care for and take responsibility for the environment. This paradigm builds on the idea of Christian stewardship and entails understanding three very important concepts: (1) God as ultimate owner, (2) Humans' relationship with nature, and (3) Humans' call to dominion and service.

The world is not for people to own; it belongs to God. Humans are to exercise their dominion over these things not as though entitled to exploit them, but as things borrowed or held in a trust. Implicit in this responsibility is the realization that the value of something is not in itself autonomous, but because God made it. It deserves this respect as something that was created by God, as humans themselves have been created by God. In examining this point further Francis Schaeffer has put forth what he calls God's covenant with creation.

> The covenant of creation rests upon the way God made things. God will not violate this covenant. He will always deal with a plant as a plant, with an animal as an animal, with a machine as a machine, and with a man as a man, not violating the orders of creation. He will not ask the machine to behave like a man, neither will he deal with man as though he were a machine. Thus, God treats his creation with integrity: each thing in its own order, each thing the way he made it. If God treats His creation in that way should we not treat our fellow-creatures with a similar integrity? (1970, 56)

To fulfill their role in this covenant humans need to understand their unique two-sided role in creation.

First, humans like stars, seas, whales, fish, and birds are simply part of God's creation. Humans were formed from the dust of the earth which reiterates what contemporary biologists and ecologists have been trying hard to tell us: "Whatever else they are, humans are also earth: they share their nature with its soil, its animals" (Wilkinson 1980, 208). Yet there is another side of humans in that they are described as being special in creation: they are made in the image of God.

> We are different, then, from the beasts of the field and the birds of the air. Let us not be naive and imagine that we can just melt into nature. We have a reflective side that the other creatures do not have. It is harder for us to die than it is for them. We have always to choose, or to be victims of our lack of choice. But the purpose of all this is that we should "have dominion": that is, that we should be servants, keepers, and priests in relation to the others. (Hall 1990, 211)

Seeing dominion as service is not the typical definition of the word by today's standards. Webster's dictionary defines dominion as absolute ownership and authority; this definition may be one of the reasons why by today's standards humans' dominion over nature is unacceptable. Yet by examining how the word dominion is used in the Old Testament we can see that biblical dominion is much more than absolute ownership. Humans are called to cultivate and keep the earth (Genesis 2:15). The Hebrew verbs used here imply a kind of tilling which is a service to the earth. In this context, human dominion should be exercised in such a way as to serve and preserve the beasts, the trees, the earth itself. Throughout scripture the lesson of dominion becomes clear: unless such dominion is used for the benefit of the dominated it is misused.

Such an attitude would accomplish two things. First, it would recognize the unique abilities of humans and attempt to direct their abilities toward caring for the earth rather than exploiting it for personal gain. Second, it would create a blend of philosophy and religion (of which Leopold spoke) in an effort to create a new land ethic which recognizes the frailty of our ecosystem and our responsibility to ensure its long-term survival.

Hall summarizes this *Humans with nature* approach by using the example of a steward as a metaphor for creating an environmental ethic in Christians because it encapsulates the two sides of human relationship—with God and with the nonhuman creatures of God. The human is, as God's steward, accountable to God and responsible for its fellow creatures. Such a commitment requires that stewardship becomes a part of who we are rather than something we do.

> The stewarding of a world on the brink of a catastrophe, like the care of a patient in the crisis of a dread illness, must be moment-to-moment, a matter of intensive care. . . . But as Christians we can do something—can be some-

thing—far more significant in the long run; something which, if it is not done, will prevent all the other, practical things from happening. It is this: we can determine that we shall not any longer be amongst those who are ambiguous about the world, who withdraw from it, and whose withdrawal results in an almost demonstrable loss to the world. . . . If as stewards of the mysteries of God we make this first and most rudimentary step towards tending God's garden-become-wilderness, by declaring our love for it, we shall have leapt over a chasm that has long [kept Christians from being true stewards of God's wondrous world]. (Hall 1990, 230–31)

In presenting the concept of stewardship as a foundation to build a land ethic, we have dealt strictly in the religious realm, dealing with the problem at its religious roots. But in today's pluralistic society is this enough? For although the western world may still be based on Christian axioms, it is no longer Christian, and an environmental ethic based solely on being a steward for a just God may be difficult to implement. Christians should advocate for their position but they must also be willing to work with other groups to find common ground in solving the ecological crisis of today. The question that we now turn to is how can we as Christian educators, working in secular institutions, advocate for our views as well as build common ground with others who are committed to the care of this world?

Promoting a Christian Environmental Ethic in the Midst of Secular World

Before one can commit to promoting an environmental ethic, let alone a Christian ethic, one needs to be convinced that this is an appropriate mission for professors, especially those teaching in park and recreation departments. Although the park and recreation field has long been concerned with protecting the environment, the field has moved away from its roots in outdoor recreation and public recreation to areas like tourism and commercial recreation. Yet, despite this shift I truly feel that all aspects of our diverse profession are tied to the environment. If not directly, then the indirect linkages cannot be overlooked. For example, many towns and cities (including commercial recreation operators) rely on the tourism dollars produced by visitors to our national parks. In the twenty years between 1960 and 1980, visits to our National Parks have increased from 136 million visitors to 282 million visitors per year. Maintaining the quality of the environment is necessary for the survival and quality of many outdoor and adventure experiences.

As a result of these linkages, we must all acknowledge these connections with the earth and encourage them. Perhaps the greatest contribution we can make as professors in park and recreation departments is to help our students develop an environmental ethic. Yet the question remains: What should be the framework from which we, as Christian educators in the park and recreation departments, can transmit this ethic to students?

Dan Dustin (1990) in his article entitled, "Looking Inward to Save the Outdoors" puts forth a three-point agenda that he would like to see the park and recreation profession pursue in the face of the current environmental crisis.

> First, I expect us to put our heads together and try to reach consensus about the kind of world we live in. Second, I expect the park and recreation profession to serve as this society's environmental conscience. Third, I expect each and every one of us within the park and recreation profession to set an example, to demonstrate environmental wisdom in the conduct of our own lives.

I would like to suggest that these three points represent the basis for a Christian educator who is committed to teaching values and promoting environmental ethics in the classroom and thus will serve as the framework for developing specific actions.

What Kind of World do we Live In?

In essence, what is our vision of man's relationship to the earth? Without such a guiding vision there is little hope of building consensus about what an environmental ethic should be. An ethic demands a worldview in light of which we are obliged to behave in certain ways. Dustin presents his worldview as framed by the assertion that

> the morality of an act is a function of the state of the system at the time it is performed. I believe the state of our system compels us to act in less consumptive ways. I believe the park and recreation profession's primary mission is to encourage recreational conduct that is compatible with that reality; hence my call to assess the moral propriety of our recreational pleasures in this world of increasingly limited resources. (1990, 89)

I like what Dustin has to say; yet, I find it lacking because it encourages us to action as a call for self-preservation. I think we need to go one step further and develop a worldview which encourages us to live more lightly because it is the right thing to do. The development of such a worldview is dealt with in the first portion of this paper. I would propose that the biblical symbol of a steward presents Christian educators with a powerful metaphor for explaining humankind's relationship to the earth. For Hall, the concept of the steward is a symbol which defines what it means to be a Christian:

"For too long we have emphasized the *doing*, with the superficial, short-term results. We need to reverse our strategy and put the emphasis on *being*, for more authentic, long-term effects" [T.S. Horvath]. . . . Stewardship does not describe any one dimension of the Christian life; it describes the whole posture called "Christian." Through this metaphor, the biblical authors with their genius for images found a single term that could point simultaneously to all three foci of Christian faith: its orientation to the one whose sovereignty the steward acknowledges; its orientation to humans, who participate in the universal stewardship of "the speaking animal"; and its orientation to otherkind and to the earth, our common home. . . . "As a worldview, the stewardship doctrine demands of the faithful an uncompromising adherence. . . . The new concept is that dominion is stewardship rather than ownership and conservation rather than exploitation. . . . *This new emphasis on stewardship is providing the foundation for the emergence of a second Protestant reformation and a new covenant vision for society*" [J. Rifkin]. (1990, 232–33, 239–40)

The steward is indeed a powerful concept on which a worldview can be developed. More importantly Hall contends that it is a concept that is perceived positively by non-Christians. The concept of a steward is understood outside of Christianity as someone who serves by taking care of something that belongs to another. Thus the concept of a steward may serve as a starting point whereby some consensus (between both Christians and non-Christians) can be built for developing an environmental ethic for all.

Setting an Example: Learning to Live More Lightly

The first step in implementing any vision is living it ourselves. As Christians we must regard stewardship as something we are, not something we do. The concept of stewardship must be an overarching metaphor in our entire lives. We can begin by asking ourselves some of the questions presented in Appendix A. These questions can also be asked on an organizational level, and as faculty members we should be encouraging our institutions to create more "earth friendly" campuses.

The questions presented in Appendix A could go on forever and in the end make us all feel guilty for our failings, but that is not their intention. Instead, the purpose of exercises like this is to challenge us to begin to make these kinds of questions part of our lives and subsequently make changes in our behavior. Some of these things are very easy to start, while others are more difficult, but once we begin, we can get into the habit of striving to live more responsible lives. We can always improve our behavior, so think of this as a process of becoming more aware of the lifestyle decisions we make. Remember to think globally, act locally, be personally.

This personal implementation is an important first step to ultimately teaching values in the classroom for we teach values through our actions as well as our inactions. In fact, the most effective teaching is often not what is said or taught in formalized classes, but what is done and taught through example. A popular story about Ghandi highlights this important point. One day a woman came up to Ghandi and asked him if he would talk to her son about decreasing the amount of sugar the boy ate. Ghandi thought for a moment and said he would do what she asked in two weeks. At the end of this time Ghandi spoke with the boy and obviously had quite an impact. Upon the completion of their talk the woman thanked Ghandi but asked why they had needed to wait two weeks before he would speak with her son. Ghandi replied that before he could tell the boy to stop eating so much sugar he had to get sugar out of his own body first and this process had taken two weeks. If we're going to challenge our students to respond to today's environmental crises, we must first begin the struggle of making our own lives more "earth friendly."

Serving as Society's Environmental Conscience

Once we have a model (or vision) for a preferred world and are attempting to live this vision on a daily basis, we are in a position to share this vision with others through the educational process. Kurt Hahn, the founder of Outward Bound, once wrote, "The aim of education is to impel people into value-forming experiences." We must develop in students the foundation upon which moral decisions can be based. In essence, we need to help students achieve moral literacy. Such moral literacy can be defined as the ability to make conscious moral decisions and to understand how and why those decisions are being made and how these behaviors are affecting the earth and other people. Developing moral literacy in students demands that values must enter the classroom.

In promoting such values in the classroom, I feel that Christian educators must be willing to do three things. First, they must be willing to stand up for what they believe. Second, they must be willing to promote moral development through their classes. Third, Christian educators must be willing to take specific stands on difficult issues.

Over the last twenty years many people have pushed the issue of separation between church and state in our educational field into the forefront. Issues such as banning prayer in the public schools and limiting religious music in Christmas programs make many Christian educators reluctant to share Christian perspectives in the classroom. Yet we have seen the ideas and values of non-Christian groups creep into curriculums. Although I understand many of the reasons for the separation of church and state, this issue should not stand in the way of presenting Christian ideas as one unique perspective for interacting with our world. In this light, Christian ideas can and should be presented in the classroom, yet many times I still find myself reticent to promote such values as one viable approach to dealing with our world. In examining this phenomenon in my own life I realize that it is a desire to avoid conflict which prompts this reticence. This reluctance was brought home to me on a hike in Smokey Mountain National Park when I encountered a woman feeding a wild chipmunk Mary Jane candy—this, despite repeated efforts by the National Parks Service to get people to stop feeding the animals. I wanted to speak up, but I did not, and I felt guilty during the remainder of my hike. As I reflect back to this experience I realize my own dislike of conflict and the need to stand up for what I believe by presenting my own values whenever possible.

Sharing our values openly and honestly in the classroom is the beginning of "values education," yet to be truly effective, we must encourage students to examine their own values and begin to formulate their own views. In sharing and living our own values we give students a powerful example, but to encourage long-term changes in students' attitudes toward the earth we must help students develop their own individualized environmental ethic. One way to create lasting behavioral changes in students is to help them to internalize why they need to relate in morally responsible ways to the environment. Thus, Christian educators need to understand the moral development of students. Lawrence Kohlberg's theory of developmental stages provides a framework to help us identify stages of moral development and design appropriate classes and assignments.

Kohlberg outlines three levels of moral development, each consisting of two stages. In stage one, *punishment and obedience orientation*, individuals select behavior based solely on avoiding punishment. In stage two, *instrumental relativist orientation*, individuals make decisions based on what is beneficial to themselves and making sure that their own needs are satisfied. In stage three, *interpersonal concordance*, individuals seek approval from others and conform to what is considered "nice behavior" by others. In stage four, *law and order orientation*, individuals believe in an inherent value to rules, authority, and order. In stage five, *social-contract legalistic orientation,* individuals examine and agree to rules for the entire society while also maintaining individual rights and maintaining personal opinions. In stage six, *universal ethical-principle orientation,* individuals develop abstract principles which guide their moral decisions and are based on the principles of equality, justice, and human dignity.

Kohlberg's stages of moral development is a good framework to deal with values because it can be embraced by both Christians and non-Christians. For Christians, each level of development can symbolize how we relate to God and His will for our lives. For example, in stage one we obey God for fear of punishment; whereas, in stage six we obey God because He is the source of what we understand to be "right" and "just" (see Micah 6:8). For non-Christians, the theory's appeal should be in developing ethical behavior in individuals.

Educators must address the level of moral development represented by all students in the classroom. Furthermore, they must seize opportunities to aid students in progressing to higher levels of moral development whenever possible. In his research, Kohlberg discovered that people grow and develop from one stage to another when they experience a moral conflict that cannot be resolved satisfactorily at their present level of moral reasoning. The ensuing anxiety or cognitive dissonance provides the necessary incentive to grapple-with the conflict from the perspective afforded at the next stage. This struggle results in moral growth. Thus, Christian educators can foster moral growth through lectures and assignments which encourage students to deal with moral dilemmas.

Perhaps the best way to deal with moral dilemmas in the classroom is to examine the role of recreation and leisure professionals in difficult environmental issues. As students confront these issues they can begin to understand their complexity and deal with the moral and ethical questions associated with such issues. To illustrate this principle I would like to return to the debate alluded to in the opening section of this essay. The central question of this debate is whether park and recreation professionals are obliged to serve popular tastes for recreation or should try to elevate them.

In the majority of my classes, students' initial response is that recreation professionals should serve popular tastes because recreation and leisure is a matter of personal preferences (freedom), and we, as professionals, should serve such preferences. A second, more emphatic response, is that they worry about who is making these judgment calls. For example, who is to say a motorhome is a bad form of recreation when it is the only means by which some people can get out and enjoy the great outdoors. We are back to the values question. Who should make these kinds of decisions? But if we truly believe we have a responsibility to create an environmental ethic in people, should we not only educate them but also encourage them to recreate in ways that reflect a more sensitive, more caring attitude toward the earth? According to Dustin: "To do anything else, would be an act of professional irresponsibility" (1984, 50).

Grappling with such an issue demands putting thoughts into action. It demands going the step beyond a simple verbal commitment to the environment to forcing professionals into action. It demands that we get beyond the "paradox of preservation." This paradox is that everyone wants to preserve and save the environment, but we enjoy (and don't want to give up) our materialistic lifestyles. In essence, we want it all and we refuse to see how our actions contribute to the overall problem.

Discussions such as this one helps students to understand the needs for values within their own programs and takes them to the next level of discussing what park and recreation professionals can do to elevate popular tastes for recreation. At this point, unique programs for encouraging a more caring attitude for the earth can be discussed, options such as providing intensive experiences for participants and helping participants achieve the maximum of well-being with the minimum of consumption.

Joseph Sax, in his book *Mountains Without Handrails,* advocates using education to promote intensive experiences for visitors. Sax feels that the more visitors know about a setting, the greater their interest and enjoyment of the area. The more knowledgeable and engaged visitors become, the less they want or need to pass through the parks quickly or at high speed. The quantity of resources visitors need to consume shrinks as they discover the secret of intensiveness of experience. In this scenario the parks perform their function without being used up at all. According to Sax,

> We do not increase our enjoyment of an alpine meadow by picking its flowers, but by leaving them where they are. The more we understand that they are part of a larger system the more we appreciate them in their setting—rather than being perceived as things to possess or to be used up—they become inexhaustible. (112)

This is similar to the idea that Thoreau presented in his book *Walden* when he stated, "My vicinity affords many good walks; and though I have walked almost everyday. . . . I have not exhausted them. . . . The limits of an afternoon walk. . . . will never become quite familiar to me."

Connected to the idea of creating intensive experience for people is maximizing people's quality of life while minimizing consumption of natural resources. We are in the business of enhancing people's overall quality of life. In today's world quality of life is often mistakenly associated with the idea that more is always better. However, this idea has come under closer scrutiny of late with the realization that the quantity of experiences is less important than the quality of the experience. With this realization comes the opportunity for our profession to increase people's quality of life without increasing (and perhaps even decreasing) the need to consume resources. Perhaps Thoreau had it right when he wrote, "A rich man is rich in proportion to the things he can afford to let alone."

Connected to the idea of enhancing people's quality of life is humanizing our complex world. John Naisbett in his book *MegaTrends* predicts the emergence of a high-tech/high-touch world. As the world gets more complicated there is a need for park and recreation professionals to provide more experiences that keep people in touch with the earth and the simple experiences that we will value.

Helping students realize that the programs we offer are value-laden is a valuable lesson and helps them see that they, too, can make a difference in dealing with today's environmental crisis. For Christian students this teaching does even more as they realize that they are not only stewards of God's world but also of people's leisure time, and they need to take these responsibilities very seriously. Inherent in this task is helping people slow down enough to watch a sunset and stroll by the water's edge, in essence, to slow down enough to "glorify God and enjoy Him forever." Herein lies the ultimate goal of teaching values in the classroom.

Conclusion

There is no denying the complexity of the issues surrounding today's environmental crisis. There are trade offs involved in answering many of the questions presented in Appendix A. What is right in one circumstance may not be right in another. In many cases the answers to these questions may not be as important as continually asking the questions and striving to make ourselves and our classes as earth-friendly as possible. One of the unique aspects of dealing with the environment is that it requires eternal vigilance and commitment, for we as individuals and organizations can always do more to lessen our impact on the world in which we live. We no longer have the luxury of letting economic costs outweigh environmental costs; we must stop making excuses and start taking responsibility. As park and recreation educators, it is time to be pioneers, striving to get our programs, ourselves, and our students into the loop where we are individually and collectively challenging ourselves to change our behavior in order to protect the earth. In the words of Dr. Seuss's Once-ler (1971): "UNLESS SOMEONE LIKE YOU CARES A WHOLE AWFUL LOT, NOTHING IS GOING TO GET BETTER. IT'S NOT."

APPENDIX A: THE LIVING MORE LIGHTLY PROFILE
(Taken from *Earth Education: A New Beginning*)

Circle the response that most closely represents your lifestyle. Don't try to do "well." Just be as honest as you can. You may be surprised. Please pay close attention to your choice for each statement as the sequence of your options will vary (R = Rarely, S = Sometimes, U =Usually). If an item is definitely not applicable, just leave it blank. Instructions for scoring appear at the end. (Please note . . . we have included some items in this list primarily to promote further thought and reflection. We hope you won't let any single statement cloud your perception about the importance of the overall profile.)

ENVIRONMENTAL HABITS

Food consumption and packaging

I take my own paper sacks (or other containers) to the grocery store	U	S	R
I avoid purchasing things in plastic containers	U	S	R
I purchase food in bulk quantities and containers	U	S	R
I eat red meat (high on the food chain) more than twice a week	R	S	U
I avoid eating animals raised in modern factory-farm production	U	S	R
I avoid snacks and other food with lots of packaging	U	S	R
I prepare meals without using processed foods	U	S	R
I grow or buy organically produced food	U	S	R
I belong to a food co-op in my community	U	S	R
I use paper towels and/or napkins	R	S	U
I read the labels before buying food	U	S	R
I eat food grown locally and in season	U	S	R
I grow some of my own food	U	S	R
I compost organic food waste	U	S	R
I use styrofoam products	R	S	U
I eat at fast-food restaurants	R	S	U
I make use of leftovers	U	S	R
I eat on airplanes	R	S	U

Impact Points _____

Honsehold Energy and Supplies

I turn off electric lights and appliances when no one is in the room	U	S	R
I heat a portion of my home with renewable energy	U	S	R
I run the dishwasher only when it is full and then let them drip dry	U	S	R

I decide what I want from the refrigerator before opening it	U	S	R
I set a thermostat at no higher than 68 degrees during the day and 55 degrees at night	U	S	R
I use air conditioning in the summer	R	S	U
I avoid using non-essential electrical appliances (i.e. can opener, electric toothbrush, hair dryer, hedge trimmer, etc.)	U	S	R
I turn the pilot lights off on my stove	U	S	R
I check the insulation and caulking in my house and improvewhen necessary	U	S	R
I keep the windows closed when cooling or heating my home	U	S	R
I make my own household cleaners out of non-toxic materials	U	S	R
I use storm doors and windows	U	S	R
I use a non-motorized push lawnmower and/or avoid cutting the lawn	U	S	R
I avoid washing clothes before they really need it	U	S	R
I wash my clothes in cold water	U	S	R
I let my washing drip dry	U	S	R
I avoid using decorative lighting	U	S	R
I use low wattage and/or energy saving bulbs wherever I can	U	S	R
I use facial tissues	R	S	U
I use natural cleaners and grooming agents	U	S	R
I use pesticides	R	S	U
I avoid buying plastics of all kinds	U	S	R
I purchase well-made, functional clothing	U	S	R
I avoid purchasing a daily paper	U	S	R
I share things with my neighbors	U	S	R

Impact Points _____

Water and Waste Water

I bathe everyday	R	S	U
I limit my showers to five minutes or less	U	S	R
I turn off the water when brushing my teeth or shaving.	U	S	R
I install regulators on shower heads to reduce the water used	U	S	R
I use phosphate free detergents	U	S	R
I place something in my toilet tank to reduce the amount of water used	U	S	R
I avoid pouring toxic substances or unknown chemicals down the drain	U	S	R
I purchase scented, imprinted paper	R	S	U
I use naturalistic landscaping	U	S	R

Impact Points _____

Transportation

I purchase internal combustion vehicles with more than four cylinders	R	S	U
I drive a vehicle that achieves 25 miles or more per gallon	U	S	R
I regularly walk or ride a bicycle somewhere rather than drive	U	S	R
I car pool or use mass transit	U	S	R
I keep my vehicle properly tuned and serviced for energy efficiency	U	S	R
I purchase radial tires and keep them properly inflated	U	S	R
I drive the same car for eight or more years	U	S	R

Impact Points _____

Recycling and Reusing

I recycle aluminum	U	S	R
I recycle paper	U	S	R
I recycle glass bottles	U	S	R
I recycle metal cans	U	S	R
I recycle motor oil	U	S	R
I use returnable bottles whenever possible	U	S	R
I reuse envelopes	U	S	R
I use both sides of paper	U	S	R
I do not throw away items which could be repaired or reused	U	S	R
I give unnecessary clothing and furnishings to charity	U	S	R
I reuse plastic bags and bottles	U	S	R
I buy throw-away pens	R	S	U
I refuse paper or plastic sacks for my purchases	U	S	R
I use disposable diapers	R	S	U

Impact Points _____

Natural Contact and Respect

I visit or take a walk in a natural area each week	U	S	R
I notice the changing phases of the moon	U	S	R
I share my love of nature with others	U	S	R
I seek support within my spiritual views for living more lightly on the earth	U	S	R
I pay attention to the natural changes in the seasons	U	S	R
I make an extended visit to a natural setting at least once each year	U	S	R
I recreate within 50 miles of where I live	U	S	R
I treat all things with respect	U	S	R
I eat baby animals (veal, lamb, etc.)	R	S	U
I bell my cat	U	S	R
I kill things for recreation	R	S	U
I practice minimum impact techniques when I go camping	U	S	R
I purchase products made from wild animals	R	S	U

Impact Points _____

Miscellaneous

I engage in (low energy) recreation activities	U	S	R
I spay or neuter my dog or cat	U	S	R
I work at learning more about ecological processes and what they mean for me	U	S	R
I examine any financial investments I make in terms of the environmental impact produced	U	S	R
I purchase simple, durable, low energy things whenever possible	U	S	R
I work consistently at improving my own habits	U	S	R

Impact Points _____

Environmental Participation

I discuss pending environmental legislation with people around me	U	S	R
I ask my workplace to engage in more environmentally sound practices	U	S	R
I help restore natural areas	U	S	R

I keep abreast of current environmental issues	U	S	R
I actively support an environmental group	U	S	R
I inform my elected officials about my environmental concerns and recommend actions	U	S	R
I contribute 1% or more of my annual income to environmental causes	U	S	R

Impact Points _____

Standard Additions

Number of rooms in my dwelling	1-3	4-6	7+
Number of automobiles I own	0	1	2+
Number of recreational vehicles I own	0	1	2+
Number of houses I own or rent	0	1	2+
Number of miles I travel to work/school	0-4	5-14	15+
Number of medium to large pets I own	0	1	2+
Number of pounds I am overweight	0	10-20	21+

Total Standard Additions _____

Reproduction Surcharge

Number of children I have had or am planning to have: _____

Standard Subtractions

I wash my dishes by hand (5 points) _____
I use a composting toilet (5 points) _____
I buy used clothing or make my own (5 points) _____
I wash my clothes by hand and let them drip dry (5 points) _____
I have made arrangements for a natural burial (5 points) _____
I do not own my own car (5 points) _____
I buy very few material things (10 points) _____
I do not use air conditioning to cool my home in the summer (5 points) _____
I teach my children how to live lightly on this earth (10 points per child) _____
I have relatives, friends, etc. living with me (10 points per person) _____

Total Standard Subtractions _____

Scoring

First, go back and tally up the number of points you have for each section. Circles in the left column are worth 0 points, those in the middle column are worth 2 points, and those in the right column receive 5 points. Enter the total points for each Environmental Habits section below.

Environmental Habits _____

Food consumption and Packaging _____

Household Energy and Supplies _____

Water and Waste Water _____

Transportation _____

Recycling and Reuse   _____

Natural Contact and Respect   _____

Miscellaneous   _____

Environmental Participation   _____

Total Environmental Habits _____

Second, tally the number of points you should add to the above totals. In the standard additions section circles in the left column are worth 0 points, those in the middle are worth 10 points and those in the right gain 25 points each. Next, figure out the surcharge for the number of children you have produced. (We don't mean to denigrate the value of human life, but that is probably the greatest impact you will personally ever have on the planet.) To do this you should multiply the total number of children you have produced by 100. Finally, total up the number of points you have under standard subtractions. Now you can enter the totals below and finalize your score:

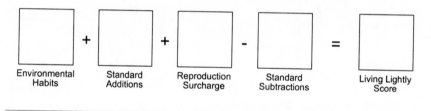

| Environmental | Standard | Reproduction | Standard | Living Lightly |
| Habits | Additions | Surcharge | Subtractions | Score |

References

Chief Seattle. 1987. Chief Seattle's challenge. *Off Belay* (February) 15–19.

Dr. Seuss. 1971. *The Lorax.* New York: Random House.

Dustin, D. 1990. Looking inward to save the outdoors. *Parks and Recreation* (September): 86–90.

Dustin, D. 1984. Recreational limits in a world of ethics. *Parks and Recreation.* (March): 49–51, 70.

Hall, J. 1990. *The Steward: A Biblical symbol come of age.* Grand Rapids: Eerdmans.

Klein, J. 1992. Whose values? *Newsweek* (June 8): 18–22.

Kohlberg, L. 1976. The moral atmosphere of the school. In *Moral education: It comes with the territory,* edited by D. Purpel, 196–220. Berkeley, CA: McCutchan.

Leopold, A. 1966. *A Sand County almanac.* New York: Oxford University Press.

Nash, R. 1982. *Wilderness and the American mind.* New Haven: Yale University Press.

President's Commission on Americans Outdoors. 1987. New York: Island Press.

Salholz, E. 1992. Values in the classroom. *Newsweek* (June 8): 26–27.

Schaeffer, F. 1970. *Pollution and the death of man: The Christian view of ecology.* Wheaton: Tyndale House.

Thoreau, H. D. 1973. *Walden.* Garden City: Anchor Press.

Van Matre, S. 1990. *Earth education: A new beginning.* Warrenville, IL: Institute for Earth Education.

White, L. 1967. The historical roots of our ecologic crisis. *Science* 155, 1203–1207.

Wilkinson, L., ed. 1980. *Earthkeeping: Christian stewardship of natural resources.* Grand Rapids: Eerdmans.

SECTION FOUR

Play, Sport, and Athletics

It's ironic that the aspect of leisure in the North American culture which has experienced the greatest participation rates has been neglected the most by Christian scholars. With few exceptions, play, sport, and athletics have not been scrutinized as to their appropriateness for Christian involvement. Consequently, we run the risk of adopting secular standards for our participation in this area. Clearly, what is needed is a philosophical basis for participation in play, sport, and athletics that is firmly rooted in the Holy Scriptures.

It is to the task of establishing a biblically based understanding of play, sport, and athletics to which the writers of this section direct their work. The approach each writer takes varies. Shirl Hoffman develops a foundation for sports participation based in the leisure experience. Visker and Zuidema propose that a biblical understanding of play is the foundational element in a Christian approach to sports participation. John Byl makes a substantial contribution to this task by helping the reader come to an understanding of the terms play, game, sport, and athletics which, in many cases and perhaps incorrectly, have been used inter-changeably. Jim Mathisen provides a fascinating look into the use of sport as a tool for evangelism. His historical account and critique of muscular Christianity provide valuable insight into the relationship between Christianity and sports participation. Sterling, Keller, and Naylor investigate competition in church sport leagues to determine its affect on attitudes and the importance of winning to those who participate. Finally, Murry Hall demonstrates the need for Christians to develop ethical standards for participation in sport and suggests a model for ethical behavior in sport.

Tom Visker

Chapter Eleven

Sport, Play, and Leisure in the Christian Experience

SHIRL J. HOFFMAN

Those venturing drafts of a Christian philosophy of sport risk yielding to two contradictory temptations. On one hand is the temptation to make too little of sport, to reduce it to existentially irrelevant therapy or a form of work that has little personal meaning for participants. Those who succumb to this temptation are quick to point to sport's value in promoting health or fitness, or in the case of colleges and universities, to its benefits in attracting students, money, and alumni support.

At the other extreme is the temptation to make too much of sport by attributing to it qualities and expectations that it can never realize. For example, theologian Michael Novak, in his much discussed book *The Joy of Sports* (1976), described sport as a "natural religion." The rituals of sport speak of communal realities that Novak labeled as collective experiences of a higher order. These, said Novak, testify of sport's religious character. Sports "feed a deep human hunger" and "place humans in touch with dimly perceived features of human life within the cosmos" (20). Religion scholar Charles Prebish identified sport as the newest and fastest-growing religion in America, "far outdistancing whatever is in second place" (1984, 318).

Scholars in the evangelical Christian community who have written on the role of sport in the Christian life have tended to succumb to the former temptation. The result has been the promulgation within the Christian community of a rather degraded view of sport. In an essay, ironically intended by its author to elevate the status of athletics in the Christian college, a historian summed up his argument with the crisp dualistic assertion that "games are things of the body, and thus of a lower order than things of the spirit" (Wilson 1987, 5). The same tone was heard from the editors of *Christianity Today*: "Among the various things we can relax with, athletics are low on the scale of demonstrable religious significance" (Sport: Are we overdoing it, 1972).

Given such a disparaging view, perhaps we shouldn't be surprised to discover that few attempts have been made to integrate the sport experience into a Christian outlook on life. Although the literature abounds with biographies of popular Christian athletes, such works tend to be designed to evangelize and inspire rather than seriously evaluate the role of sport in the Christian life. Christian scholars in the humanities and social sciences have generally avoided the subject altogether, even where these same professors remain glued to their television sets for hours during the Super Bowl, or hold reputations on their own campuses as avid fans of the college team.

This tendency for Christian scholars to diminish the impact that sports have on the way we think and act and feel in favor of their presumed utilitarian effects probably has much to do with a pernicious dualism that associates sport more with the body than with the spirit, and the dubious status that body has been accorded in the minds (if not the theologies) of Christian academics. Rendering sport "a thing of the body" relegates it to a common class of perfunctory human activities. When no distinctions can be discerned between the human experiences of dribbling a basketball, climbing a mountain, or driving a golf ball, and such routine chores as fixing a family car, mowing the lawn, or mending a broken water pipe, it is understandable why good minds have chosen to concentrate on other, more interesting topics.

Obviously sound anatomies and physiologies are essential to playing sports, but they are no more critical to sport than they are to all of the performing arts. One must be fit to play sports, just as one must be fit to sculpt, to dance, to paint, or to play the piano, activities which, like sport, rely heavily on skillful and often exhausting human performances. Biological integrity is the key to producing human action, but it is merely a *condition of the action, not the action itself.* In neither case—sports or the arts—should the condition be offered as the organizing principle around which to develop a Christian perspective.

Sport as Play

Getting off on the right foot toward a Christian philosophy of sport requires that we position it accurately within the entire range of activities known to humanity. I believe sport is most appropriately positioned within the family of activities known as play. As used by scholars, the term play denotes the broad range of activities—theater, music, art, gardening, boating, etc.—that we intentionally bracket off (literally or imaginatively) from "the real world." Sport is best viewed as a variety of this general class. Daryl Siedentop has wisely noted that "the weekend golfer is motivated by the same impulse that activates the weekend painter, the member of the community theater or the amateur musician; each is at play, and it is only the species of play that distinguishes one from the other" (1980, 260–261).

Most important for consideration here is not the types of activities that comprise the family of play but the nature of "playfulness," the unique cast of soul that characterizes those at play. Playfulness is that something "in play" which, as Johan Huizinga pointed out, "goes beyond the confines of purely physical or purely biological activity." "In play there is something 'at play' which transcends the immediate needs of life and imparts meaning to the action," said Huizinga (1950, 1). It is this "something at play" in sports that was described by the late Bart Giammatti as "part of our artistic and imaginative impulse" (1989, 38), and by Arthur Holmes as that which has "aesthetic and intellectual potential" (1981, 47). And it is this "something at play" which offers hope for integrating sports with the Christian faith.

By positioning sport within the family of activities called play we acknowledge that sport is more than perspiration and heart rate and muscle endurance; it impacts the human spirit and gives access to untranslatable expressions of the soul. There is a world of difference between the experience of hitting a golf ball or running a mile or serving a tennis ball and the mundane experience of repairing broken pipes. Plumbing is a useful and important activity that can be performed to the glory of God, but there is nothing inherent in the *experience* of fitting pipes together that quickens one's imaginative impulse or sharpens one's spiritual vision. If this distinction between these two vastly different realms of human experience is denied, any attempt to integrate sport with Christian thought and belief is doomed from the start. Christian philosophies of sport will hold no more water than will Christian philosophies of plumbing.

The suggestion that sport has the potential for touching our minds and emotions and spirits in ways denied us in everyday life, or that it, like art, poetry, and the dance, can be an avenue of religious expression is radical only because of the distance we have allowed to occur between sport and religion. Sport and games made their appearance in culture in connection with religious rituals and festivals orchestrated to celebrate the mythic origins and imagined destinies of primitive peoples (Barasch 1970). Richard Mandell has suggested that historians "may be making artificial separations if we remove sport very far from the ritual, the dance and the theater" (1984, 5). Properly blended with the Christian life, sport aims not at physical fitness or refreshment for work, but at the same quality of expressive potential we customarily associate with other forms of play such as art, poetry, music, and dance.

Unfortunately, the *potential* is not the *reality*. In *From Ritual to Record*, Allen Guttmann traces the historical transformation of sport from a rite which emphasized qualitative distinctions quite appropriate for religious expression to contests that have become fascinated with quantitative records and self-aggrandizement. Says Guttman: "The bond between the secular and the sacred has been broken, the attachment to the realm of the transcendent has been severed" (1978, 26). This is not to say that modern sports have been gutted of their expressive potential. Indeed, they are extraordinarily rich contexts for expression. When people gather for sport, values will be instilled and visions nourished. But these needn't be *Christian* values or visions that illuminate the Christian experience; in my view, they usually aren't. For this reason sports can be deceptively dangerous experiences for Christians and Christian institutions, not all that unlike art, to which Seerveld has noted Christians are vulnerable because "it catches people at ease" (1964, 29). Thus, it is important to recognize that sport, both as a participant and spectator activity, inherently reinforces values, celebrates symbols, invokes passions, and casts up visions, not all of which lend themselves to an articulation with Christian thought and belief. Thus we should not take our cues from what we've allowed sport to become, but on what it might be, given proper direction by the Christian community.

Sport as Leisure

When sport is viewed as play and as part of the expressive domain, it nudges up against traditional concepts of *leisure*, a term which bears a close and often indistinguishable resemblance to play. A careful analysis of philosophers' descriptions of the cast of mind and soul of the person "at leisure" and the person "at play" lead one to conclude that the disposition called leisure is the same disposition others call "playfulness." Elegant arguments have been made for both leisure (Pieper 1962) and play (Huizinga 1950) as seedbeds of culture. Both have been credited as essential avenues for human expression, and both have been shown anthropologically, historically, and sociologically to have longstanding ties to religion. Thus, any comprehensive Christian apologia for sport must be anchored in a careful analysis of both leisure and play. In what follows, special emphasis is placed on sport's ties to leisure, although I am not certain that a similar essay drawing on the vast literature on play would arrive at any different conclusions.

The Ethical Problem of Free Time

When mention is made of leisure, attention automatically turns to the notion of free time, even though many leisure theorists are quick to dismiss any important connections between the two. Leisure is an attitude of soul, we are told. It has no reference to time. Without blunting the force of this critical truth, I believe some concessions can be made to an intermediate position that posits free time as a condition which has special potential for nurturing and amplifying the spirit known as leisure. Calls for leading all of one's life in a "leisurely fashion" (Vos 1979) miss the mark, not because it is impossible to experience the spirit of leisure when one is chained to the desk at the office, but because proponents underestimate the way unencumbered time conditions the spirit for this special attitude of soul.

Before considering the implications of viewing sport as a leisure pursuit, we should clear up one ethical dilemma seemingly posed by casting sport as a "free time" activity. Sports are activities we have invented to pursue in our *discretionary* time, time over which we have maximum control. It is the time left after completing tasks we feel an obligation to do—meeting *existence needs* (those occasioned by one's biological integrity such as eating and sleeping, for example) or meeting *subsistence needs* (those related to obtaining the basic essentials of food, shelter, clothing, etc.). The concept of discretionary time can be extended to mean freedom from any obligations that compel us, contractually or psychologically, to do anything in a measurable block of time. Free or discretionary time is the time during which we are freest to determine what we will do, with whom we will do it, where it shall be done, and under what conditions. Thus, positioning a Christian conception of sports within the framework of leisure and drawing tight connections between leisure and leisure time seem to create a thorny ethical dilemma concerning Christians' responsibility for being good stewards of their time. Time is our most valuable commodity. The story is told of a student who, upon hearing that the great runner, Pavlo Nurmi, had set the world record for the mile run, dashed into philosophy class and told his professor: "Sir, Nurmi has just knocked two seconds off the mile record!" The professor fixed a cold eye on the student and asked: "And how does the distinguished Finnish runner propose to employ the time he has saved?" The professor's point was that time "freed up" raises unavoidable questions concerning how that time should be "spent." "Spent" is an especially apposite term to use here, because time is a zero sum commodity. That is, one can't really "split" time in any meaningful way. Hours and minutes and seconds once "spent" can never be reclaimed.

Thus, a decision about how one *will* spend his or her time is, in the same instant, a decision about how one *will not* spend it. Choosing to spend an afternoon on the golf course, for example, is at the same time a choice *not* to spend the same time visiting the sick, helping the poor, or participating in the religious experiences of private or communal worship. Theologian Lewis Smedes described the foil in penetrating fashion: "Every child of God is expected to repeat each night: 'Forgive us the good we have left undone'" (1975, 55). This notion of stewardship, encapsulated in the New Testament's twice repeated admonition to "redeem the time," necessarily conditions a Christian view of sports. We may not wish it were so, but the cold fact of the matter is that an afternoon on the golf course or tennis court or on the couch watching a football game is a choice freely made from among the entire panoply of alternative activities which might have been chosen to do.

Now we can begin to see why health and fitness have figured so prominently in popular apologias for sport. Casting sport in a utilitarian perspective moves it out from under the long ethical shadow cast by the notion of discretionary time. If we can show that sport is essential for the health or psychological release it offers to participants, it takes on the character of all activities we do to satisfy existence or subsistence needs. That which we tell ourselves we *must* do (to maintain our biological integrity) is much easier to justify than that which we *choose* to do in our free time.

But utilitarian arguments for sport aren't really defensible. For example, sports—in their popular contexts in American society—are not effective means to physical fitness or psychological development, nor do they contain any inherent character building value. To make matters worse, the ends brought about by sport often are precisely the opposite of those we often claim for it. For example, those who hail sport for its health benefits and as an activity that "builds the body-temple" are finding it increasingly difficult to balance a conception of the body as a sacred trust with the plague of debilitating injuries associated with sports participation (Hoffman 1991). A long career spent playing sports—from the obviously violent interpersonal sports like football, boxing, and hockey, to the deceptively violent individual sports like marathon running, gymnastics or baseball—is virtually guaranteed to produce permanent debilitation. On what grounds can Christians involve themselves in high school and college sports events at which state regulators mandate the presence of a fully equipped ambulance? Those who seek to justify sport as a facilitator of psychological release are confronted with a growing body of research which suggests that sports stimulate rather than sooth angry passion. It seems clear, for example, that fans are much more likely to leave certain athletic contests more hostile and aggressive than when they walked into the stadium (Goldstein 1971). And claims for sport as a moral tutor ("sport develops character") can easily be deflated by a growing body of research which shows its effects on value formation in young people to be dismal, even alarming (Weiss and Bredemeier 1990).

Even if it could be demonstrated that sport produces positive effects in these areas, there is no reason to believe that sport is the only activity by which these effects could be realized. For any practical benefit one claims for sport, other less ethically problematic means can be proposed for achieving it. If one is after physical fitness how much better to seek it as a by-product of mowing a neighbor's lawn, or building houses for the poor than through the apparently serif-indulgent act of playing? If psychological release and relaxation or character development is the desired goal, why not seek them through quiet devotions and meditation than through the agitation of sport? At its very best then, sport is an indirect route to achieving anything of practical importance. This is hardly a novel suggestion. It was a point Santayana thought so obvious that only a "barbarian" would fail to recognize:

> Essentially sport has no purpose at all: it is an end in itself, a part of that free fruition of life which is the purpose of other things, when they are good for anything, and which, when present, can make a long life better than a short one. Its possible uses are incidental, like those of the fine arts, religion or friendship. (Shaughnessey 1977, 180)

Thus the defense of sport within the Christian life, if it has a defense, will not be by showing that it serves some important ends, but by demonstrating how it graces and enriches moments of free time in which productivity is not a consideration.

Leisure and Christian Identity

Conceiving sport as a human activity that can grace and enrich free time is one and the same as conceiving it as a "leisure activity," or an activity done to support and sustain a spirit of leisure. Leisure theorists describe leisure as a special disposition characterized by moments when we free ourselves from a sense of care, worry, and obligation. Sebastian de Grazia has described it as "a state of being freed of everyday necessity" (1962, 246) and, like many others, has linked it to activities that we perform "for their own sake," that is, not as a means toward another end. From the days of its earliest illumination by the ancient Greeks, leisure has been portrayed as the condition that spawns the highest expressions of culture (O'Loughlin 1978).

It shouldn't surprise us then, that those examining leisure from the perspective of religion locate it quite close to the spirit that accompanies worship. Josef Pieper contended that the celebration of worship constituted the "deepest springs by which leisure is fed and continues to be vital" (1962, 76). Pieper's point becomes clearer when we appreciate the fact that leisure is not only the spirit that derives from being *free from* claims and obligations, it also is *freedom to* do what one wants to do and be the type of individual one wants to be. Leisure is the mind, body, and spirit joining in a sensing and expressing of the deep desires of the heart.

Writer Leland Ryken has described leisure as an innate human pursuit of what a person regards as a desirable identity (Ryken 1987). Put another way, leisure moments offer Christians opportunities to be the kind of people they really want to be. For Christians struggling under the daily pressures and obligations of earning a living or caring for a family, sport—as a leisure experience—offers a truly remarkable sphere of existence. Here, in a world set off from the "real world," Christians are free to be the kind of people they know they could be in all walks of life were it not for the unrelenting pressures of a cold, cruel world that so easily masks their Christian dispositions. At leisure, released from the crushing demands of daily life, time can be set aside to shed the camouflage of natural man, to polish up the *imago Dei,* to regain spiritual balance, and to show others and themselves who they really are. As a feature of leisure time, sport offers Christians the greatest opportunity they have this side of eternity "to be and become the new man after Christ's own splendid example" (Dahl 1972, 70–71).

This notion of freedom denies Christians all their clumsy excuses for not being the kind of people they say they really want to be. For those who would have followed a higher ethical plane were it not for the need to survive the competition of the business world, leisure time offers a chance to think and act in peaceful, cooperative surroundings. For those who claim they would have been more honest or more civil were it not for the press of deadlines and an impossible agenda, leisure time offers opportunities to seek out social situations where honesty and courtesy are valued. For those who, like the Psalmist, yearn to "bless the Lord at all times," but recognize that praising the Lord with timbrel and dance is not likely to be appreciated by one's co-workers or boss (especially when done on company time), sport *as leisure* presents unlimited possibilities. If it is indeed the case that inside every furrow-browed, culture-constrained, work-manipulated Christian, there is a more ethical, sensitive, radiant, vibrant, joyous, worshipful Christian trying to get out, the logical expectation is that if it comes out at all it will come out when one has "free time."

Applied to sports this is a fairly radical notion. Entrenched within the Christian community's conception of sport is the nearly subliminal mindset that sports represent a kind of mardi gras for Christians, a time for harmlessly yielding to the inescapable impulses of one's fallen nature. One can point to many examples of this from Christian literature. An especially poignant example is found in Daniel Jenkin's otherwise marvelous book *Christian Maturity and Christian Success*. Jenkins contends that all humanity suffers from "the hangover of evolution, possessing deeply rooted within ourselves aggressive, combative, and competitive urges, which often make us anything but gentle in spirit, makers of peace, and magnanimous, even when we set out with the best intentions to be so" (1982, 112). While we might hope Jenkins would view leisure-centered sport as the unique opportunity to "sober up" from the "hangover of evolution," instead he views it as an occasion for its cathartic expression. In his view, sport offers Christians an opportunity to channel and release these regrettable urges "in a harmless, enjoyable, and sometimes socially constructive way." "[We] need games in which it is right to want to win and to be disappointed if you lose, to be shamelessly and cheerfully partisan, and even to show off a little" (113).

A leisure-oriented philosophy of sports moves you in the opposite direction. As a free-time activity, sport offers Christians unique opportunities to be the kind of people they would really like to be. Moments of free time offer opportunities for making contact with our religious zones. These "ruptures in the paramount reality" (Berger 1980) can be brief respites from the spiritually alienating forces of daily life. They promise peace and security, and opportunities for exercising the imaginative and religious impulses. More than this, leisure moments can be the means—no, they logically *should be* the means—for recovering lost spiritual identities that have been distorted by a pressurized existence. We recover them in their best and purest form in that leisure which is worship. But we can recover them in other compartments of our lives as well, especially during those moments we bracket off as "free from" the distractions of the never ending list of "shoulds." Leisure theorist Richard Kraus put it nicely when he said, "The religious person who is part of the Judeo-Christian tradition will therefore view leisure time as time reserved by God, which must be filled with spiritual meaning—not necessarily worship, but spent according to divine intent" (1977, 159). Sport is not worship, but, when designed as a *leisure experience*, it offers potential for encouraging the same quality of spirit which exhibits its highest expressions in worship.

Sport as a Leisure Opportunity

All of this has convinced me that a sport can legitimately draw on a Christian's reservoir of time, energy, and emotions, only to the extent that such activities cultivate that state we have described as leisure. That is, at their best and in their most defensible forms, sport activities—as personal recreation or as institutional programs—are "leisure opportunities." Played in proper contexts by those motivated by the spirit of leisure, sports offer the *potential* for enriching and extending the leisure state. However, sports do not guarantee leisure. The sports people choose to do have at least as much of a chance to starve as to strengthen, to weaken as to amplify, to dampen as to energize the leisure state. At best, a game (or any other activity done for the sake of leisure) merely nurtures-in those that play or watch it the leisurely disposition that people bring to the playground. It also would be a mistake to think that we can play ourselves into a leisurely frame of mind. At most, sports are a spiritual response, a way of expressing the remarkable feelings of spiritual security.

How should we characterize this ideal state which Christians might logically be expected to aspire while participating in sports? The question is important because of its obvious centrality to devising any criteria for evaluating the effectiveness of activities intended to be leisure activities. The desired spiritual state, for example, would be a key consideration in addressing such questions as the following: Is football a game that should be sponsored by Christian institutions? How should church-league basketball games or Christian college athletic programs be structured? What is the role of competition in sports; is it possible to compete and, at the same time, manifest the Christian distinctives? The answers to all such questions hinge upon what we envision to be the role of leisure and leisure time in the Christian experience, and specifically upon our expectations for such experiences on the human spirit.

As a way of "trying on" a couple of the more important characteristics of leisure to see if our current models of sport "fit," I have chosen two characteristics that leisure theorists would consider to be indispensable features of the leisure spirit: contentment and contemplation. Where disjunctions are found between these dispositions and those that are nurtured by our sport activities, I think our sport activities need to be carefully reexamined.

Leisure as Contentment

In his monumental work on leisure, Sebastian de Grazia positions a spirit of striving at the opposite pole from a spirit of leisure because "striving means you want something badly, that you are in a state of necessity, the state opposed to leisure" (1962, 353). An attitude of contentment, of peaceful resignation, is at the heart of leisure. It is an inward tranquility, an attitude of rejoicing in *how things are* rather than what they might be. Leisure is an affirming attitude which, as Dahl reminded us, "liberates us from our illusion of striving and performance by enabling us to be open to the presence of grace and peace in our daily walk" (1977, 26).

Contentment is not consumed with worry about how things will turn out, and it is not sensing the need to prove one's worth by bringing about a predetermined result. Contented people do not hitch their sense of identity to contingencies. Not that contentment is incompatible with uncertainty (for uncertainty is a critical feature of play) but leisure doesn't embrace uncertainty to the point of being consumed by it. And it is not allowing events, neither wins nor losses, personal defeats nor triumphs, to alter the underlying peace that lies at the heart of leisure. In his marvelous little book *Wellness, Spirituality and Sports*, Thomas Ryan confesses: "Whenever the god of success looms up in front of me, if I can recognize it as an idol, can recognize that I am already saved by the grace of God's free gift, then I am freed from the tyranny of having to perform and achieve and produce in order to prove my worth" (1986, 179).

Characterizing leisure as contentment comes very close to traditional characterizations of the Sabbath. Arthur Holmes has described the Sabbath as "a picture of leisure and play replacing fear of what will happen if we are not productive" (1981, 46). The Sabbath not only celebrates the resurrection, but it also incorporates many insights from the older Jewish Sabbath. Daniel Jenkins was reminded of Karl Barth's observation that what was the Sabbath day for the Creator was the first day for the Lord's creatures. This understanding casts light on the Sabbath, not as a day of rest earned by a week of work, but as Jenkins said,

> a day on which we are to stand back from our everyday occasions and look at them in the perspective of eternity, taking heart from the knowledge that God's kingdom is our home and rejoicing in the way in which things are moving toward the fulfillment of God's original intention in creation. (1982, 110)

Taking one's cues from the Sabbath means that one doesn't pursue leisure activities as a refreshment for another six days of work. Rather the Sabbath heightens our sensitivity to leisure as a special form of consciousness, a day for the people to stop and remember, as Harvey Cox pointed out, "that there will be a time, as there once was a time, when toil and pain will cease . . . when we will no longer require the rhythm of work and repose because there will be no difference between them" (1977, 71–72).

There is an undeniable playful ingredient in this conception of leisure and the Sabbath, a kind of pretending that we are already in the heavenly country, already glorified, but not in a way that causes us to retreat from reality. Rather, as Jenkins notes, "It is an imaginative apprehension of a life fuller than our present capacities are able to express, so that there has to be a pretense of play, in our attempts to anticipate that life" (1982, 111). But there is a connection between the Sabbath and leisure that goes far beyond this. As a model for leisure, celebration of the Lord's day should be normative for the way in which Christians enjoy sports and games, for "it is on the Lord's day above all else that the Lord's people should be those of gentle spirit, peacemakers, magnanimous, generous, and joyful" (110). Cultivating the contentment of leisure is acquiring a Sabbath consciousness. No more, no less.

It is apparent that a spirit of contentment is ill-suited to those who seek success within the framework of modern models of sport. Modern competitive psychology thrives on states of discontent and uneasiness, and, where players are judged to be "too content," the smart coach unpacks his bag of psychological gimmicks in order to create perceived needs which only victory in a competition can satisfy. During the 1991 football season a player for the San Francisco 49ers sported a T-shirt emblazoned with the motto: "Contentment Stinks: Stay Focused." It was his way of reminding his teammates not to let down in their drive to attain the NFL Championship. The spirit of the motto along with the familiar locker room rhetorical question—"How badly do you *want* it?"—underscore the enormous gulf separating the notion of leisure from the dominant ethic driving modern sports.

When games are approached as tests of personal or institutional honor, or when the significance of winning or losing a contest is allowed to embody a symbolism that goes far beyond the confines of the athletic field, court, or gymnasium, the logical outcome is creation of a dissonance that can only be resolved by the players' actions. As such, sport events are not intended for expressive purposes: they are intended to "prove" a team's superiority, and by reflection, the superiority of those who feel the players in some inexpressible way "represent them." Most social contexts in which we have embedded our sports virtually insure that players will approach contests with an acute sense of need rather than the contentment of leisure, and the reasons are obvious. Given the goals of modern sport and the conditions we appear willing to tolerate to insure their attainment, the motivation derived from a contrived, yet deeply sensed need, is genuinely effective. It works well on the battlefield, and it works well in sports. The leisurely state is not a disposition that lends itself to "preserving the school's honor" on the basketball floor or winning the Super Bowl. It is not an attitude of soul that contributes to any discernable, practical end. Rather it is the irrepressible response of a soul temporarily freed from the daily chain of obligations.

Leisure as Contemplation

The contentment of leisure is closely related to a contemplative disposition. This association can be traced back to the ancients who considered contemplation to be the most important leisure activity because it, more than any other human endeavor, marked humanity's uniqueness. Only humans and the gods could contemplate; hence when humans contemplated, they came as close as they could come to the divine. The Christian tradition also accorded an important role to contemplation, not because it mimicked God, but because contemplation was a way of seeking God and reflecting on the truth. The contemplator is one who has taken to heart the admonition of Psalm 46:10: "Be still [have leisure] and know that I am God." Early church architecture featuring cavernous cathedrals with enormous heights, domes, and spires had its basis in engendering a contemplative attitude in churchgoers. Contemplation was the chief activity of the monastery. It was assigned a priority over everything else. Work was something to be done in one's spare time, and those forms of work which least distracted the spiritual faculties (manual labor) were the most favored. Commenting on Aquinas' views in *Summa Theologica*, de Grazia notes, "Religious activity stands above secular activity but contemplation above all else. The act itself crowns man's highest faculty, the power to know the truth" (1962, 28).

Forces unleashed by the Protestant Reformation eventually elevated work over the simple act of contemplation as the highest and best use of the Christian's time. It has had an enduring effect on our perception of leisure and its relationship to contemplation in the Christian life. When the work spirit filters our vision of what is important, the focus invariably shifts to a consideration of ends rather than means. In leisure activities such as sports, the purely secondary considerations of human accomplishment, health, well being, and human development become goals for our "leisure pursuits," rather then the overriding question of whether such activities have helped sharpen our spiritual insights.

Of course Christians are called to work, and it would be foolish to deny that in certain circumstances work can be performed with a certain contemplative disposition. Douglas Steere wrote an excellent book, *Work and Contemplation* (1957), largely to show the reality of this proposition. Acknowledging this, however, does not detract from the wisdom known to ancients—that we are freest to contemplate, to ponder an eternal existence of leisure, to have our spirits soar their highest and to sound out our deepest spiritual longings when freed from the compulsion to produce.

Contemplation is largely a matter of harboring a disposition that opens us up to realities too easily obscured by the busyness of everyday life. Writers have invoked metaphors of seeing (Aquinas spoke of "a simple unimpeded gaze on truth") or listening (Heraclitus talked of "listening to the essence of things") as a way of capturing the essence of contemplation. It differs from work in this important respect: effort paves the way to a successful work end, but effort is not a companion of contemplation. Enlightenment is not something one can produce; it is a gift. In an essay on art appreciation, C.S. Lewis once complained that "the many *use* art and the few *receive* it" (1961, 363). His point was that if you want a work of art to speak to you, you merely have to open yourself up to it. Not to recognize that the first demand a work of art makes on us is surrender, said Lewis, is to behave "like a man who talks when he should listen or gives when he should take" (363).

Finally, we need to note the close ties between the contemplative spirit and the spirit of contentment. Contentment, we have said, comes when we are not driven by a sensed need to accomplish or produce. Those who elevate attainment of an end to outrageous levels are, by definition, driven by their search for a satisfaction of a need and hence not dispositionally suited to a spirit of contemplation.

Sports and Expectant Alertness

All of this sounds well and good, you might say, as a standard to apply to our approaches to the arts, literature, camping, gardening, music and other forms of leisure pursuits, but it doesn't work very well as a standard for evaluating our approaches to sport. Attaining a leisurely disposition while meditating on a work of art or trimming back a rose bush or sightseeing on a motor trip is one thing; attaining it in the midst of exciting and exhausting physical activity is quite another. Yet, vigorous movements tailored to mastering complex skills, even when accompanied by heightened enthusiasm, are not prima facie grounds for dismissing sports as activities that might nurture a contemplative disposition.

Festive occasions, because they free us from the demands of everyday life, can be effective ways of seeing the broader and more subtle dimensions of life. The contemplative act in this case is not as deliberate as contemplation in the context of worship; it is masked and more subdued here. The key is a receptive attitude on the part of the players. Josef Pieper has shown how a receptive spirit can penetrate to the heart of a joyous, even raucous, celebration of a religious festival. "We cling to the feeling that a special spice, essential to the right celebration of a festival, is the kind of *expectant alertness*. One must be able to look through and, as it were, beyond the immediate matter of the festival, including the festal gifts; one must engage in a listening, and therefore silent, meditation upon the fundament of existence" (1965, 13).

Can sports, like religious festivals, really nourish an attitude of expectant alertness in players and spectators? Under the right conditions I believe they can. I don't think it is possible in cases where simple games are converted into sport spectacles which are touted as opportunities to satisfy personal or institutional needs. "School spirit," as expressed in athletic contests, is not a promising route to expectant alertness. I think expectant alertness is unlikely to follow in the wake of hype and promotion that distract us from the basic point of the game: to keep alive, and perhaps to nurture in us a spirit of contentment and contemplation. And expectant alertness will not grace our more combative sports, if only because the "kill or be killed" ethic of such contests force on participants a psychological state (essential for success in such sports) that precludes their remaining open to anything other than delivering and receiving physical assaults. Neither will it accompany any sport activities in which competition (the essential structure of games) gives way to rivalries in which spectators identify with the fortunes of one team or participant and root accordingly.

Finally, expectant alertness will probably escape the growing numbers of well-meaning Christian athletes who have been influenced by the teaching that God is glorified in proportion to the effort they expend in the athletic arena. Those who propagate such messages understand quite well what it takes to win contests but overlook the purpose of leisure activities in the Christian life, and effort is unrelated to this purpose. Regrettably, "sports-faith organizations" continue to propagate the view that the grounds for integrating sport and faith intersect the dominant ethic that drives popular sport; thus what seems best suited to bring about victory also seems best suited for spiritual expression. This view has led to the ill-advised notion that sport performances, like mowing the lawn or fixing broken water pipes, are best viewed as tributes to be offered to God. Not surprisingly, it has worked well for teams bent on satisfying needs fulfilled only by success.

But Christians would do well to reconsider such notions. As leisure, athletic contests are not times for *giving glory to God* as much as they are times for *receiving insights* from God. They are not worship but they can be occasions for sensing the greatness and goodness of God. This awareness happens, however, only when the circumstances surrounding the contest permit it. In my view, our traditional models of sport fall far short of this objective.

Renown Christian educator Frank Gabelein (1979) was once asked if he regarded his pastime of mountain climbing as a means of grace. He replied,

Yes, providing that we do not equate it with such means of grace as the Lord's Supper and do not confuse a kind of mountain mysticism with true religion. But that climbing can uplift the spirit and give one a sense of the greatness of God in creation is undeniable.

Mountain climbing, yes, and I believe it can be the same for other sports as well.

References

Berger, P. 1980. *The heretical imperative: Contemporary possibilities of religious affirmation.* Garden City, NY: Anchor Books.

Cox, H. 1977. *Turning east.* New York: Simon and Schuster.

de Grazia, S. 1962. *Of time, work and leisure.* New York: The Twentieth Century Fund.

Gabelein, F. 1979. Striving for excellence. *Christianity Today* 11. April 20.

Goldstein, J.H. and Arms, R.L. 1971. Effects of observing athletic contests on hostility. *Sociometry* 34, 83–90.

Hoffman, S.J. 1992. Nimrod, Nephilim and the *Athletae Dei.* In *Sport and religion,* edited by S.J. Hoffman, 275–285. Champaign, IL: Human Kinetics Publishers.

Holmes, A. 1981. Towards a Christian play ethic. *Christian Scholar's Review* 11(1): 41–48.

Huizinga, J. 1950. *Homo Ludens: A study of the play element in culture.* Boston: Beacon.

Jenkins, D. 1982. *Christian maturity and Christian success.* Philadelphia: Fortress Press.

Kraus, R.G. 1977. *Recreation today* (2nd ed.), New York: Goodyear.

Lewis, C .S. 1961. How the few and the many use pictures. In *The Christian imagination,* edited by L. Ryken, 359–365. Grand Rapids: Baker.

Mandell, R. 1984. *Sport: A cultural history.* New York: Colombia University Press.

Novak, M. 1976. *The joy of sports.* New York: Basic Books.

O'Loughlin, M. 1978. *The garlands of repose.* Chicago: University of Chicago Press.

Pieper, J. 1965. *In tune with the world: A theory of festivity.* New York: Harcourt, Brace and World.

Pieper, J. 1962. *Leisure: The basis of culture.* New York: Pantheon Books.

Prebish, C. 1984. "Heavenly father, divine goalie": Sport and religion. *Antioch Review* 42 (3): 306–318.

Ryan, T. 1986. *Wellness, spirituality and sports.* New York: Paulist Press.

Ryken, L. 1987. *Work and leisure in Christian perspective.* Portland, OR: Multnomah Press.

Seerveld, C. 1964. *A Christian critique of art and literature.* Toronto: The Association for the Advancement of Christian Scholarship.

Shaughnessey, E. 1977. Santayana on athletics. *Journal of American Studies* 10 (2).

Siedentop, D. 1980. *Physical education: An introductory analysis.* Dubuque: Wm. C. Brown.

Smedes, L.B. 1975. Theology and the playful life. In *God and the good*, edited by C. J. Orlebeke and L. B. Smedes, 46–62. Grand Rapids: Eerdmans.

Sport: Are we overdoing it? 1972. *Christianity Today* (August 11): 23.

Steere, D. 1957. *Work and contemplation.* New York: Harper.

Vos, M. 1979. To take life leisurely. *The Reformed Journal* (May): 14–16.

Weiss, M.R. and Bredemeier, B.J.L. 1990. Moral development in sport. In *Exercise and sport science reviews*, edited by K. B. Pandolf (18) 331–378). Baltimore: Williams and Wilkens.

Wilson, J. 1987. Dilemmas of the Christian college athlete. *Imprimis* 16 (5): 1–6.

Chapter Twelve

Coming to Terms with Play, Game, Sport, and Athletics

JOHN BYL

"There are few words in the English language which have such a multiplicity of divergent meanings as the word sport" (Graves 1990, 877). When words such as play, game, and athletics are added to the discussion, the confusion of meanings seems to increase exponentially. What does it all mean when someone says, "They showed good sportsmanship playing a game of basketball at the Athletic Center." Were they just playing, like two children playing with dolls? If they were just playing, is that not incongruous with an athletic contest? Statements such as "playing a game at the Athletic Center" open up a multitude of questions.

The need to carefully define play, game, sport, and athletics is important in at least two respects. The first concerns the confusion of language. Millar suggested that the term play had become a "linguistic waste-paper basket badly in need of being cleaned up" (1968, 11). Keating commented: "Basic terms such as play, game, sport have been extended by common and careless usage to the point of meaninglessness" (1978, i; also Giddens 1964, 81). This confusion needs to be addressed.

In the second respect academics need clarity. Tangen notes: "Both the historians and sociologists need a definition that manages to include all the activities—both ancient and modern—that they intuitively will accept as sport and exclude all those they consider as non-sport" (1985, 18; see also Metheny 1969, 59). Meier stated that the "plethora of postulations previously forwarded. . . are most often fraught with numerous inadequacies." Nevertheless, he argued that it "should be possible to critically analyze the concept, make some sense of the complexity and variability of the term, and overcome limited or myopic views to produce an adequate and precise definition of sport which is acceptable, beneficial and, hopefully, stimulating to further sport sociology research" (1981, 81).

There are some, particularly phenomenologists, who feel such an endeavor cannot be done. Neale suggests: "Play is as illusive as the wind and can no more be caught by theory than the wind can be trapped in a paper bag" (1967, 68; Kleinman 1968, 33; Steen 1978, 59). From a non-essentialist perspective, McBride argues that the term sport is "both vague and ambiguous" and that it is "logically impossible to define the concept" (1975, 9–10). To this he adds,

> Perhaps we should rejoice that "sport" is not a precise concept. If it were, we would probably not be considering matters such as this and it is highly unlikely that there would exist a society such as ours. As Michael Scriven puts it: "When a precise definition is possible, one may be sure the term defined is either a new, technical term or one not of great importance for scientific or philosophical issues . . ." (Scriven, 1966, p. 8). Justus Hartnack, in speaking of Wittgenstein's attack on essentialism, puts it even stronger when he says, "It is arguable that no concept of philosophical interest can be defined" (Hartnack, 1965, p. 71). (10)

But just because it is not of philosophic interest does not mean it cannot be done or that a definition would not be helpful. Finally, Ziff criticizes the drawing of conceptual boundaries by stating: "That's a dull matter left to linguists and lexicographers. . . . Drawing boundaries and fixing conceptual limits is generally unproductive. Anyway, examples of sports are easy to come by" (Ziff 1974, 93). Then there are those like Vander Zwaag who argue that a "philosophy is characterized most by the formulation of its problems than by solution of them" (1969, 56). Yet, for the non-academic and academic, it would be helpful to define play, game, sport, and athletics for the two reasons stated earlier. But perhaps I should do as Suits did in his 1977 Presidential Address to his fellow philosophers and give a 15-second pause for terminal Wittgensteinians soundly opposed to constructing definitions, an opportunity to leave the room (Suits 1977, 115).

In developing a definition, I used several principles. The definition needed to be simple, honest, and accurate. Reductionistic perspectives that look at these concepts from only a psychosocial, biological, anthropological, or other perspective were considered too narrow. The definition should be understood by non-academics and be both precise and ambiguous. Thomas declared: "It is noteworthy that such a largely semantic venture cannot be limited entirely by common usage of these terms, and neither can this usage be totally ignored since it may reflect the evolutionary status of sport in culture" (1976, 37). Or as Champlain posits, our definition should "be responsible to the community of users" (1977,

105; Morgan 1977, 29). McBride advises: "A definition is too narrow if it excludes instances that would ordinarily (conventionally) be included. A definition is too broad if it includes instances that would ordinarily (conventionally) not be included" (1975, 6; and 1979). Morgan warns against becoming "definition mongers" who "simply insist on essences and precise definitions while ignoring altogether any problems of ambiguity" (1977, 28). Though Schmitz argues that "ordinary usage is the usage of ordinary men, and not that of scientists or philosophers" (1979), it is the intention of this paper to develop a definition in conventional language that will be useful to academics. What do we mean then, when we say play, game, sport, or athletics?

Based on my experiences with, my reading about, and my reflecting on physically active play, games, sport, and athletics, I propose the following model (see Figure 1).

FIGURE I: PHYSICALLY ACTIVE PLAY AND GAMES

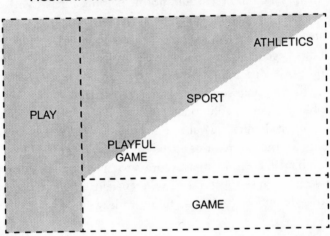

Play = A freely chosen consciousness intent on the enjoyable and non-traditional use of resources primarily committed to instrumental purposes. This is best realized when personal conflicts have been resolved.

Game = "The voluntary attempt to overcome unnecessary obstacles-hindrances" (Suits 1973, 55).

I = Level of commitment to overcoming unnecessary obstacles.

Playful Game = A greater commitment to play than to successfully overcoming unnecessary obstacles.

Sport = A roughly balanced commitment to play and to successfully overcoming unnecessary obstacles.

Athletics = A greater commitment to successfully overcoming unnecessary obstacles than to play.

The model submitted is meant to represent physically active play and games, or bodily contests. The definitions for play and game are most influenced by Suits (1973; 1977) while the model is a significantly revised version of Salter's (1980). The dashed and open lines around the model indicate that these concepts are not boxed in to be understood exclusively in the context of the model; there are more games than physically active ones. There are no lines separating the continuum from playful games, sport, and athletics, because it is not always clear when exactly a playful game becomes sport, or sport becomes athletics. Therefore all these lines have not been drawn to permit reasonable ambiguity. There is a dashed line separating play from games because when play attempts to overcome unnecessary obstacles it becomes a game.

Play is perhaps the most important topic to deal with. Neale notes that the church historically equated play with immaturity and perhaps ungodliness. "They could not permit themselves to be irreverent. And like David's wife, their lives were made barren by the Lord. Despite a clear call, man has refused to delight in and enjoy his God" (Neale 1969, 175). He added:

> The Christians who work out their salvation with fear and trembling before their fellow men are secular workers . . . they work for their own sake. The reward is hell, the hell that is eternal work. It is no wonder many believers have noted that they would be bored and unhappy in heaven. They are too well adjusted to the future eternity which is their likely lot. Who could be more reverent before God than the working Satan, and who could be less reverent than the playing cherubim? (175–176)

But what does scripture say about play? When God promised Israel he would return to bless Jerusalem, a sign of that blessing was city streets "filled with boys and girls playing there" (Zechariah 8:5). Isaiah (11:8–9) recounts for us that in the new heaven and new earth children will be playing at the mouth of the hole of the asp and not be injured. Jesus himself states that "unless you change and become like little children, you will never enter the kingdom of heaven" (Matthew 18:3). Furthermore, God opens scripture in a garden and closes it in a city filled with gardens. In the middle of the Bible there is a note about the Leviathan which God had made to "frolic" where the "ships go to and fro" (Psalm 104:26). Based on this, why do we play? Not to recapitulate our ancestors. Not in an autotelic sense, as if to absolutize an aspect of creation, but to honor and enjoy a playful God, for "from Him and through Him and to Him are all things. To Him be the glory forever! Amen" (Romans 11:36).

Though I have tried to refrain from a reductionistic approach, the proposed definitions, particularly of play, most closely fall into the realm of psychology. This acceptance is largely because I see play as an attitude, or what Roochnik (1975) and Hyland (1984) refer to as a "stance."

Giddens argues that games "are not always play" (1964, 73). I would argue that they never are. Play and game are related as singing is to song. One can play a game, or sing a song, but one cannot game a play or song a sing, and song is never sing, in the same way as game is never play. In this connection the model also deals with Meier's suggestion that "although not all games are sports, all sports are games. . . . It has not been demonstrated that sports cannot also be games simultaneously" (Meier 1981, 91 and 94). To illustrate these points a game of basketball can be participated in as an athletic contest (for example, professional or college ball), as a sport (for example, most recreational leagues), or as a playful game (for example, an informal pick-up game over lunch), but never as pure play.

The model also helps deal with conflicts over the importance of competition. If play is defined as autotelic and absolutized as an inherent good, then the further we move away from it, as we usually do in an athletic contest, then the less good would be the game, or as Banham referred to it, "a swaggering barbarism" (1965, 64). We should therefore do away with competitive games or at least de-emphasize the importance of overcoming the unnecessary obstacles of a game. But it seems wiser to accept what Bowen proposed that "perverted play is a possibility just as much so as beneficial play" (1923, viii). I would suggest the same is true at all levels of game playing. Therefore, the point is for competitors in a game to agree beforehand what level of game they are participating in. Too often people accuse each other of being too competitive or not serious enough when what they are really talking about is the kind of game they are playing. The purpose of a game is not simply to outdo someone else, but it is to overcome obstacles in a mutually acceptable manner. Though games at all levels have the potential for good, not all levels are helpful to the participants. The question one needs to answer is what emphasis on overcoming unnecessary obstacles is appropriate in different situations. Having decided on a level for a particular situation does not necessarily mean that all other levels in other situations are bad. It simply means that you feel that you made the most helpful choice in your specific situation. One way athletic associations often do this is by specifying the length of the season—though coaches and players find ways to circumvent this by entering a team with all the same players in a different league.

It might be helpful for a moment to deal with the competitive purpose in a game. In this connection, Metheny's suggestion, though Weiss refers to it as exaggeration (1969, 151), is, I think, helpful. She writes: "The word competition, as derived from *cum* and *pedere*—literally, to strive with rather than against. The word contest has similar implication being derived from *con* and *testare*—to testify with another rather than against him" (1965, 40). This is a view that was later shared by Kretchmar (1973, 74). As Suits later put it: "In games one approves of one's goal being contested by an opponent precisely because one wants that goal to be contested" (1982, 758).

The model can also be applied individually to participants, or to groups or subgroups of participants. A player or a group of players may enter into a trophy-winning end-of-the-season final game with an athletic disposition—this season would be complete with try-outs, practices, special diets, exhibition games. . . . At half time a team is comfortable in the lead and each move matters less to the final outcome of the game; participants then begin to move the game to the level of sport. If the score gets too close, participants will likely focus more on successfully overcoming the unnecessary obstacles. But while the team moved the game from athletics to sport, perhaps one athlete, who wished to impress a spectator, continued to participate at an athletic level, because the athlete felt the successful resolution of unnecessary obstacles was more impressive. A romantic relationship that ended prior to a game may also have a reverse effect, when the athlete's "head is not in the game." In other words, the athlete is not committed to efficiently overcoming unnecessary obstacles because her or his mind is focused on other "more important" matters.

There are various influences that incline people more towards athletics than play, or vice versa, for example: the presence of spectators, level of rewards, institutionalization, and rationalization. But these influence the commitment to overcoming unnecessary obstacles; they are not defining characteristics of game, sport, or athletics.

One argument against the proposed model could come, not surprisingly, from McBride. He points out:

> Fishing, fencing, skiing, wrestling, track and field, swimming, auto racing, scuba diving, rock climbing, and thoroughbred racing are sports—they are not games. Badminton, football, curling, baseball are sports and they are, also, games. . . . The instances of the extension of "sport" are varied in at least two fundamental ways, some are games and some are not games. (1975, 5)

But the model I have presented deals with that accusation both operationally and in common language. Is fishing not a game? Surely there are more efficient means to catch fish than with a little hook? Does it not become sport when the element of display is emphasized by the participants? Does it not become athletics when participants increase the importance of the outcome, as in a high-stakes fishing derby? The fact that we might not customarily refer to some of these activities by what they are does not mean that is not what they are. Suits makes this point when he talks about

> watching the earth dip—which anyone can do by facing east at dawn on a clear day. But we find that this activity is never called, nor is it customarily thought of, as watching the earth dip. It is always called, and almost always thought of, as watching the sun rise. So very often we call things by the wrong names because of cultural lag. (1981, 72)

To this he concludes that not all games, for example, need not be called games, "just that, in the absence of some further distinguishing property, they be acknowledged, upon further reflection, to be games" (Suits 1981, 72).

I have not mentioned play in opposition to or as part of work. The focus of this paper has been on physically active play and games. But if I may, I would be inclined to agree with Burke when he notes that "the most satisfying kind of work, shares in the freedom and plasticity of play" (1971, 33). But this paper is not about work, it is about play.

Where do we go from here? In the context of the proposed model one must ask if it succeeded. That depends on whether or not the terms play, game, sport, and athletics, and their relationships to each other, are made more clear to non-academics and academics. This evaluation I leave for others to determine. It is my hope that this model will provide a common language when we talk about play, game, sports, and athletics, so that the important discussion concerned with pleasing the Lord in each of these categories can be more fully realized.

References

Bowen, W.P., and Mitchell, E.D. 1923. *The theory of organized play.* New York: A.S. Barnes.

Burke, R. 1971. "Work" and "Play." *Ethics* 82, 33–47.

Giddens, A. 1964. Notes on the concept of play and leisure. *Sociological Review* 12 (March): 73–89.

Graves, H. 1990. A philosophy of sport. *Contemporary Review* 77 (December): 877–

893.

Hyland, D. A. 1984. *The question of play*. Lanham: University Press of America.

Keating, J. W. 1978. *Competition and playful activities*. Washington: University Press of America.

Kleinman, S. 1968. Toward a non-theory of sport. *Quest* 10 (May): 29–34.

Kretchmar, S. 1973. Ontological possibilities: Sport as play. In *The philosophy of sport: A collection of original essays*, edited by R.G. Osterhoudt, 64–78. Springfield, IL: Charles C. Thomas.

McBride, F. 1975. Toward a non-definition of sport. *Journal of the Philosophy of Sport* 2 (September): 4–11.

McBride, F. 1979. A critique of Mr. Suits' definition of game playing. *Journal of the Philosophy of Sport* 6, 59–65.

Meier, K.V. 1981. On the inadequacies of sociological definitions of sport. *International Review of Sport Sociology* 16, 79–102.

Metheny, E. 1969. *Connotations of movement in sport and dance*. Dubuque: Wm C. Brown.

Millar, S. 1968. *The psychology of play*. Harmondsworth: Penguin.

Morgan, W.J. 1977. Some Aristotelian notes on the attempt to define sport. *Journal of the Philosophy of Sport* 4 (September): 15–35.

Neale, R. 1967. Religion and play. *Crossroads* July/September.

Neale, R.E. 1969. *In praise of play*. New York: Harper and Row.

Roochnik, D. 1975. Play and sport. *Journal of the Philosophy of Sport* 2 (September): 36–44.

Salter, M. 1980. Play in ritual: An ethnohistorical overview of native North America. In *Play and culture*, edited by H. Schwartsman. West Point, NY: Leisure Press.

Schmitz, K. 1979. Sport and play: Suspension of the ordinary. In *Sport and the body: A philosophic symposium*, edited by E. W. Gerber and W. J. Morgan (23). Philadelphia: Lea and Febiger.

Steen, B. 1978. *Let's play—all our lives*. Grand Rapids: Calvin College.

Suits, B. 1973. The elements of sport. In *The philosophy of sport: A collection of the original essays*, edited by R. G. Osterhoudt, 46–63. Springfield, IL: Charles C. Thomas.

Suits, B. 1977. Words on play. *Journal of the Philosophy of Sport* 4 (September): 117–131.

Suits, B. 1982. Sticky wickedness: Games and morality. *Dialogue* 21 (December): 755–760.

Tangen, J.O. 1985. Defining sport: A pragmatic contextual approach. *International Journal of Physical Education* 22, 17–25.

Thomas, D. 1976. Sport: The conceptual enigma. *Journal of the Philosophy of Sport* 3 (September) 35–41.

Vander Zwaag, H.J. 1969. Sport: Existential or essential? *Quest* 19 (May): 47–56.

Weiss, P. 1969. *Sport: A philosophic inquiry*. Carbondale: Southern Illinois University.

Ziff, P. 1974. A fine forehand. *Journal of the Philosophy of Sport* 1, 92–109.

Chapter Thirteen

Play, Game, and Sport in a Reformed, Biblical Worldview

TOM VISKER

Play, game, and sport have a greater impact on our lives today than at any other time in modern history. Whether it be through participation in a physical fitness or competitive sports program or as a spectator of sporting events, this phenomenon is increasingly impinging upon our time, energy, and financial resources. People are adjusting their schedules to make room for the necessary time to "stay in shape." Youth athletic programs are at an all-time high in terms of both the number of participants and programs that are offered. Sporting goods manufacturers are enjoying record profits from the sale of their goods. Despite a dramatic increase in the price of admission, new attendance records are being set regularly at major sporting events. The major television networks have not only increased their allotment of air time for sporting events, but are also implicitly promoting a lifestyle devoted to the consumption of televised sporting events. Indeed, the "couch potato" has become the ultimate in sports consumerism.

While some benefits have resulted from this phenomenon, a serious problem has emerged for the Christian community. For the most part, we have allowed this phenomenon to permeate our lives without giving adequate attention as to how it ties into a biblically directed life style. Little effort has been made to determine the proper place for such activities or just how a Christian ought to behave while participating in sport events. The attempts to integrate one's faith life with sports participation has too often resulted in nothing more than a pre-game invocation.

As Christians we must conscientiously wrestle with this problem. We can do so by allowing the wisdom of the Scriptures to shed light on the study of play, game, and sport. Although there is little, if any, *direct* instruction regarding play, game, and sport in the Bible, it is still our most valued and necessary source for discerning God's will for play, game, and sport.

The purpose of this study is twofold: first, to identify and describe the context (a reformed, biblical worldview) in which play, game, and sport will be studied; second, in that context, to explore what it means to live obediently before our Creator when we are involved in play, game, and sport.

The Context for the Study of Play, Game, and Sport

In order to study play, game, and sport in the context of a reformed, biblical worldview, we must understand what worldview is, and what makes a worldview "biblical" and "reformed."

Simply stated, a worldview is the way we look at, or view, the world. It is our attempt to make some sense out of the life we live in this world. It is something which gives meaning to one's life. It provides organization and logic to the way we think of and experience this world. A worldview also serves as the basis for the decisions we make. It is the underlying element that forms all we think, say, and do.

Hoffecker defines an individual's worldview as a "collection of his presuppositions or convictions about reality, which represent his total outlook on life" (1986, ix). This definition is helpful in that it establishes our presuppositions and convictions about reality as the foundation of a worldview. Those things that we assume to be true about life, those things which we are willing to stand up for or defend are the soil out of which our understanding of reality grows. This definition also establishes the scope of a worldview. It is something which forms our thinking about "reality" and is representative of our "total outlook on life." It is all-encompassing. Our thoughts, actions, and speech are a reflection of our worldview.

One inherent difficulty with this definition is with the word "collection." Collection implies a gathering or an accumulation of something. In this case it is a gathering or accumulation of presuppositions and convictions. While it is true that a worldview brings our basic beliefs and convictions together, it must also bring them together in a coherent or systematic way. The word "collection" may or may not mean that there is a relationship among our presuppositions and convictions.

In light of that weakness, Wolters' definition of worldview is more helpful. He defines a worldview as "a comprehensive framework of one's basic beliefs about things" (1985, 2). This definition establishes the same foundation of basic beliefs and indicates the broad scope of a worldview ("things" is to be understood in the broadest possible sense). In addition, the word "framework" denotes the interdependence of our basic beliefs. There is more of a sense that our basic beliefs are "hinged together" to form a whole. Just as our bones are joined together to form the human skeleton which supports and protects the various systems of our body so, too, our basic beliefs are joined together to support and protect (defend) the way in which we experience "things."

It is important to note that each of us functions with a worldview. However, not everyone is able to articulate or is aware of their worldview. This principle can be demonstrated by using the example of hostile aggression in sports. Hostile aggression is the act of intentionally causing harm to an opponent with the purpose of inflicting pain or injury. As Christians, we would agree that this is an unethical act, although not everyone would be able to articulate why it is unethical. Some would say that injuring or hurting others intentionally is always wrong and leave it at that. Others would be able to identify the basis of that decision as the fundamental belief that all people are created in the image of God and are therefore deserving of our respect. The point is that each of these persons is operating with the same basic beliefs about life even though one is unable to articulate that belief.

The purpose or function of a worldview is navigation. It is our guide to life. With it we can steer our way through the realities of the imperfect world we inhabit. Wolters elaborates on the purpose of worldview as follows:

> A worldview, even when half unconscious and unarticulated, functions like a compass or a road map. It orients us in the world at large, gives us a sense of what is up and what is down, what is right and what is wrong in the confusion of events and phenomena that confront us. Our worldview shapes, to a significant degree, the way we assess the events, issues, and structures of our civilization. It allows us to "place" or "situate" the various phenomena that come into our purview. (1985, 4)

The next question which must be dealt with is, "What makes a worldview biblical?" If a worldview functions as our guide in life, a biblical worldview is one in which our pathway through life is illuminated by the Scriptures. It is only in the light of the Bible that we can see life the way God has intended. Greidanus reiterates this belief while addressing the use of the Bible for Christian scholarship. He writes: "It is in the light of the Bible that the creation can once again be seen as a revelation from

God. Or, to use the familiar imagery of John Calvin, the Scriptures are like 'spectacles' that enable us to view reality aright" (1982, 140). Even the best road map is useless if it is distorted by a poor, dimly lit vision. With the proper illumination and corrective lens, we can read the map as it was intended to be read. So it is with our worldview. We must constantly shine the light of Scripture on the world we live in, for without it, we cannot experience life as God intended.

The final question which must be addressed is, "What makes a worldview reformed?" A reformational worldview recognizes the Lordship of the Creator God over all aspects of life. It does not allow for a distinction to be made between the "secular" and the "sacred." Since God created all things and created them good, even though they have fallen prey to the effects of sin, all things are subject to God's ordinances. It is by God's grace that all things can be restored to their original, creational goodness. All areas of life are sacred. Not only are matters of church and religion considered to be sacred, but so, too, are business, politics, education, sports, and all other areas of life. As such, they fall under the blanket of God's grace and are redeemed because of Christ's victory over sin.

In a biblical, reformational worldview all of life is shaped and tested by Scripture. Our thoughts about world politics, our idea of family, the conversation we have at the coffee shop, the way in which we play games, figure our income tax, and worship in church all come under the jurisdiction of Scripture. It alone has the final authority. All of life falls under the creation-fall-redemption motif. For Christians who hold this worldview, the task is to bring to fruition the restoration that has taken place in Jesus Christ. It is only by the grace of God that we will accomplish this task.

Since a reformed, biblical worldview sees all of life in a creation-fall-redemption motif, it is necessary to briefly elaborate on each of these categories. This clarification will allow us to see more clearly how play can be studied within this context. Wolters, in his book *Creation Regained* (1985), presents an excellent discussion on creation-fall-redemption as an essential ingredient in a reformational worldview. Most of what follows in this section is a summary of his work.

At the heart of creation is the belief that God both created and sustains the cosmos. He not only brought into being all that is but He also continues to uphold and rule over the cosmos. Wolters uses the phrase "the law of creation" to stand "for the totality of God's ordaining acts towards the cosmos" (13).

The law of creation can be of two types: (1) the law of nature and (2) norms. The primary difference between the two is the way in which God imposes His law upon the cosmos. When He does so directly without the help of human beings, it is the law of nature He is imposing. These are frequently referred to as the natural laws, the laws which dictate the order of physical things. Gravity, force, motion, and the changing of the seasons are all examples of how God is directly ruling over the cosmos.

When God gives the responsibility to human beings to carry out His orders in society, it is His *norms* that He is imposing on the cosmos. In this sense, we become "co-workers" with God in carrying out His will for the cosmos. Stewardship of natural resources, business transactions, sexuality, medicine, and play are all examples of aspects of the creation that God has entrusted to humans to execute his commands. It is our responsibility to see to it that His will is done in all areas of life.

A second aspect of creation which is fundamental to this study is the scope of creation. If we accept the fact that the law of creation contains both the natural laws of the cosmos as well as the norms for culture, then it is obvious that the scope of creation is to be understood in the broadest possible sense. Not only did God create the heavens and the earth, water, plants, animals, and so forth (laws of nature), but He also created the structures of our society. These include such things as marriage, family, civil authority, business, and education (norms). Simply stated, God created *everything*! There is nothing in the cosmos (excluding God Himself) which falls outside the parameters of creation. Therefore, everything lies within the jurisdiction of God's sovereignty.

A third aspect of creation which is significant to this study is the "revelation of creation." Through creation God imparts knowledge about His will for the cosmos. The Bible makes it very evident that this revelation is the case (Psalm 19:1–4, Acts 14:17). In fact, we have no excuse for *not* knowing His will (Romans 1:18 and 2:14–15). It is because of sin that we do not always properly hear what He is saying, but nonetheless, God speaks clearly through His creation. Even when God doesn't explicitly tell us His will, we can still know His will through our "intuitive atunement to creational normativity" (25), or our conscience. Our conscience will not allow us to be deaf to the revelation of the Creator. The point is that "the creational order is knowable" (28). Whether it is through nature (general revelation) or the Scriptures (divine revelation), we can know God's will for His creation and will be held responsible for its implementation.

An understanding of the development of creation will also be beneficial to this study. The biblical account of creation is found in Genesis

1 and 2. However, creation did not end when God rested on the seventh day. In fact, there is a real danger in thinking that God discontinued His creational activity after the first six days. In doing so we are placing institutions outside of the scope of creation, institutions such as education, business, politics, media, and sport, and therefore are positioning them outside of the creational order. They would no longer be areas of our responsibility as stewards of creation and therefore would be secular.

To avoid this danger we must see creation as an ongoing process. God created, He is creating, and He will continue to create. As His imagebearers, we have been given the task of unfolding and developing the creation that God began. "We are executing God's blueprint for the completion of His masterpiece" (38). The positive implications of this view of the development of creation are exciting.

> If we see that human history and the unfolding of culture and society are integral to creation and its development, that they are not outside God's plan for the cosmos, despite sinful aberrations, but rather were built in from the beginning, were part of the blueprint that we never understood before, then we will be much more open to the positive possibilities for service to God in such areas as politics and the film arts, computer technology and business administration, developmental economics and skydiving. (38)

Finally, a comment about the goodness of creation. The point here is simply that all God created is good. His creation as we are discovering it today is good. Whether it be plant or animal, family or business, politics or play, they were all created good. It is only when we are disobedient to the creational norm that these things become corrupted. It is only through obedience to the law of creation that we can experience God's good creation. We can experience the goodness of marriage if we adhere to the norm of monogamy. Our farmland will be productive if we farm it obediently. Our play will be "playful" if we play obediently. Our freedom to experience the goodness of God's creation comes from living by the creational laws and norms as they are revealed to us by God.

There are two points which must be made regarding the fall into sin. The first concerns the scope of the fall. Just as the scope of creation includes everything in the cosmos (excluding God), so too, the scope of the fall includes everything in the cosmos (excluding God). That which is subjected to the laws of nature and that which is subjected to God's norms are tainted by the effects of sin. Regarding the physical world we read in Genesis 3:14 that the ground is "cursed" because of Adam's sin. It no longer displays its creational goodness. Similarly, the goodness of creation is no longer reflected in the human world. We do not have to look far to see numerous ways in which God's norms for society have been violated. Excessive eating and drinking and the lack of moderate physical exercise demonstrate abuse of our bodies. Apartheid, racism, and segregation are antithetical to the harmonious human relationships God intended in His cosmos. The scope of the fall is universal—nothing has been left untouched by humanity's fall into sin.

The second point concerns the relation ship of sin and creation. In a biblical worldview, sin must never be seen as a part of God's good creation. Sin was never a part of His plan. The responsibility for sin lies with human beings, not with God. We may experience creation and sin simultaneously but we may never view them as one; they must remain distinct.

To clarify the relationship between sin and creation it is helpful to picture sin as a caricature of creation (Wolters, chapter 3). A caricature is something that is a distortion of the object, but is not that object. A caricature of George Washington would have a resemblance to him but it would not be an accurate likeness of him. Similarly, "dirty" politics is still politics, hedonistic leisure is still leisure, and pornographic literature is still literature. Each has been distorted by sin but still continues as part of God's sustaining work in His creation. Despite the perverse effect of sin on creation, God remains faithful to His creation. He will not give up any of it to sin.

In this context, Wolters' concepts of "structure" and "direction" become important. "Structure" is the form in which things are created. In its original form, creation was perfect. "Direction" refers to the pull of sin and grace on the creation. If, by grace, we live in harmony with the goodness of creation, our direction is toward God. Conversely, if, because of sin, we live contrary to the law of creation and distort its goodness, our direction is away from God..

The implications of structure and direction for a biblical, reformed worldview are obvious. Since, in structure, everything created is good and it is only through misdirection (sin) that they become evil, there is the possibility that by grace and through Christ's redemptive work, we can reverse the direction and once again restore creation to its original goodness.

Redemption, in a biblical, reformed worldview, is synonymous with restoration. When something is restored it is returned to its original condition. Antique furniture is restored to look like new again. Older automobiles are meticulously revived to their original showroom condition. In each case, something which had fallen prey to the ravages of time or abuse is lovingly returned to its original goodness. So it is with God's creation. What once was made good had become tainted by disobedience to the Creator. However, sin is not the final word. God has mercifully and graciously made possible the restoration of His creation through the person and work of Jesus Christ. All of creation will be returned to its original "showroom condition."

It is crucial to a reformed worldview that redemption be understood in its broadest sense. Through Christ's death and resurrection all of the violations of the law of creation have been forgiven. Too often we focus only on the redemption of humanity and forget that Christ's victory over sin applies to the entire cosmos. Recognizing the universal scope of sin and redemption is a distinguishing characteristic of a reformed world-view.

Based on this understanding of the universal nature of sin and re-demption, the task of reformed Christians is clear. We are to be working towards the restoration of all creation. There is nothing that we encoun-ter that lies outside this mandate. Someday, by God's grace, we will see the entirety of God's creation restored to its original state of goodness.

In order to investigate play, game, and sport in the context of a re-formed biblical worldview, we must see it in terms of the creation, the fall, and the redemption. This can be accomplished by returning to Wolt-ers' concepts of "structure" (the essence of something) and "direction" (the deviation from or restoration of the created structure). When we investigate the structure of play, game, and sport, we will be attempting to discover their creational dimension. The question which needs to be asked is, "What is the essence of play, game, and sport?" The impact of sin on play, game, and sport and our efforts to restore them to their origi-nal state of goodness refer to the direction of play, game, and sport. The questions needing answers are (1) How has sin affected play, game, and sport? and (2) What can be done to restore play, game, and sport to their creational conditions?

The Structure of Play, Game, and Sport

Although there is not a universally accepted definition for play, there is a consensus regarding the characteristics of play. A review of the litera-ture on the nature of play reveals eight characteristics of play on which most play theorists would agree. One could argue for additions or dele-tions from the list since it doesn't propose to be an all-inclusive list. It is, however, a representative gathering of the opinions of some of the major play scholars.

One of the characteristics of play on which there is near unanimous agreement is that it is freely chosen (Huizinga 1950, Hyland 1984, Johnston 1983, and Caillois 1961). When we play, we play because we choose to do so. No one can tell us we must play. If the activity is imposed upon us, it is no longer play.

Roger Caillois (1961) modifies the characteristic of "freely chosen" to "freely accepted." Play is free in the sense that you are willingly engaged in the activity you have been told to do. Accordingly, a child can be told to "go play" and be playing even though it was against his wishes, so long as the child "accepts" the directive to play.

Play also must function in its own space and time. Huizinga (1950) refers to this aspect of play as being outside "ordinary" or "real life." Van Asch (1977) calls it a "stepping out of real life." Each of these authors indicates that play is something we can experience only when we can get away from our normal daily routines. Play is to function parenthetically in our lives. Johnston writes:

> ... play has a new time (a playtime) and a new space (a playground) which function as "parentheses" in the life and world of the player. The concerns of everyday life come to a temporary standstill in the mind of the player, and the boundaries of his or her world are redefined. (1983, 34)

We must be careful, however, in our description of this characteristic of play. Describing it as "stepping out of ordinary or real life" may relegate play to a lesser, even secular, sphere of life. Play is to be as much a part of our life as our work and our worship. Therefore, although the intent is the same, allowing play to occupy its own space and time within a person's life frees us from the temptation to banish play to the realm of the secular. Furthermore, it is consistent with the reformed, biblical worldview context in which we are exploring play.

The third and fourth characteristics of play can best be understood together. Play is, at the same time, both serious and non-serious. Although these characteristics appear to be in direct opposition to each other, they are both essential to the understanding of play. Lewis Smedes provides an explanation of how play is both serious and non-serious and demonstrates the essential position of these characteristics in play when he writes:

> In order to be playful, one has to be serious in playing a non-serious game. Being serious is being involved, committing oneself to the game, and playing as

hard as one can. If a player lacks seriousness, he spoils the play. It is not fun to win against an opponent who does not try to beat you. And if he does not try to beat you, he is not really playing. On the other hand, if he takes winning as serious business, he also spoils the game by not really playing it as a game that has no important consequences. The dialectic of playful seriousness consists of being seriously involved in something we do not interpret as serious business. (1975, 50)

The fifth characteristic of play is that it is autotelic. Autotelic activities are those which are engaged in for their own sake. Play, then, is to be characterized by intrinsic motivation. One is to play for the sake of playing. Play "is an activity connected with no material interest, no profit can be gained by it" (Huizinga 1950, 13). When play is entered into for extrinsic reason, the quality of the play experience will be diminished.

This leads quickly to a sixth characteristic of play—the outcomes of play. At first glance, there appears to be a contradiction in that play is autotelic and outcome-oriented at the same time. However, it is possible and, in most instances, likely that play can be engaged in for its own take and yet have outcomes or consequences attached to it. A golfer, for example, can play golf solely because of his love for the game, but yet may have as by-products of his golfing experience relief from stress, development of social relationships, and the satisfaction of acquiring a physical skill.

A comprehensive listing of the outcomes of play is beyond the scope of this study. However, identifying a few of the major outcomes is in order. For Johnston the primary consequences of play are "the joy and release, the personal fulfillment, the remembering of our common humanity, and the presentiment of the sacred, which the player sometimes experiences in and through the activity" (1983, 34). Broadus and Broadus (1987) emphasize the personal renewal that play offers. Smedes (1975), although listing it as a separate characteristic, points to experiencing pleasure through play.

For players to experience these outcomes they must not focus their attention on attaining them. This is precisely the point at which play is no longer play. When the motivation for playing shifts from intrinsic to extrinsic, the play experience dissolves. Johnston summarizes this when he writes,

> Play has. . . an external value that reaches far beyond the boundary of the play world. But this is the case only when the player "forgets" play's consequences and focuses solely on the intrinsic value of the play. (1983, 49)

The seventh characteristic of play is that it has order. By order we mean that play has spatial, temporal, and movement restriction. Huizinga (1950) refers to this quality as "secludedness" and "limitedness." Johnston (1983) refers to a "playtime" and a "play space." Van Asch (1977) and Caillios (1961) refer to this as "rules." Whatever the terminology, they are all making the essential point that even our play has restrictions. There are certain time, space, and movement lines in play which cannot be crossed if we want to continue playing. Furthermore, as we shall see later, rules become more restrictive as we move from play to game and game to sport. When we play, then, we are not freeing ourselves from restrictions, but rather subjecting ourselves to a new set of mutually agreed-upon restrictions.

The final and often overlooked characteristic of play is that it is fun. Play is fun in that it entails a sense of adventure and uncertainty of outcome. Neale (1969) calls adventure the mark of play. It is this quality which draws people to play. From child's play to professional "play" the uncertainty of what will happen next or what the final outcome will be enhances the play experience for players and spectators. Conversely, when we know what will happen next or what the final outcome will be, our interest in playing is drastically diminished.

The Structure of Game and Sport

One of the assumptions of this study is that play is foundational for game and sport. Therefore, the characteristics of play previously identified should be found in game and sport. As we proceed to discover the structure of game and sport, we will assume the presence of play and focus on the distinguishing features of game and sport.

One feature of game is that the time, space, and movement limitations of play become more restrictive than play (Frey et al. 1986, 36–59). For example, a group of children could be playing during their recess by chasing each other around the playground. A second group of children could be chasing each other as well but within the rules of a game of "tags" In the first instance, the children are limited only in terms of the boundaries of the playground. In a game of tag, the "playing field" normally has more restrictive spatial limitations as well as rules limiting movement (for example, must tag above the waist, can't tag the person who just tagged you, and so forth.)

A second distinguishing feature of game is the use of goals and obstacles (Frey et al.) When playing a game there is normally an objective or an end product on which the players focus their attention. The purpose of the game is to accomplish that objective. When playing the game of "Sorry" with my children, the goal of the game is to get all tokens to "home" before another player does. All of the strategies (including some very creative ones from my children!) are dedicated to reaching that goal. However, to keep us from reaching that goal in the most efficient manner, there are obstacles or hindrances to our progress. These obstacles are in the form of rules which limit the number of spaces we can move during a turn, dictate when a token can be moved from the starting position onto the board, force us to move backward instead of forward, and so on.

A third feature of game is what Van Asch (1977) calls "bellicosity" or the will to outdo each other. It is important to note, however, that this feature is not always found in games but frequently is part of the games we play. The games which have this feature are referred to as "competitive" games. Games which do not have this feature are termed "noncompetitive" games.

Several features of sport can distinguish it from game. First, there will be a difference in the rules. Just as there were more restrictive rules as we moved from play to game, the move from game to sport entails even more restrictions in time, space, and movement (Frey et al. 1983). Generally, the rules and regulations which govern sport are so numerous that they are put into rule books. The demands of enforcing the rules becomes so great that often a nonplayer is relied upon to enforce the rules. The rules which govern little league baseball or AYSO soccer are much more restrictive and strictly enforced than the "pick-up games" of baseball or soccer which kids play at the local playground.

The goals, or the attainment of goals, become more complex in sport as well. In order to accomplish the objective of a sport, time must be devoted to practicing the various aspects of the sport so that a higher level of proficiency can be attained. Interscholastic basketball teams devote a lot of time to drills aimed at developing the fundamental skills needed to compete. Conversely, seldom do we see individuals drill on fundamentals to play in a pick-up game played in the backyard.

Sport is also characterized by physical skill and physical exertion. Sport involves training the body to move skillfully so that the goal of the game can be achieved. This movement is normally large muscle movement requiring adequate levels of strength, endurance, and flexibility. This feature is obvious when you compare the physical skill and exertion requirements of participating in "Monopoly" to those of participating in soccer.

Finally, whereas competition was an optional feature of game, it is an essential element of sport. All sport is characterized by some type of competition—individual or team, or what Reuben (1986) calls "auto-comps" (competing with yourself).

It is the competitive feature of game and sport which is the most controversial. More discussion is needed regarding the nature and use of competition. However, this would go beyond the purpose of this study and will therefore be left to another time.

In summary, the structure of play was described by eight characteristics: (1) freely chosen; (2) has its own place and time; (3) is seriously engaged in; (4) is tran-serious; (5) is autotelic; (6) has outcomes such as pleasure, joy, fulfillment, and renewal; (7) creates order; and (8) is fun. Game has all the characteristics of play in addition to more restrictive rules, established goals, obstacles to achieving goals, and possibly competition. The structure of sport entails all the characteristics of play and game with some modifications: more restrictive rules, more difficulty in achieving goals, the development of physical skills and use of physical exertion, and the necessity of competition.

Direction of Play, Game, and Sport

Based on a reformed, biblical worldview, we understand that the structure of play, game, and sport is good since it is part of the created order. We also recognize the fact that play, game, and sport, like all other aspects of creation, have been affected by our fall into sin. Our playing is distorted because it no longer reflects the form in which it was created. However, our distorted play is not play's final form. Through the death and resurrection of Christ our Savior, our playing can be restored to its original perfect form.

In this final section we will investigate the direction of play, game, and sport. The direction of these concepts refers to the pull of sin and grace on them. The pull of sin is the violation of the creational order. The pull of grace is the restoring of the creational order.

It can be difficult to discern the pull of sin from the pull of grace in regard to play, game, and sport. The Bible does not directly give us standards by which we should play. There are no "proof texts" justifying our play nor can we cite, chapter and verse, God's guidelines for playing. In the absence of any explicit directives for play, game, and sport, how can God's expectations for our play be identified?

While we may not find specific directives for playing, it is possible to discover general biblical *norms* which should guide our playing (Greidanus 1982). General biblical norms are themes throughout Scripture which should characterize our behavior in all the dimensions of being human. When applying general biblical norms to the structure of play, game, and sport, we are allowing the light of Scripture to dictate the way in which we play. We are seeing play, game, and sport through the "spectacles" of Scripture. In doing so, we remain true to a reformed, *biblical* worldview.

To identify these norms it is helpful to think in terms of relationships. In developing a Christian play ethic, Arthur Holmes (1981) stresses the importance of what it means to play in all of life's relationships. He identifies our relationship to God, to others, to nature, and to ourselves as areas in which we must live obediently to our Creator. I suggest that in the context of these relationships we can discern the pull of sin from the pull of grace in play, game, and sport. It can also be demonstrated that by violating biblical norms for these relationships, we also eliminate one or more of the characteristics which constitute the structure of play, game, and sport.

What determines the direction of play, game, and sport, then, is obedience to the biblical norms for these relationships in our play experiences. In the paragraphs which follow, some of the norms governing these relationships will be identified and specific applications to play will be made. This is not intended to be a comprehensive coverage of the norms as they apply to play, game, and sport. The intention is to offer these suggestions as a starting point from which we can proceed in unfolding God's will for our play.

Nowhere in the Scriptures will the norms for our relationship to God and to others be spelled out more clearly than in the Ten Commandments (Exodus 20:1–17, Deuteronomy 5:6–21). This point is demonstrated in Lord's Day 34, Question and Answer 93, of the Heidelberg Catechism:

Question: How are these commands divided?

Answer: Into two tables.
            The first has four commands, teaching us what our relationship to God should be.
            The second has six commandments, teaching us what we owe our neighbor.

In these commandments are found the standards for obedience and disobedience in our relationship with God and others. We can proceed, then, to apply these standards to play, game, and sport.

In our relationship to God, the first four commandments set the norms. The first command dictates that we may not have any other gods before God. It is God and God only that we love, trust, fear, and honor. He, alone, will provide everything which we require. Therefore, idolatry, magic, superstition, and prayer to saints, etc., need to be avoided since they displace our trust and confidence in God to provide for our needs (Heidelberg Catechism, Lord's Day 34).

In terms of our playing, this commandment indicates that we recognize God as the source of our play. Play is God's gift to us (Ryken 1987). Play is a necessary part of living a healthy life. As such, God has provided for one of our basic needs. Conversely, we must not let play, game, and sport rival God for being the provider for our needs. Only God is capable of providing us with what we need to live as He intended for us to live. While play is part of His gracious provision, it can never replace Him as the provider for our needs.

When play, game, and sport become the primary source for our physical, social, and emotional needs, they lose their autotelic nature. We no longer play because the activity is intrinsically pleasing, but rather for the external benefits that we receive from play. This dependence is an abuse of play.

The second commandment forbids the use of idols as representative of God or in the place of Him. Seldom do we see physical images representing God in our play activities; however, there are numerous ways in which play, game, and especially sport have replaced God as the object of our worship. The time, money, and effort we willingly devote to sport is often out of proportion to that which we willingly give to our Creator. In this respect, sport has become the object which we worship, and we have demoted God to a lesser status. When this occurs, sport receives greater importance (seriousness) in our lives than it is meant to have. This, too, is a perversion of the structure of sport.

The third commandment requires that we use the Lord's name only with reverence and respect. We are forbidden to blaspheme the name of God. The implications of this for play are obvious. The words spoken during participation in play must demonstrate the reverence and awe we have for our Lord. Too often our Lord is called upon (even by those who do not know him) to "damn" something or someone. Flippantly calling upon our Lord's name is something for which we will not be held guiltless. Once again, this action is most likely to take place when we give our playing a more serious role than it is intended to have.

The fourth commandment instructs us to "remember the Sabbath day by keeping it holy." To keep the Sabbath holy we must use the Sabbath as God intended it to be used. What is the proper function of the Sabbath? Based on the slightly differing instructions for the Sabbath found in Exodus 20 and Deuteronomy 5, Johnston (1983) suggests a twofold purpose of the Sabbath: (1) it is a time to reflect upon God's goodness and faithfulness to His creation, and (2) it is to be a time of rest from our daily routines. The concept of Sabbath has profound implications for play. First, our play must heighten our awareness of God's faithfulness and goodness to His creation. It is meant to draw us closer to our Creator, not to distance us from Him. How often in our play have we experienced the presence of the Divine? Too often we play as if God were not present or was disinterested. The second implication of the Sabbath commandment is that it calls for a balanced approach to life, or what Johnston calls a "rhythm of life." Our life is not to be all work or all play, but rather, there is to be a balance of work and play. There are to be periods of work which are followed by periods of play.

When we follow this rhythm, we are providing play with its own space and time, therefore, remaining true to the nature of play. When we get out of that rhythm by working at our play, or playing at our work, we violate the balanced approach to life that is called for in the Sabbath day concept.

Beginning with the fifth commandment the focus shifts to norms regarding our relationships with others. The fifth commandment specifically guides our relationship with our parents. It is a relationship in which we are to honor, love, and obey our parents in the Lord. Explaining this commandment, the Heidelberg Catechism (Lord's Day 39) extends this directive to include all those in authority over us. With this expanded understanding of the fifth commandment it is clear that not only are we to honor our parents in and through our play, but we are also to submit to the authority of those who have valid jurisdiction over our play. Fishing can be a healthy play activity, but not if it is done in an area posted "no fishing" or if we choose to disregard size and limit restrictions imposed by civil authorities. Similarly, when we participate in recreation softball leagues, we are obligated to respect the umpires and their decisions. In effect, when we disobey those who have authority over our play, we violate the spatial, temporal, and movement restrictions of the play environment and therefore are violating the structure of play as well.

The sixth commandment instructs us not to murder. Obviously our play cannot include killing. It is generally understood, however, that in forbidding murder, God is also forbidding the root of murder. Such things as hate, envy, anger, and revenge are also forbidden. Furthermore, our thoughts, words, and gestures can make us guilty of murder. How often do we hear phrases like "We're going to get them next time" or "Kill the Ump" uttered at sporting events. Coaches often rely heavily on the motivation of revenge to get their players ready for the "big game." Obviously, play in these instances has been translated to the realm of the serious. The outcome (winning) has become the motivation. Once again, the nature of play has been violated.

In the seventh commandment, God is calling us to sexual purity in both our actions and our thoughts. At first glance, there appears to very little here in terms of establishing norms for play. What is forbidden, however, is not only the actions, but also anything which incites unchastity (Heidelberg Catechism, Lord's Day). Anything in play which arouses sexual desires (outside of marriage) is sin. One type of play which has been accused of this is the dance. While not condemning all types of dance as sinful, there are some dances which are specifically designed to arouse sexual desires. The "dirty dancing" craze, for example, is a dance activity which has submitted to the pull of sin. Here again, when the purpose of the activity is to arouse sexual passion, play's autotelic nature is lost. It becomes a means to an end rather than the end itself.

The eighth commandment instructs us not to steal. Stealing, too, is meant in a broader sense to include cheating and swindling (Heidelberg Catechism, Lord's Day 42). Anything acquired or gained illegitimately is stealing. In our play it is often the end product or goal of the game that we try to gain through illegitimate methods. We deliberately violate the rules of the game in an effort to increase our chances of winning the game. When we do this we not only "steal" the game from our opponents, but we also "rob" them and ourselves of the adventure which makes our playing fun. This practice, too, is motivated by the end product of winning rather than the intrinsic joy of playing. Once again, the nature of play is denigrated.

In the ninth commandment we are told not to give false testimony against our neighbor. Included in this instruction is that we refrain from gossip, slander, lying, and deceit. Instead we are to love the truth and guard and advance our neighbor's good name (Heidelberg Catechism, Lord's Day 43). In our play we must speak positively of our fellow players and do what we can to protect their reputation. Here is the basis for what it means to be a humble winner and a gracious loser. If we win a game or contest we must speak admirably of the effort and skill of the other team or individual. If we lose, we must give them the credit they deserve, without qualifying it as "lucky" or playing "above their heads." This commandment does not require us to give undue credit or to whitewash the truth—it simply means we must speak the truth in love as we speak of others.

When we fail to speak lovingly in our play experiences, it is often due to the fact that we have pinned too much of our self-esteem on the outcome of the game. If we win, we're okay; if we lose, we're nothing. In an effort to reclaim self-esteem we belittle our fellow players' skill, effort, or person. Once again, we have engaged in play primarily to boost our egos and not because we have an intrinsic love for the activity. Therefore the game is placed in a much more serious realm than it should be. Thus, we have eliminated two characteristics of the structure of play.

The final commandment warns us not to covet our neighbors' possessions. Covet means to want ardently—usually something others have. The evil in coveting is not so much that we appreciate what others have as it is that we are not satisfied with what God has provided for us. In play, coveting statements often begin with "I wish . . .": "I wish we could win the championship." These statements indicate a dissatisfaction with the lot God has given us. We need to refrain from coveting others' abilities and possessions when we play or we will seriously jeopardize the joy, pleasure, fulfillment, and renewal that we can experience through our playing.

Next we need to apply God's norms for our relationship to nature to our play. Before God rested from his creating activity he gave to Adam the mandate to "be fruitful and increase in number; fill the earth and subdue it. Rule over the fish of the sea and the birds of the air and over every living creature that moves on the ground" (Genesis 1:28). God has appointed Adam and his descendants as caretakers of His creation. As His image-bearers we are to be responsible stewards of His handiwork. We are to be "God's hands in God's world."

Arthur Holmes clearly articulates what our role as caretakers of creation has for play:

> We can play responsibly in God's world or we can play destructively and profligately, spending our natural resources on riotous living. I question the use of scarce energy resources in auto racing. I question the stewardship in roaring around a placid lake in a gas-guzzling motor boat that exhales noxious fumes. I question not only bullfighting and cockfighting, but also hunting animals for "sport alone", not for food or other responsible purposes. I question play that needlessly defaces nature's beauty or upsets its eco-balance. Such "games" disregard the stewardly purposes and consequent limitation of man's "dominion"

over nature. (1981, 47)

Finally, what do God's norms for our relationship to ourselves say about the way we play? Scripture clearly tells us that we are to love ourselves (Matthew 22:39). Yet, at the same time, it warns us about excessive self-love (Galatians 5:26, Philippians 2:3). It is through a healthy self-love that we will care for our physical, social, emotional, mental, and spiritual needs. Although we participate in activities primarily because we enjoy them, we can also select activities which will enhance our total health. Playing can provide avenues for increasing bodily health, developing social relationships, establishing a positive self-concept, challenging our cognitive abilities, and increasing our awareness of the faithfulness of our Creator.

Conversely, excessive self-love in play can only lead to experiences which rob play of its value. We will not play for play's sake, but to prove ourselves better than others. Cheating and slandering become the necessary tools for us to be "one up on" our fellow players. Play becomes a very serious activity because it can establish or preserve our dominance over others.

In summary, it has been demonstrated that we can know God's norms for play through examining His norms for our relationship to Him, to others, to nature, and to ourself. If we live in obedience to these norms the direction of our play is toward God and we are reclaiming play from the clutches of sin. If we live in disobedience to these standards we allow the goodness of this part of God's creation to become a perverse distortion of what He intended.

Conclusion

Investigating play, game, and sport in the context of a reformed, biblical worldview allows us to place these concepts in the framework of the general biblical theme of creation, fall, and redemption. We can unfold the beauty and goodness of play as God created it. We can also discover the distorting affects which the fall into sin has had on play, yet rejoice in the fact that play is restored to its creational goodness through the redeeming work of Jesus Christ.

We have studied the structure of play, game, and sport to see what God has intended these to be. In investigating the directional dimension of play, game, and sport we have attempted to demonstrate the effects of sin and redemption on our playing. It was suggested that the direction of play could be determined by applying the norms for our relationship to

God, others, nature, and ourself to our play experiences. To live in violation of these norms is sin. To live in accordance with these norms is to be busy restoring play to its original beauty and goodness.

The answers to the questions of what is structural and what is directional about play in this study are presented to stimulate further study and dialogue. It is only through these activities that, by God's grace, we will be able to discover God's beautiful design for play and how we can live obediently to Him in our play, game, and sport.

References

Broadus, C., and Broadus, L. 1987. *Play, it's not just for kids*. Waco, TX: Word Books.

Caillois, R. 1961. *Man, play and games*. Glencoe, NY: The Free Press.

Frey, B. L.. Ingram, W. E., McWhertor, T. E., and Romanowski, W. D. 1986. *At Work and Play*. Jordan Station, Ontario: Paideia Press.

Greidanus, S. 1982. The use of the Bible in Christian scholarship. *Christian Scholars Review* 11(2): 138–147.

Heidelberg Catechism. 1987. In *The Psalter Hymnal* (860–925). Grand Rapids: CRC Publications.

Hoffecker, W. A. 1986. Perspective and method in building a worldview. In *Building a Christian world view*, edited by W. Hoffecker and G. Smith, ix–xvi. Phillipsburg, NJ: Presbyterian and Reformed.

Holmes, A. 1981. Towards a Christian play ethic. *Christian Scholars Review* 11 (1): 41–48.

Huizinga, J. 1950. *Homo Ludens: A study of the play element in culture*. Boston: Beacon.

Hyland, D. A. 1984. *The question of play*. Lanham: University Press of America.

Johnston, R. K. 1983. *The Christian at play*. Grand Rapids: Eerdmans.

Neale, R. K. 1969. *In praise of play*. New York: Harper and Row.

Reuben, H. L. 1980. *Competing*. New York: Lippencott and Crowell.

Ryken, L. 1987. *Work and leisure in Christian perspective*. Portland, OR: Multnomah Press.

Smedes, L. B. 1975. Theology and the playful life. In *God and the good*, edited by C. Orlebeke and L. Smedes, 46–62. Grand Rapids: Eerdmans.

Van Asch, J. C. 1977. *Physical education from a Christian view of anthropology* (K. J. Boot, Trans.). Sioux Center: Dordt College Press.

Wolters, A. M. 1985. *Creation regained: Biblical basics for a reformational worldview*. Grand Rapids: Eerdmans.

Chapter Fourteen

Athletics from a Christian Perspective

MARVIN A. ZUIDEMA

Basic Statement

The interscholastic athletic program in schools should be an integral part of the total school offering. The essence of the educational function of the athletic program is the "joy of sport as game; the detachment of movement; the release of many tensions; the testing of self-control, honesty, perseverance, concentration, intelligence, skillfulness and sense of community" (Van Asch 1977, 32). Athletics are a form of play, play which can serve an educational function and play which can promote choices and commitment of values. The goals of the athletic program, particularly in Christian schools, should be expressive, celebrative play and responsible action education. A Christian athlete is one who engages in sport for the excitement and creative drama that is vested in sport and for the values that can be developed, refined, and tested through participation.

Philosophical Foundations

Central to Christian education is the belief that the student is an indivisible normative being created by God for a life of service and commitment to God. Human beings are creatures called by God to praise their creator. This is particularly true for the redeemed persons who are set free to use their wholeness of being to serve their Redeemer.

The sporting experience is important for the forming of a person if the biblical view of the human being is taken seriously. Sports, like all expressive activities, influence us either for good or evil. Sport can be used to serve self or serve God. Sports, if such activities are to be part of Christian education, must be used to develop a unity of person in which God's plan for life is fulfilled.

The goal of Christian education is the transformation of living. Athletic activities focus on certain aspects of this living: namely health, skillful movement, wise movement decisions, willing and doing, releasing self to go beyond self, beauty and drama, perfecting and enlarging, joy and disappointment, joyful busyness, and dramatic expressions. Athletics, thus viewed, focus on people becoming the persons and community the Lord wants His creatures to be.

The athletic experience, from a Christian perspective, should focus on students discovering avenues of God-glorifying self-expression, on students experiencing the excitement and drama of play, and on students building and mirroring Christian lifestyle values. Athletics belong in Christian education because participants and spectators are led to focus on decisions of how the Christian life can be lived in contemporary society.

As previously stated, a Christian athlete should engage in competitive sport for its inherent expressive and competitive play and for values that can be developed, refined, and tested.

Key Elements in Athletic Play

I submit that there are three important elements in educational athletics conducted from a Christian perspective: 1) Expressive play; 2) Competition; and 3) Responsible action. (See Figures 1 and 2)

FIGURE I: ATHLETICS

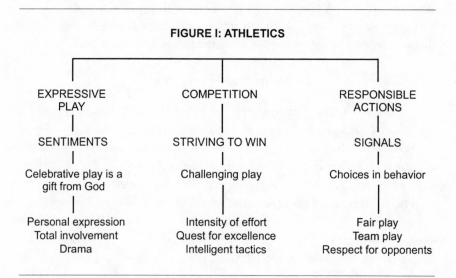

FIGURE 2: ATHLETICS, AN OVERVIEW

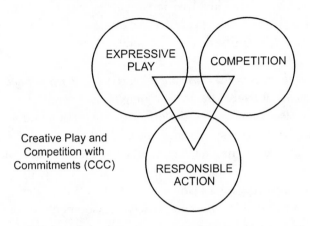

Athletics as Expressive Play

The athlete is a player! Athletes know the beauty of intensity of effort, the motivation of pursuit of goals, the feeling and being of fitness, the expressiveness of movement, the creativity of play, the excitement of total involvement, and the joy of sport.

Play is celebration, a revelation of the joyous nature of a Christian's existence in God. Christians are free to relax, to play, to enjoy God. Work is not holier than play. However, play, as an activity, should not dominate life. Both work and play must be part of the life of celebration to the Lord.

Athletics must focus on the play experience. The discipline, regimentation and drive for victory found in interscholastic athletics need a playful spirit if athletics are to remain a part of the celebrative life.

Athletics as Competition

Interscholastic athletics have competition as a basic ingredient. "Play is 'tense,' as we say. It is the element of tension and solution that governs all solitary games . . . and the more play bears the character of competition the more fervent it will be. In . . . athletics it is at its height" (Huizenga 1955, 11). There are various ways competition can be used. It is even possible to see differing views of competition within the Christian community.

1. *Competition is morally wrong because it pits one player or team against another in rivalry which often results in hate.* And doesn't God demand love for others?

However, competition in itself is neither right nor wrong; it is the use of competition that can be right or wrong. The athletic event in which each team or player is totally involved in play, the contest is close, and each participant feels the celebration of the game does not lead to rivalry or hate. Competition can bring out cooperation, celebration, respect, and even love.

2. *Competition is a duel, a bitter struggle between two players or teams each trying to beat the other.* "We must beat them tonight" is a common locker room or dinner table reminder. The net effect of such competition is often a dog-eat-dog battle for supremacy. "We killed them tonight" is heard in the winner's locker room after such struggles. But bitterness and hate are hardly part of the Christian life (Leviticus 19:17). The athletic contest which totally involves each team or player in expressive, exciting action must be kept free of bitterness and self-pride. Competition for the Christian must flow from a respect and appreciation for others as image-bearers of God.

3. *Competition is a pursuit of a prize.* A quest for victory is at the heart of athletic play. No one can play responsibly to lose. The Bible even promotes running "in such a way as to get a prize" (1 Corinthians 9:24). Yet, the quest for achievement must be evaluated in terms of what the means are and what effect the results have. The winning of a game or championship or the receiving of a trophy or all-conference award is a thrilling experience, but such achievements do have a temporal focus. Christians are enjoined to "not store up treasures on earth, where moth and rust destroy" (Matthew 6:19). Compete to win! But remember the prize does not have eternal significance nor should the search for a prize be at the expense of Christian commitments.

4. *Competition motivates players to pursue excellence.* And God would have people use all their talents (Matthew 25:14–30). Surely, a pursuit of excellence is at the heart of competition for the Christian. "There is no doubt that this spirit of competition has certain healthy effects on the individual. It often makes [one] more determined to do [one's] very best" (Admiraal 1978, 6). Yet, the search for excellence must be evaluated from the perspective of priorities. Should players practice from 8:00 A.M. to 3:30 P.M. every day and not go to class? Such action might allow for a pursuit of excellence but would fail to consider total personal development. Athletes have a responsibility to pursue excellence but they also must make important decisions about time and priority in all of life's aspects. The same is true for those who direct educational learning in schools.

5. *Competition is fun, challenging, and it helps players think about Christian personal and social habits and commitments.* Celebration, intensity of effort, and responsible actions are to flow from the competitive experience. Athletic competition for the Christian seeks an integration of celebrative, intense play with Christian response patterns. This integrative view gives ethical and developmental qualities to competitive play. It puts athletics in proper place as a part of education and life to use rightly.

How then should a Christian view competition? A de-emphasis on competition is not necessary unless competition is used to serve selfish ends. Competition must not become a bitter duel. Pursuit of a prize and excellence are honorable goals but they must be evaluated according to the standards of time and priority. Yet, such judgments must not distract from intensity of effort and total involvement, which are at the heart of competitive athletics. Athletic competition may best be defined as challenging, intense play with Christian response. Intensity of effort and pursuit of excellence are essential—but so are "love, joy, peace, patience, kindness, goodness, faithfulness, gentleness and self-control" (Galatians 5:22–23).

A Christian response to competitive play is focused competition which encourages the athlete to be an expressive player in celebration to the Lord, to give God thanks for the gift of play, to play intensely, to pursue excellence and test the limits of abilities, and to develop and act with Christian commitments.

Athletics as Education for Responsible Action

Athletic competition can also focus on the development and mirroring of Christian actions. I judge that the following specific responsible actions seem important for athletics as education for Christian responsible action:

1. Commitment to a celebrative play lifestyle.

2. Choices and commitments in personal conduct; such as intensity of effort self-control under stress, fair play, handling success and failure, accepting responsibility with concern and love, God-glorifying self-esteem, developing the fruit of the Spirit.

3. Choices and commitment in social conduct; such as joy of team membership, relations with teammates, coaches, the student body, opponents, and officials.

I believe the elements of personal and social conduct in athletics that have Christian responsible actions include at least the following decisions:

Personal decisions:

Perseverance   Pursuit of excellence and total involvement but with a balance of priorities

Self-Knowledge   Knowledge of my tendencies to act under stress

Integrity   Sense of fair play following from a heartful commitment to the truth

Self-Respect   Belief in self flowing into true thankfulness for God-given talents (Fruit of the Spirit)

Stewardship   Acceptance of responsibility from a commitment to love others

Social decisions:

Cooperation   Caring and sharing versus jealousy, rivalry, and back-biting (such as roasting coach)

Responsibility   Leadership and fellowship actions

Respect   Opponents as enemies or friendly "co-petitors"? Belittling of official? Roast coach? Roast player?

Justice   Wrath and anger over bad calls? Ranting and raving? Spectator conduct?

Competition   A duel or a motivation, challenge, and test?

Guidelines for Action

Christian coaches, parents, players, and fans must act from a value belief structure if athletics is to be properly conducted from a Christian reference. I feel the following guidelines are important considerations in shaping Christian coaching attitudes and behaviors:

A. The activity should build up the people involved—a lasting celebrative experience.

B. Programs should be developed so all students might enjoy the challenge of competitive play (intramural, clubs, and athletics).

C. Athletes should be helped to understand the differences between the games they play and professional games watched in person or on television.

D. Play for the student in interscholastic sports should be different from the play of the win-at-all-costs professional athlete.

E. Athletes are first of all organized for participants and only secondly for spectators and parents.

F. Players must be prepared for interschool competition by first being provided with good instruction in the techniques and tactics of the game and in conduct decisions.

G. Christian sports conduct should be congruent with the Christian lifestyle.

H. Players must be led to understand the responsibilities and implications of the freedom to choose between ethically fair and unfair play.

I. We can expect modeling of Christian virtues from those conducting and supporting athletic programs. The activity must be under the guidance of leaders who understand that the chief end of athletes is to serve God.

J. Athletic participants and spectators should come to appreciate all good plays, whether your team's or your opponents' team.

K. Our bodies should be developed, not destroyed.

L. The interscholastic program must be conducted so the physical welfare and safety of the participants and spectators are protected and fostered.

M. Realistic expectations for athletes should proceed from an understanding of growth and developmental factors.

N. To view sports competition as challenging, intense play with an evaluation of Christian virtues does permit athletics to be pursued with all the vim and vigor of youth. Athletes should be challenged to test the limits of their abilities.

O. Players have other tasks in life besides participating in athletics. We must be reasonable in our demands on energy, time, and enthusiasm.

P. Cooperation between directors, coaches, athletes, parents, and supporters is crucial.

Q. Officials should be regarded as support persons—not adversaries.

R. There are some alarming trends in athletic sports programs. Among these are the stress on winning-at-all-costs, the increasing incidence of violence, a stress on the combativeness, the promotion of games as only entertainment for fans, and an overemphasis on personal glory.

S. The budgetary system of funding is essential to maintaining a sound educational perspective in the interscholastic athletic program. Funds for the program should be placed in the regular school operational budget and revenue placed as an income source in the budget. It almost goes without saying that we must deal discreetly with resources.

The "Bill of Rights for Young Athletes" found in Appendix A also provides guidelines that may be useful for Christians to adopt. Finally, I submit for your evaluation and discussion a list of questions that parents and athletes should consider (see Appendix B). By applying these principles and using other sources such as those listed below, Christians will be able to develop responsible athletic sports programs that truly reflect our calling to redeem this area of our society.

References and Additional Readings

Admiraal, H. 1978. A Christian looks at competition. *Christian Home and School*, 56 (9).

Huizinga, J. 1955. *Homo Ludens: A study of the play element in culture*. Boston: Beacon.

Interscholastic Athletics. Grand Rapids: Christian Schools International.

Open letter to athletes, parents, and fans: Guidelines for Christian action in athletes. Grand Rapids: Christian Schools International.

Van Asch, J.C. 1977. *Physical education from a Christian view of anthropology*. (K. J. Boot, Trans.). Sioux Center: Dordt College Press.

APPENDIX A

Bill of Rights for Young Athletes
(National Association for Sport and Physical Education)

1. Right of the opportunity to participate in sports regardless of ability level.

2. Right to participate at a level that is commensurate with each child's development level.

3. Right to have qualified adult leadership.

4. Right to participate in safe and healthy environments.

5. Right of each child to share in the leadership and decision-making of their sport participation.

6. Right to play as a child and not as an adult.

7. Right to proper preparation for participation in the sport.

8. Right to an equal opportunity to strive for success.

9. Right to be treated with dignity by all involved.

10. Right to have fun through sport.

APPENDIX B

Questions Parents Raise, or Should Raise, About Athletics

1. Should the school sponsor athletics? Shouldn't athletics be sponsored by community agencies so that schools can focus on academics?

2. What qualifications should a good coach have? When should a coach be released?

3. Should there be cuts?

4. Should all members on a team play?

5. Is winning everything in athletics?

6. How should opponents be treated? Officials?

7. How should an athlete be educated to handle personal glory?

8. What sports should be included in the athletic program?

9. What are the rights and roles of male and female athletes?

10. What happens when athletics and formal studies conflict?

11. How should the program be financed (general budget, booster clubs, pay-to-play)?

12. Can athletic participation help build character?

13. What kind of conduct should spectators model?

14. Has the Christian school placed too much emphasis on team and individual competitive sports at the expense of family-type recreation?

15. Do sports encourage athletes to serve self more than others?

16. What is competition? Can participation in a competitive sport be a celebration to honor God? Or does competition encourage rivalry and hate?

17. Do you want your son or daughter to win an athletic scholarship? Do you speak with great admiration about the athlete who wins such a scholarship?

18. Have you ever had "roast coach" for dinner?

19. Should we pray for wins?

20. Aren't sports an idol?

21. Can a Christian be a professional athlete?

22. How should coaches treat athletes?

23. Can a coach demand that an athlete go to a sports camp? Should we pay for our children to go to sports camp?

24. Are expensive uniforms and super-slick equipment needed?

25. Are some sports too dangerous?

26. Why shouldn't every scholar in a school receive a school letter? Why do only athletes receive letters?

27. Don't we have an over-emphasis on sports in our schools?

28. Should we have female yell-leaders?
29. Must an athlete be punished if he or she elects to go on family vacation rather than stay home to practice or play?
30. What are the rights of my son or daughter as an athlete?
31. Aren't some sports given the status of minor sports?
32. Don't sports place too much pressure on young adults?
33. How do we handle personal conflicts?
34. Should athletes get out of physical education classes?

(Guideline answers based on Christian principles for these and like questions are found in a self-study manual written by this author and published by Christian Schools International, 3350 East Paris Avenue, Grand Rapids, Michigan 49508.)

Chapter Fifteen

Toward an Understanding of "Muscular Christianity": Religion, Sport, and Culture in the Modern World

JAMES A. MATHISEN

In 1946 the reigning American mile champion, Gil Dodds, reentered competitive running after retiring in 1945 to work for the new Youth for Christ organization. Upon coming out of retirement, he broke the U.S. mile record one more time, adding to his accomplishments of winning 39 consecutive races in the 1940s and being voted the Sullivan Award in 1943 as the Amateur Athlete of the Year.

Later *Life* magazine commented on his amazing comeback, and the author included an anecdote about Dodds complying for autographs when besieged by youngsters. He would sign his name and then add "Phil. 4:13" because his favorite Bible verse was "I can do all things through Christ who strengthens me" from Philippians 4:13. Apparently some fans were having difficulty trying to solve the code. Why would Dodds refer to winning a mile in 4 minutes and 13 seconds in Philadelphia? (Farmer 1948).

That was 1948. In early 1990 I was in Moscow and attended a Sunday service at the Moscow Baptist Church. After being squeezed together into the balcony with other visitors, I eagerly made my way out of the sanctuary when the service concluded. I noticed one small group of fellow visitors and thought, "They're not Russians; they look like Americans, and they look like American athletes." Some stereotypes do work, which can be the advantage of stereotypes. Looking at these young men in knit cotton sweaters, unbelievably I recognized one of them. "This is incredible. This is Tom Roy from the church my brother attends in Indiana. What in the world is he doing in Moscow?"

Then I recalled that Roy directs a small sport evangelism organization called "Unlimited Potential Incorporated." He takes American professional baseball players into other cultures to put on clinics and to give witness of their Christian faith. And here he is when I run into him on a Sunday morning in Moscow. This is incredible; what a coincidence! But no, this is not a coincidence at all. This makes perfect sense. Tom Roy and I are both active Protestant lay churchfolk in the 1990s. Although I was in Moscow working with Soviet sociologists and he was there with baseball players, we knew each other through the network of sport ministry groups and incidentally through my brother. So it was neither incredible nor a coincidence.

My point is that to go from Gil Dodds "running a mile in Philadelphia in 4 minutes and 13 seconds" to running into Tom Roy in Moscow 45 years later in one sense illustrates some of the dramatic changes both within the sport evangelism movement during that period but also in the increasing cultural awareness of the interaction between religion and sport in American life. Fewer people today would make the mistake of looking at "Phil. 4:13" and thinking, "That means Philadelphia in 4 minutes and 13 seconds." They may not know Philippians, and even if they do, they may not know how to spell it, but at least many know it is a Bible verse because of the signs they have seen displayed at numerous televised sports events. Not only have other Christians become familiar with such displays, but the larger culture also has seen these people and now almost expects them to appear at sports events, even though they also may ridicule them for their efforts to articulate their Christian commitment in such a setting.

This leads to a two-fold discussion in this paper. The first part is a review of the "muscular Christian" movement, with emphasis on its modern reemergence and development since the days of Gil Dodds. The second goal is a preliminary evaluation—both positive and critical—of the movement as it has evolved in the past four decades. Hopefully the combination of historical description and assessment will provide some insight into the current state and possible future directions of the movement.

An Overview of the Development of Modern Muscular Christianity

The first point I wish to assert is that since the 1940s and the days of Gil Dodds, evangelical Protestant Christianity and modern sport have developed a relationship that might best be depicted as one of "symbiosis" or "elective affinity" in which evangelicalism and sport have created points of commonality and mutual benefit. Secular journalist Carol Flake observes,

> The resurgence of evangelicalism in America had brought with it a revival of muscular Christianity and a return to the social Darwinism of the athletic arena. Jesus the teacher had become Christ the competitor. . . . From the pulpit, preachers prayed for winning seasons, sprinkling their sermons with so much athletic symbolism that they sometimes sounded like color commentators on TV sports broadcasts. (1984, 93)

Historically this affinity was not always so, at least not prior to the modern, post-World War II era. Then this new relationship developed, and Flake is correct. There is something about the resurgence of evangelicalism—or of fundamentalism in the 1940s and 1950s on its way toward today's evangelicalism—that resulted in sport and this brand of Christianity finding each other. The relationship is not an exact symbiosis, because alongside the benefits that each partner derives are also some losses and risks. Nor are the benefits equally shared, as each partner has altered both itself and the other as a result of their interaction.

Next, I give some necessary long-term historical background. The term "muscular Christianity" probably originated in 1857 in an English book review. Charles Kingsley and Thomas Hughes were authors of popular-level novels that incorporated their ideas about how sport and athletic participation in the British public schools could be a means of inculcating morals and ethics. In 1857 a reviewer used the term "muscular Christianity" when writing pejoratively about Kingsley's novel *Two Years Ago* (Guttmann 1988, 73). About that same time, Hughes wrote *Tom Brown's Schooldays* (1857) in which he idealized the kind of athleticism that his hero Thomas Arnold had begun at Rugby School in the 1820s–30s. Inadvertently, Hughes and Kingsley were also reversing long-held negative positions within the church about its relationship to sport and athleticism, as they sought to Christianize the ancient Greek ideal of *mens sana in corpore sano*, a sound mind in a sound body. The label "muscular Christianity" then came to describe the kind of mix of sport and values, usually within English public schools, that Hughes and Kingsley advocated and wrote about.

What followed historically was the rapid development of pluralistic types of muscular Christianity. What Kingsley and Hughes originated was simply the first, "classical muscular Christianity," of several versions, depending on different combinations of attitudes different people held toward sport, religion, and culture. That is, Hughes and Kingsley held strong ideas about the intrinsic value of sport. Sport and athleticism have value in and of themselves with no other reasons for their being necessary. They were communal and ethical in their approach to religion, quite unlike today's evangelicals trying to convert people via sport, and they viewed Christianity as the key to creating a kind of shared ethical ethos. They also held rather negative views about British culture. Their long-term goal was one of restoring the values of British life to their former dominant status, and they hoped to do this through the public schools. So for lack of a better term, this was the "classical" version of muscular Christianity, blending an intrinsic attitude toward sport with a communal, ethical approach to religion and a negative position toward culture.

Shortly after, Baron de Coubertin read *Tom Brown's Schooldays* when he was twelve years old. It made a tremendous impression on him that became both a part of his motivation as well as a model for his reviving the modern Olympic movement. Coubertin was not Christian in an orthodox sense. He was a Deist who was influenced by the French social philosopher Auguste Comte; one of Comte's goals was the creation of a "new religion of humanity." Coubertin decided that the alternative new religion of "Olympicism," a term he coined, could be a means to a new international, spiritual ethos emphasizing fair play and transmitted through quadrennial athletic competitions. Fuse the secular philosophy of Auguste Comte and the Deistic religious emphasis of Coubertin's own life together with the athletic influence of *Tom Brown's Schooldays*. Add a personal mystical experience Coubertin had when he stood at the grave of Thomas Arnold near Rugby School,[1] and out came an "idealist" muscular Christianity—a second type—which is similar to Hughes' and Kingsley's, but much more positive about culture. Thus Coubertin's model for shaping the Olympic movement was indirectly supplied through the British public schools. Like Hughes and Kingsley, Coubertin was intrinsic toward sport and ethical about religion but differed in his positive attitude towards British life and culture.

Meanwhile, the YMCA was coming into being in the 1840s–50s. It began in Great Britain as a means of urban evangelism to young boys in the garment industry. Early on, it had nothing to do with sport or recreation and leisure, but sport soon became an integral part of the YMCA movement, both in England and in the United States. In 1869, for example, the New York YMCA was the first to add a gymnasium when building a new structure (Hopkins 1951). That decision was also something quite controversial. Thus as a means to urban evangelism, the YMCA added the gymnasium as a way of reaching young boys alongside the Bible studies and the traditional evangelistic and revivalistic means of transmitting Christianity.

The YMCA differed from the two other forms of muscular Christianity, however, by its decidedly more extrinsic view of sport. Its utilization of sport as a tool for attracting youth was an approach unlike what Hughes, Kingsley, or Coubertin were doing. They were more intrinsic, valuing sport on its own terms, whereas the YMCA people viewed sport as but one means of communicating Christian ideals. But the approach of the Y religiously was similar to theirs, emphasizing an ethical and communal approach to Christianity. The YMCA also was positive about culture and went on to export cultural values alongside Christian values in its work beyond England and the United States. Thus it represents a third type of "urban-secular" muscular Christianity—extrinsic about sport, communal about religion, and positive toward culture.

A fourth type of muscular Christianity was that of C.T. Studd. Studd's father converted to Christianity in the 1870s when D.L. Moody preached in London. The senior Studd had three sons, all of whom were outstanding cricket players, and they followed in their father's footsteps and converted to Christianity shortly after. C.T. Studd's younger brother Kynaston went on to become the Lord Mayor of London, while C. T. Studd was one of the famous "Cambridge Seven" athletes who set out for China and used their athleticism and notoriety from sport as a way of evangelizing people outside a western European setting. C.T. Studd became involved with J. Hudson Taylor and the China Inland Mission in the 1880s, while Kynaston came to the United States to join Moody in the YMCA movement and his Northfield conferences (Grubb 1933). C.T. Studd's version was an "evangelical" muscular Christianity that was virtually the opposite of the classical type of Kingsley and Hughes. Studd was extrinsic about sport, viewing it largely as an evangelistic tool for the conversion of souls to an individual, salvationist Christianity as mirrored his own experience, while on the basis of his heroic role as an athlete, maintaining positive views of Anglo-American culture.

What happened in the following decades is that the whole of muscular Christianity in both its British and subsequent American variants waned, so that at about the end of World War I, little remained in any organized sense. Thomas Hughes tried to bring his classical version of muscular Christianity to the United States by establishing a commune in Rugby, Tennessee, but he was undermined by real-estate speculators (Worth 1984). The project failed, so classical muscular Christianity never transferred to the American scene. The idealist vision of Baron de Coubertin, however, had something of an American counterpart in the career of Amos Alonzo Stagg. Stagg attempted an idealist muscular Christianity, particularly through coaching football at the University of Chicago. But big-time American football was increasingly less-than-conducive to his ethical ideals, and eventually Stagg's coaching lessons lost much of his original Christian vision (Lucia 1970). The YMCA, particularly through Luther Gulick in the 1880s and 1890s, popularized a version of the urban-secular muscular Christianity in the United States (Hopkins 1951). But as the physical culture within the Y increased proportionately, the YMCA's earlier commitment to muscular Christianity gradually secularized and fell apart. Also in part because of the fundamentalist modernist schism among American Protestants, the YMCA lost much of its previous mission of using sport for overtly Christian purposes. And C.T. Studd simply had no U.S. counterpart in the World War I era, despite a visit to America in 1896–97; thus his evangelical version of muscular Christianity faded from sight.

But there was a fifth, indigenously American version of muscular Christianity represented by Billy Sunday, the professional baseball player, who converted to Christianity in 1886 near the Pacific Garden Mission in Chicago. He left baseball in 1891 to become a full-time worker with the YMCA. When the YMCA asked Sunday to leave its evangelistic branch to take over the gymnasium, he said in effect, "I can't do that; that's not real evangelism." Then in 1893 he published a brief article on the ten reasons why he left baseball. Sunday's position after his conversion was "separatistic," and he was not able to bring together the principles of Christianity with an ongoing athletic involvement. This position meant instead that the only way that he felt he could respond was to leave professional sport. Although in his subsequent career as an itinerant evangelist, Sunday often used sport metaphors in his preaching, those sermons reflected an extrinsic view of sport to achieve individualistic Christian conversions, while he viewed much of the larger culture including the subculture of organized sport quite negatively.

What resulted was that muscular Christianity virtually disappeared in the United States in the post-World War I era. It either secularized or accommodated to the culture, as in the cases of the YMCA and coaches like Amos Alonzo Stagg, or conversely, it developed a dualistic and separatistic view represented by Billy Sunday. Unfortunately, the evangelical version of C.T. Studd's muscular Christianity did not transfer from England, partly because of the schism among American Protestants, as well as the increasing secularity of organized sport. So within about seven decades of its origins, muscular Christianity was no longer on the agenda of American Christians.

If one were to move ahead about one generation to the 1940s, an indirect, but a key figure in the serendipitous rediscovery of muscular Christianity was a youth evangelist named Jack Wyrtzen in New York City. After previous careers as a dance band leader and a used car salesman, Wyrtzen began frequent youth evangelism rallies in Times Square in the early 1940s, about the same time that Gil Dodds was the reigning American mile champion. Wyrtzen was interested in athletics, had been a high school trackman, and invited Dodds to talk about his Christian commitment at the youth rallies. Apparently, on some Saturday evenings Dodds appeared first with Wyrtzen at Times Square and then dashed over to run a competitive mile at Madison Square Garden (Sweeting 1961; Larson 1948). In 1945 Dodds went to Wheaton College in Illinois as the track coach and attended graduate school there, while employed by the new Youth for Christ organization that originated formally in August 1945 in Winona Lake, Indiana.

There Youth for Christ announced it existed and had four full-time employees—one of them was Gil Dodds and another was Billy Graham. On Memorial Day 1945, the Youth for Christ leader from Chicago, Torrey Johnson, led a Youth for Christ rally at Soldier Field. Sixty-five thousand people appeared, many of them teenagers, and Dodds ran a lap around Soldier Field before giving his testimony about his Christian conversion while still in his track suit ("Wanted: A Miracle," 1945). Thus Dodds emerged as the prototypical muscular Christian of the day, reviving a modern version of the C.T. Studd type of evangelical muscular Christianity. That is, Dodds' approach was an individual, salvationist one particularly oriented toward attracting young males to a fundamentalist-Protestant Christian message. Dodds also held to an extrinsic view of sport, being eager to use it to attract listeners to a Christian message, with little sense that sport has much intrinsic worth. And Dodds' view of culture was increasingly positive, with little evidence of the earlier Billy Sunday type of separationist attitude.[2]

For the next several years, Dodds was employed by Youth for Christ while continuing to coach track at Wheaton until 1957. Youth for Christ sent him to Europe and then to Korea in 1950, and out of that came an invitation in 1952 from Dick Hillis, the Youth for Christ representative in Taiwan. Hillis requested that Youth for Christ send a U.S. basketball team to Taiwan to play exhibitions against local teams and help in evangelism ("Bibles and Basketball," 1952). So the "Venture for Victory" basketball team—including Dodds's friend Bud Schaeffer, an all-American from Wheaton—coached by Don Odle from Taylor University in Indiana became the prototypical organized form of modern muscular Christianity. Venture for Victory became Sports Ambassadors (SA), and Hillis left Youth for Christ to found Orient Crusades (now OC International), a new missions organization with Sports Ambassadors as the athletic division of Orient Crusades. With its 1952 origins, SA was the first organization given to the goals of modern evangelical muscular Christianity. Incidentally, in 1975, the daughter of James Naismith, the "inventer of basketball," wrote a letter to Sports Ambassadors, thanking them for using basketball not as a means to make money, but in a way that her father would have appreciated (Dodd 1975).

Following these origins of SA in 1952, via Gil Dodds, Billy Graham, and Youth for Christ, the Fellowship of Christian Athletes (FCA) appeared soon after in 1954, and then Athletes in Action (AIA) emerged in 1966 within the existing Campus Crusade for Christ organization. These became an early "Big 3" of organizational muscular Christianity, totally committed to the assumptions about using sport for evangelism and missions, with the unintended effect of defining how many Christians today continue to think about the real value of sport in terms of ministry.

Some years later, a second derivative form of organizational muscular Christianity appeared to meet the distinctive needs of a growing sub-culture within elite sport. With organizations such as Pro Athletes Outreach in 1971 and Baseball Chapel about that same time, a number of groups arose that target elite professional athletes ("Training," 1990). These groups were a response to the perception that elite athletes have special needs, and specialized ministries are necessary to reach this increasingly visible and culturally significant subculture of professional athletes, especially in baseball and football. This variation differs from simply using sport as a means to evangelism, such as SA or FCA were doing, and addresses the more narrow subculture of elite professional athletes. This second type of muscular Christianity has expanded of late and is attracting widespread popular and journalistic attention.

A third version of muscular Christianity followed as a response to selective opportunities for social action involvement. One example is the work of Bill Glass, the former football player with the Detroit Lions and Cleveland Browns, who in the 1970s developed a prison ministry. Glass incorporated the evangelistic emphasis of FCA/AIA groups, but he is also oriented indirectly toward prison reform and thus uses sport as a means of access for direct contact with prisoners and prison officials ("Basic Counselor Training"). A second example of social action is provided by Cris Stevens among the women golfers of the Ladies Professional Golf Association (the LPGA). Besides Stevens's work as chaplain to the golfers, her organization also sponsors a Habitat for Humanity chapter (personal communication, April 26, 1990). The women are part of a group that takes time to build houses for people in economic need. These two examples of prison involvement and building houses are the kinds of social action that compose a third, but relatively less-developed, variation of muscular Christianity.

Finally, a fourth version of muscular Christianity lies within the Christian college movement. During the late 1960s, the National Christian College Athletic Association (the NCCAA) arose as a kind of "sacred alternative" to secular organizations such as the NAIA and the NCAA to provide opportunities for athletic competition among smaller Christian colleges unable or unwilling to compete in the larger, secular groups. Today the NCCAA has grown into two different divisions—one for church-related liberal arts colleges and one for Bible colleges with two divisions within the Bible college division according to student enrollments.[3] The NCCAA provides individual and team competitions, including national tournaments, for the Christian colleges. Another direction that Christian colleges have gone is in building a pedagogical base by offering coursework in sport evangelism. The most formal program is for students attending The Master's College in suburban Los Angeles where one can get a bachelor's degree in sport ministry ("Sports Ministries," 1990). This fourth version of muscular Christianity within an academic setting ironically looks more like Thomas Hughes's vision than it resembles that of C.T. Studd. But the overall emphasis remains that of an "evangelical" muscular Christianity using sport as a means to evangelism.

Predictably, the muscular Christian movement became more institutionalized in 1986. Depending upon the perspective one takes, this institutionalization occurred either because these groups were increasingly threatening to each other as competitive rivals or because they really wanted to achieve some kind of coherence and cooperation within the movement. Perhaps the real answer is a combination of these motives. They formed the International Sports Coalition (ISC) in 1986 and then Sports Outreach America (SOA) in 1988 ("International Sports Coalition," 1988). Both groups exist as international and national "umbrella coalitions" that have annual meetings and are trying to bring some semblance of order to what is described here. SOA also took on the sponsorship of *Sports Spectrum* magazine (formerly *Second Look*), published by Radio Bible Class in Grand Rapids, and of the "Sports Spectrum" radio broadcast on over 150 stations on Saturday mornings as a Christian version of thematic sports programming hosted by Chuck Swirsky of WGN in Chicago.

The result is that as the muscular Christian movement moves into its fifth decade in the 1990s, it retains its original, primary evangelistic emphasis, but also has diversified into at least three other, more specialized variations, and then has institutionalized into national and international coalitions of organizations—all of which began with Sports Ambassadors in 1952.

Evaluating the Movement of Modern Muscular Christianity

A second goal of this discussion is a preliminary evaluation of the modern muscular Christian movement, identifying both its specific strengths and weaknesses—its benefits and risks—as the movement evolved since the early days of Youth for Christ and Venture for Victory in the 1950s.

A first important benefit of the modern sport ministry movement is that it has served the church's goal of evangelism since World War II. There is no question that sport and athletics form a distinctive subculture in American life, and the muscular Christian movement has been effective in attracting people, particularly those interested in sport, to consider the Christian message. For example, a young pastor near Minneapolis, as a part of his church's ministry, organizes local golf outings and tournaments. Men from his church cannot participate unless they invite nonchurched persons to play with them. These golf occasions have been effective as a way of introducing some people to Christianity and to the church who arguably would not be attracted through traditional, nonathletic means. There is also no question that muscular Christianity has aided the cause of the Christian mission beyond the American borders. I once received a postcard a former student who was touring in Peru with an Athletes for Action basketball team. He wrote about giving his testimony to several hundred people after his team played. Local churches and mission groups such as these, beginning with the early Orient Crusades teams, have aided significantly the cause of the Christian church in their creative use of sport as a means to evangelism and mission.

To extend the example of this former student, a second, related benefit is that muscular Christianity has contributed to individual spiritual growth, particularly among those involved in sport ministry. It provides an outlet for some who otherwise might not have an opportunity to exercise their spiritual gifts. Amos Alonzo Stagg overheard a conversation, after studying for the ministry at Yale, predicting that he would not be very effective as a minister because he simply could not speak well (Lucia 1970). That incident caused him to consider whether he might use athletics, and coaching specifically, as an alternative way of "preaching." This is even more true today. Modern muscular Christianity provides a means particularly for those with a background in sport to use their spiritual gifts and to find their niche in the kingdom.

A third benefit is that the modern muscular Christian movement has aided an overall increasing cultural awareness that the Gospel can make a difference in people's lives. I once heard former baseball pitcher Dave Dravecky talking simply about how his career had been cut short by cancer and a succession of surgeries. He spoke to a group of about 3,500 men on a Saturday morning, and it was a powerful way of discussing the meaning of life with clarity and authenticity (Dravecky and Stafford 1990). Similarly, pitcher Tim Burke and his wife have adopted third-world children simply because they see that as something Christians should do. Athletes who take advantage of the high profile that sport provides in American culture and use that as an entrée—whether it is Orel Hershiser singing the doxology on "The Johnny Carson Show" or Darryl Strawberry explaining why he tithes in *The New York Times*—have contributed to this larger cultural awareness of the Christian message and its power to change lives (Hershiser and Jenkins 1989, Vecsey 1991). In sum, these are three important benefits resulting from the modern muscular Christian movement.

But there have been weaknesses or costs alongside these benefits. A first cost is the degree to which modern muscular Christianity has taken on and adapted the secular values of American culture. Given the ideas of "symbiosis" and "elective affinity" cited above, perhaps it has been inevitable that the practitioners of muscular Christianity too often have accommodated to the values they know best—the values that the world of sport holds up and intensifies within its American context. One easy

example of this adaptability is the glorification of competition and winning. Competing in a zero-sum setting in which there must be a loser for
every winner and the ultimate value is determining who is "Number 1"
are clearly American values exaggerated by sport. The question is whether those values have any relationship to biblical ideals, including that of
God's grace which is never based on winning and losing, but "whosoever
will may come."

A second weakness that stems from this movement is that little cross-
cultural awareness exists among muscular Christian proponents seeking
to export their message and methods into other cultures. All too often,
American muscular Christians simply export American values—or a mix-
ture of these values and the Gospel—into other cultures where they may
not be appropriate at all. That is, the movement demonstrates little sense
of the cultural meanings that sport has in other settings, unlike its meaning in the United States. As a result, Americans often dominate the local,
indigenous views of sport with little sensitivity that sport likely has significantly different cultural implications in other settings. Furthermore,
Christians in those cultures might have quite different understandings of
the role, if any, that sport should play in the furtherance of the Christian
message.

Third, let us move from cultural implications to consider the idea of
social structures and especially the relationship between institutional religion and institutional sport. Muscular Christianity has failed to bear a prophetic witness by addressing the corrupt structures of institutional sport.
Built into modern sport are such structural evils as racism, sexism, the
whole issue of cheating (often in the name of competition and winning),
academic irresponsibility, the abuse of drugs and steroids, and other serious faults. Rather than address these structural excesses within sport, the
visible and credible proponents of muscular Christianity have opted for
an individualistic ethical response, with little consideration that somehow
these evils may be built into the very structures of modern secular sport.
The modern muscular Christian movement remains unable or unwilling
to confront or even call attention to the unchristian structures that have
dominated American sport since World War II.

A fourth point of criticism is that the modern movement has toler-
ated inadequate understandings of Christian church history and theology.
In the area of church history, people within the movement should look
to the YMCA as probably the best case study of a group that started
out with very good intentions and purposes in its utilization of sport,

but within about a 50-year period it pretty much abandoned those. Using examples from bygone eras as a constructive resource for avoiding comparable mistakes typically does not occur among modem practitioners.

Probably the area of theology is more serious, and there are several sub-points here. First, what has occurred is that the modern movement has developed a kind of "inductive folk theology." Because the movement has not articulated an adequate theology as a basis for ministry, it has created this inductive theology by default, often by extrapolating from the statements that St. Paul made when using athletic metaphors. Arguably, none of the Pauline passages has as its central teaching anything to do with athletics and sport per se. Simply because Paul used a common metaphor from his day does not lead to the frequent interpretation today that he therefore was tacitly endorsing modem sport and its potential for Christian involvement. By comparison, Paul wrote about masters and slaves, but that should not be interpreted as an endorsement of a social system of slavery. Likewise Paul used several athletic metaphors illustratively but probably did not intend those as an endorsement of athletics.

What happens further is that muscular Christian speakers preach about Christian virtues such as obedience and declare that one of the characteristics of the Christian life should be our obedience to God and our willingness to be submissive to each other. Then that point is extrapolated into the athletic arena, and it results in an unthinking subservience, that a committed Christian athlete always must obey his or her coach. That idea obviously has little to do with the biblical teaching on obedience. But perhaps the most flagrant example of the inductive folk theology approaches the reverse of this kind of reasoning. A representative of the movement once began a talk by citing common clichés from sport and then extrapolating them back into Christianity for his applications. For example, contemporary sport advocates place a lot of emphasis on being "focused," so that in one's performance, one should concentrate and focus. What happened in this talk was that the speaker invoked this cliché and then shifted to the Christian life to exhort about the comparable need to "focus on Christ" for direction in one's life. One result of the absence of an adequately articulated theology is this further inductive theologizing in the form of deriving would-be biblical principles from the clichés and rhetoric of sport. Arguably, that is exactly opposite of what a proper theology should stimulate.

And a final indictment is that the current movement has distorted an equitable distribution of resources for ministry. The adjective "equitable" may not be the exact term here, but the idea behind it is apparent. If one invokes the sociological notion of "resource mobilization," one can assert that the modern muscular Christian movement succeeded in part since the 1960s because of its unusual success in mobilizing human and financial resources in the post-war era. Because it originated as a nondenominational movement with little organizational structure, for the most part, one might ask how its leaders mobilized the money and the personnel as resources on which to build what is now a well-institutionalized movement. How all that occurred—beginning with Billy Graham, the Youth for Christ people, and then Campus Crusade—is outside the bounds of this discussion, but the result makes a simple point.

As these resources were mobilized so successfully, an inequity developed that continues today in terms of the amounts of personnel and money involved in ministering to a relatively small number of people. Conceivably, today's elite athletes compose the most overly-ministered-unto subculture in American life, especially on a per capita basis. Nearly all professional and some major college teams have their own chaplains, not all of whom are full-time, granted. Multiply that fact by the relatively large number of chaplains who are involved in reaching athletes from either team or individual sports for a total audience of perhaps three or four thousand elite athletes. Add in the hundreds of millions of dollars raised on their behalf, and the result is an approximation of the wealth of resources, human and financial, that the movement has access to. If we granted above that the mission of the church has benefited by the presence of muscular Christians, then it is fair to observe that clearly a disproportionate amount of resources is being channeled toward sport ministry. At some point we as a church shall be held accountable for our stewardship these past forty years. Given all the needs confronting the modern church, this issue asks whether we can justify the disproportionate resources that have been mobilized to minister to such a small number of people in modern American life.

Thus at best, we face a mixed picture. Benefits have accrued to the Christian church and to individual participants. But the risks also have been significant—both within and beyond the American church and American society.

Perhaps the most appropriate way of moving from assessment toward a conclusion is with one eye on this brief history and another looking to the future. Does its past provide any clues to where all of this is going and what we might expect from the muscular Christian movement? First, it seems that we are in this for the long run. The relationship that has developed since World War II among religion, sport, and American culture is not likely to change much, at least not in any significant sense. The symbiosis or elective affinity is here to stay, even though some specific details are likely to change. So there is at least the possibility that some different forms of ministry may appear.

For example, the present movement has a strong masculine orientation, with little female presence, which should not surprise us. Although one can point to Cris Stevens' ministry among the women golfers, the mere fact that she has few peers highlights the need to develop other strategies, including a possible entirely separate model for women in sport ministry. Given the expansion of women's athletics, the time has come for new approaches, rather than women merely adapting the existing male model.

Somehow the cross-cultural issues are going to have to be addressed, and it is not clear what this might lead to. By and large, the movement is still based on a 1950s-style fundamentalist Protestant approach to ministry that is going to have to adapt to the post-Christian world of the twenty-first century. It is also reasonable to expect greater inner-city involvement and some variations from the largely white, middle-class, small-town, male-dominated model of evangelism to come up with more options in sport ministry. As one example, chaplain Max Helton's success among the NASCAR stock car drivers may be instructive, as his audience has some distinctive characteristics unlike earlier groups, and Helton has earned valuable attention and respect. It is difficult to be predictive beyond this. In the meantime, some of the persisting risks or losses are going to have to be addressed, or the movement also may suffer in ways that it has not anticipated.

Conclusion

Modern muscular Christianity reemerged serendipitously because of the presence of key individuals such as Gil Dodds, Jack Wyrtzen, Torrey Johnson, Billy Graham, and others. From them originated distinctive organizations dedicated to developing evangelistic ministries via sport and athletics. Over time, they took on a variety of forms and eventually were institutionalized in national and international umbrella groups that dominate the current sport ministry scene.

Inevitably, this history of over forty years has had both benefits and costs, wins and losses. The movement, however, is not likely to disappear, so the question confronting the Christian church is how best to utilize its resources as the movement shifts into the twenty-first century. American culture is not the same as it was in 1945 or 1952, and the world of sport is radically unlike what existed in the post-World War II era. So the question is also one of how best to take a movement that originated in one cultural setting and was derived from one set of assumptions about the normative relationship among Christianity, sport, and culture and adapt the resulting organizational structure and the resources to meet the needs of a changing international setting. The task is formidable, but the challenge is well worth the risks.

Notes

1. The authoritative source on Coubertin is John J. MacAloon, *This Great Symbol: Pierre de Coubertin and the Origins of the Modern Olympic Games* (Chicago: University of Chicago, 1981), esp. Ch. 3; cf. Jeffrey O. Segrave, "Toward a Definition of Olympism," 149–61 in Jeffrey O. Segrave and Donald Chu, eds., *The Olympic Games in Transition* (Champaign, IL: Human Kinetics, 1988).

2. For an overview of Dodds's contribution to modern muscular Christianity, see my "Reviving 'Muscular Christianity': Gil Dodds and the Institutionalization of Sport Evangelism," *Sociological Focus* 23, 3 (1990): 233–49.

3. The NCCAA has its headquarters in Marion, Indiana, and its current executive director is Dr. Barry May.

4. For a more complete discussion of the "myth" of modern muscular Christianity, including its inadequate theology, see my "Modern Muscular Christianity: The Movement, the Myth, and the Meaning," a paper delivered at a conference on religion and sport, Center for the Study of American Religion, Princeton University, March 1992.

References

Basic counselor training for total prison weekends. Cedar Hill, TX: Bill Glass Foundation.

Bibles and basketball aid in Formosa mission. 1952. *United Evangelical Action*, 43. March 15.

Dodd, H. N. 1975. Personal communication to Dr. D. Hillis. Special collections, Billy Graham Center Archives, Wheaton College, Wheaton, IL. June 26.

Dravecky, D. and Stafford, T. 1990. *Comeback*. Grand Rapids: Zondervan.

Farmer, G. 1948. Best indoor mile. *Life* 24 (7): 95–96, 98. February 16.

Flake, C. 1984. *Redemptorama: Culture, politics, and the New Evangelicalism.* New York: Viking Penguin.

Grubb, N. P. 1933. *C.T Studd: Athlete and Pioneer.* Grand Rapids: Zondervan.

Guttmann, A. 1988. *A whole new ball game.* Chapel Hill, NC: University of North Carolina.

Hershiser, O. and Jenkins, I. B. 1989. *Out of the Blue.* Brentwood, TN: Wolgemuth and Hyatt.

Hopkins, C. H. 1951. *History of the YMCA in North America.* New York: Association.

Hughs, T. 1857. *Tom Brown's Schooldays.* Cambridge and Macmillan.

International Sports Coalition. 1988. Boca Raton, FL: International Sports Coalition.

Larson, M. 1948. *Gil Dodds: The Flying Parson.* Grand Rapids: Zondervan.

Lucia, E. 1970. *Mr. Football: Amos Alonzo Stagg.* Brunswick: A.S. Barnes.

Sports Ministries. 1990. Newhall, CA: The Master's College.

Sunday, B. 1893. Why I left professional baseball. *Young Men's Era* 19 (30). July 27.

Sweeting, G. 1960. *The Jack Wrytzen story.* Grand Rapids: Zondervan.

Training for life's ultimate victory. 1990. Issaquah, WA: Pro Athletes Outreach.

Vecsey, G. 1991. As they look past their riches, athletes are turning to religion. *The New York Times*, Al, C7. April 29.

Wanted: A miracle of good weather and the "Youth for Christ" rally got it. 1945. *Newsweek*, 84. June 11.

Worth, G. J. 1984. *Thomas Hughes.* Boston: Twayne.

Chapter Sixteen

Competition in Church Sport Leagues

KIMBERLY A. KELLER, GARY H. NAYLOR, DAVID R. STIRLING

The selection and use of competitive and non-competitive games in school and church curricula remains a controversial subject for many educators and youth leaders. In recent years there has been a significant shift to the use of cooperative or non-competitive games in our school systems, particularly with the resurgence of violence on the community and school playgrounds. The use of competitive activities in Church Sport Leagues (C.S.L.) is well known, but not well documented. In a recent review of the literature, there were no published reports of any kind on activities related to church sport leagues. The purpose of this study was to investigate competition in C.S.L. to see how competition has affected the attitudes of participants and spectators, the importance of winning and the reputation of these leagues.

Methods

The present study involved two hundred and seventy (N=270) undergraduate students attending Trinity Western University who filled out a detailed, locally developed questionnaire concerning their views of church sport leagues. Trinity Western University is a private Christian liberal arts and science university situated in Langley, British Columbia, Canada. As a liberal arts and science institution, the university requires each student to complete courses of study across the liberal arts and science curriculum. The sample of students participating in this study was taken from those students registered in the core Health and Fitness course required as part of their liberal arts/science degree requirements in the area of Physical Education.

As part of the requirements for this course, each student attended weekly laboratory sessions. It was during one of these laboratory sessions that the questionnaire was administered. At the beginning of the session each person was given a copy of the questionnaire and, following introductory comments regarding the purpose and specific details of the survey, was asked to complete the questionnaire and return it at the end of the laboratory period.

Results

Shown in Table 1 are the data describing the age, gender, and geographical origins of the students participating in the study. The largest group of students participating in the study were between the ages of 17 and 20 years of age from the Western Canadian region. Other groups were from Ontario and Quebec, with foreign students coming primarily from the United States and China. Note: The no responses were recognized and recorded as follows: age=18, sex =7, and family origin=16.

The academic background of the students participating in the study is shown in Table 2. The largest number of students participating were either Business students or Social Sciences students, 58 students and 53 students respectively. The distribution of students reported in Table 2 is similar to the distribution of students across the academic disciplines university wide. Of the Social Science students, psychology students make

TABLE I

AGE, GENDER, AND GEOGRAPHIC LOCATION OF THE FAMILIES OF THE STUDENTS PARTICIPATING IN THE CHURCH SPORT LEAGUE (C.S.L.) SURVEY

	AGE		GENDER		PROVINCE/FAMILY ORIGIN			
	17-20	21-25	Male	Female	B.C. Alta. Sask. Man.	Ont. Que.	Nfld. N.B. N.S. P.E.I.	Other
# of Students	208	44	135	128	193	27	33	

TABLE 2

MAJOR FIELD OF STUDY

	AVIA	BUSI	EDUC	FINE	HUM	N.S.	PHED	RELS	S.S.	G.S.	UD
# of Students	11	58	41	4	15	19	26	16	53	4	23

Aviation=AVIA, Business & Economics=BUSI, Education=EDUC, Fine Arts=FINE, Humanities=HUM, Natural Sciences=N.S., Physical Education=PHED, Religious Studies=RELS, Social Sciences=S.S., General Studies=G.S., Undeclared=UD up the largest portion.

Students' perceptions about winning are shown in Figure 2. These results are calculated and reported as percentages of the total number of students responding in each category. Comparing collectively categories 1 and 2 with 4 and 5, winning was an important motivation when competing in sporting activities.

The perceived reputations of the C.S.L. by both participants and spectators are reported in Figure 3. To illustrate the student responses, these data are calculated as a percentage of the total number of respondents. From these observations, the largest number of students participating in and spectating at the particular C.S.L. perceived the C.S.L. to have a poor reputation.

FIGURE I
DISTRIBUTION OF STUDENTS BY ACTIVITY

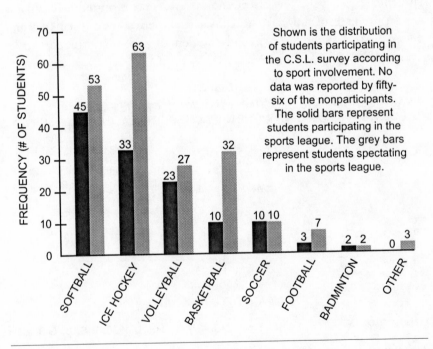

Shown is the distribution of students participating in the C.S.L. survey according to sport involvement. No data was reported by fifty-six of the nonparticipants. The solid bars represent students participating in the sports league. The grey bars represent students spectating in the sports league.

FIGURE 2

IMPORTANCE OF WINNING

Shown are the percent ratings of
the participating (solid bars) and
nonparticipating (grey bars) students on
the importance of winning when they
answered the C.S.L. survey. The ratings
were completed on a five point scale:
1=important and 5=not important.

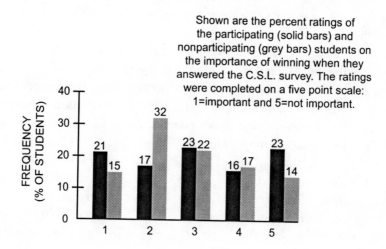

FIGURE 3

PERCEIVED REPUTATION OF THE LEAGUE

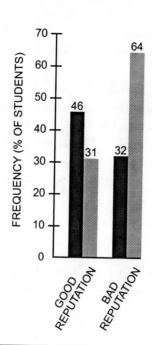

Reported is the percentage of participants
and nonparticipants rating the reputation
of the C.S.L. The solid bars represent the
students participating in the sports league,
and the grey bars represent students
spectating the sports league.

Discussion

Presently there is a dearth of information in the published literature on church sport leagues. In many regions across Canada and the United States these leagues are well-subscribed but there are few reports appearing in the literature.

In western society winning is an important goal and source of motivation (Bethe and Willis 1968, Ellis 1981, Martens 1975, Roberts 1986, Warner 1979). This attitude has filtered through and permeated many aspects of our lifestyle including physical activity and sports participation. It is then not surprising that these values and attitudes are internalized and displayed in community and church sports leagues. It would appear that the reported observations of C.S.L. in this study follow a pattern set in other community sport leagues (Dubois 1980). This correlation would be expected as most of the participants were concurrently involved in various community leagues as well as the C.S.L. As reported in Figure 2, winning is perceived to be important to both participants and nonparticipants alike. Unfortunately, the attitude that winning is all important even at the expense of performing basic sport skills was evident and has been reported elsewhere (Robinson 1982). This attitude can have many negative consequences.

For example, this study indicates that nonparticipants have a low regard for Christian Sport Leagues. The reasons given for the low regard appear to relate back to the students' basic attitudes toward winning. Timmer (1986) writes that an individual's attitude towards participation can be affected by one's perceptions of winning and one's need to win. Dubois (1980) and Timmer (1986) describe our attitudes towards winning as not just important, but the only thing that matters.

The majority of students in this study report that they have received no guidance or instruction on how to approach participation in any sports leagues whether it be a community sports league or church sports league. It is then not surprising that students do not know how to approach competition from a Christian perspective.

In our review of the literature we found no reports that describe programs of instruction that would help athletes and sports participants to develop attitudes towards sport participation and in particular towards winning. This dimension of instruction in our physical education, athletic, and sports programs appears to have been overlooked, at least in the church sport literature.

Based on comments from the participants and nonparticipants it would appear that their attitudes towards competition and winning in the church sports league have been influenced primarily by their participation in local community sports leagues and their observations of sports competition on television. In this study, 86 percent of the students competed without any instruction or guidance about competition in sport from a Christian perspective. By default these students would bring their own perspectives and ideas regarding competition and winning to each game played. This affected their actions and attitudes toward others involved as well as. Clearly, leaders of church leagues need to develop instructional programs that deal with competition and shape attitudes regarding winning. The first step may be to educate and train the pastors, Christian education leaders, and youth workers, who can train the lay workers, volunteers, and league participants.

More research is needed in the area of church sport leagues regarding organization and management, and in particular, how they can be used as a vehicle to shape and develop individual attitudes toward competition, winning, and losing from a Christian perspective.

Conclusions

There is limited published information describing the organization of and participation in C.S.L. From this study, it would appear that there is a limited range of sporting activities developed for C.S.L. This limitation is even more evident when the types of C.S.L. reported here are compared to the many public school and community sport leagues available across North America. Existing C.S.L. tend to have a negative reputation. The reason for this reputation is reportedly related to the highly competitive attitudes of participants competing in these leagues. Interestingly, the highly competitive attitude is cited as one of the main reasons why many chose to be spectators rather than active participants.

Participating and spectating students in C.S.L. have received little instruction on how to approach competition in sporting activities. In particular, students have received limited direction or instruction on how to approach sport competition from a Christian perspective. There are no reports or published curriculum on this particular issue of sport league organization and development. More reported research is particularly needed on the organization and management of church sport leagues.

References

Bethe, D.R., and Willis, J.D. 1986. Success in sport and physical activity as a function of the theory of achievement motivation. In *Contemporary psychology of sport*, edited by G.S. Kenyon and T.M. Grogg, 423–427. Chicago: International Society of Sport Psychology Athletic Institute.

Dubois, P.E. 1980. Competition in youth sports: Process or product? *Physical Educator*, 151–154. October.

Ellis, M.J. 1981. Motivational theories of play: Definitions and explanations. In *Handbook of social science of sport*, edited by R.F.G. Luschen and G.H. Sage, 479–491. Champaign, IL: Stipes.

Martens, R. 1975. The process of competition. *Social psychology and physical activity* (67–86). New York: Harper and Row.

Roberts, R.C. 1986. The sanctification of sport: Competition and compassion. *Christianity Today*. April 22–23.

Robinson, R. 1982. Sports from a Christian perspective. *The Christian Educators Journal* 21, 15–31.

Timmer, J.R. 1986. Winning is the only thing. *The Christian Educators Journal* 25, 22–25.

Warner, G. 1979. *Competition*. Elgin, IL: David C. Cook.

Chapter Seventeen

Christian Ethics in North American Sports

MURRAY W. HALL

Although recent events have brought it sharply into focus, the concept of fair play is not a 1990s trend, not even an invention of the twentieth century. Long before Ben Johnson tested positive for steroids, before Ted Green's skull was fractured during a fight in a NHL exhibition game, and even before the Chicago White Sox threw the 1919 World Series, the principles of fair play—integrity, honesty and respect—were already of great concern in sport (Fair Play Commission 1990, 2). A 1929 Carnegie Fund report identified recruiting violations, lack of professionalism, lack of educational integrity, and commercialism as serious problems in college athletics (Knight Foundation 1991).

In his drive toward the revival of the Olympic Games in 1896, Pierre de Coubertin, the founder of the modern games, envisioned not just an event, but a broadly based social movement using sport to develop the individual and to foster friendship among peoples. He summarized his vision: "The important thing in the Olympic Games is not winning, but taking part. . . . Effort is the greatest joy" (Fair Play Commission 1990). Thus, one of the aims of the Olympic movement was to promote the development of those physical and moral qualities basic to sport (Dubin 1990).

"The history of moral philosophy is largely the history of ideas about what is fair and unfair. Physical education and sport have from time to time been regarded as powerful vehicles for the inculcation of moral values and moral behavior" (McIntosh 1979, 4).

The national education commission in 1954 listed several benefits that were believed to accrue to people based on school sport participation: emotional maturity, health and happiness, social competence, moral values, learning to win and lose, building character, obeying rules, sportsmanship, fair play, teamwork, discipline, democratic process, egalitarian values, meritocratic values, competitiveness, and cooperativeness. Almost forty years later we are "not so naive as to believe that all of these behavioral and attitudinal traits are actually learned in school sports" (Figler and Whitaker 1991, 138).

Randy Roberts, professor of history at Purdue University, writes about "America's misplaced emphasis and inordinate concern for sports" and suggests that priorities are out of whack, with sports "increasingly occupying to an unwholesome degree the attention of millions of Americans" (1989, x). He relates the incident of a Denver Broncos fan who watched as his team fumbled seven times in a loss to the Chicago Bears. Apparently it was more than he could take, and after the game he attempted suicide. His suicide note read: "I have been a Broncos fan since the Broncos were first organized, and I can't stand their fumbling anymore." Or, you may have heard about the tragic incident of a top grade 12 quarterback who after a loss ran head first without his helmet into a brick wall resulting in his becoming a quadriplegic.

> For tens of millions of Americans, sport is not leisure anymore. Sport has become a national obsession, a new cultural currency, a kind of social cement binding a diverse society together. Instead of work, family, or religion, increasingly large numbers of Americans are choosing sport as the focus of their lives. In the 1970s and 1980s, modern America has worshipped sport, not only in global arenas but inside the home as well. (Roberts 1989, xii)

An article appearing in *Psychology Today* (Ogilvie and Tutko 1971) twenty years ago was titled "Sport: If You Want to Build Character Try Something Else." It decried the damage that competitive sport can do to personality development. Some say we have adopted the so-called eleventh commandment: "Do anything to win as long as you don't get caught." This humanistic worldview that there really is no right and wrong permeates sports. Michner summarizes it well when he says, "Winning is not a matter of life and death . . . it's more important than that" (1976, 421).

As long as winning remains more important than *how one plays*, there is little chance for fair play. Cheating, or at least bending the rules, is condoned if not often accepted outright, and practices which were previously regarded as cheating are accepted as an integral part of the game.

Serious sport, writes George Orwell (1986), has nothing to do with fair play. It is bound up with hatred, jealousy, boastfulness, disregard for all rules, and sadistic pleasure in violence; in other words, it is war minus the shooting. Orwell's thesis is that the very nature of sport runs directly counter to a humanistic (and Christian) concern for integrity, honesty, respect, fairness, justice, cooperation, compassion, and honor. Similarly, Robert Roos, reporting in the *Physician and Sports-medicine* (1986), addresses the question, "Do rough games hinder kids' moral growth?" Preliminary studies have found that children most experienced in organized, high-contact sports tend to be less mature in their moral reasoning and more aggressive both on and off the playing field.

In 1988 the National Federation of State High School Associations reported their concerns about what kids are learning from sports and about the educational aspects of sports. They bemoaned the lack of leadership from coaches, educators, and parents. Others have suggested that we have become morally calloused to the negative issues in sport in part because it has become a "big business." We bring the latest medical technology to heighten athletic prowess—indeed, some say that the athletic battle in world championships is not who has the best athletes but who has the best chemists. Such attitudes are reflected in the statement, "They turned play into work, and work into the worst of play, with unbridled competitiveness" (Holmes 1983, 227).

Winning seems to be the great American obsession, and our win-at-all costs philosophy has distorted our sense of values. Competitive sport does not have a good reputation today in terms of ethics and values. "The rhetoric of many colleges far exceeds the practice, and there is no shortage of moralizing and moral posturing, especially the kind that does not cost anything and does not take time or self-denial or effort" (Ostro 1987, 4).

But we are beginning to hear calls for change. Scott Crawford of George Mason University writes about the crisis of sport's integrity:

> Physical educators have a moral responsibility to speak up, speak out, and speak to young people to stress that difficult "right" and "wrong" decisions have to be made if sport is to remain as an expressive and dramatic facet of human experience dependent on ethical behavior. (1986, 42)

Crawford suggests that the tarnished image of sports needs much more than cosmetic surgery. It may well be time for the "back to basics" educational movement to jump on a new bandwagon, that of restoring the teaching of human values.

"If," as Gwynn states, "moral integrity is the supreme purpose of all worthy teaching" (1953, 54), and if we value fair play and sportsmanship as a quality, then we must work to attain it. Moral and ethical values do not accrue automatically from participation in sport but must be carefully planned.

However, although the current literature decries the ethical dilemma we face in sport, many practitioners who are most closely involved in sport seem unwilling to suggest a means of righting this "overturned cart" of sport ethics. At a recent national conference only six of 700 delegates turned up to hear an academic paper on "Fairplay in Sport." As a Christian physical educator, what concerns me most is that the church has not been widely used to call attention to the problems and unethical behaviors others have noted in sports for years. Nor have religious sport organizations taken a leadership position in dealing with these problems and unethical behaviors. It appears that few are willing to begin a process for reforming the unethical dimensions of sport.

National Reform Movements

Two recent reports provide some encouragement at least from a governmental perspective. In October of 1988, following Ben Johnson's disqualification in the 100-meter Seoul Olympics for anabolic steroid use, a Commission of Inquiry into the Use of Drugs and Banned Practices Intended to Increase Athletic Performance was established in Canada. The inquiry, which lasted a year, was very far-ranging, calling 119 witnesses whose testimony approached 15,000 pages. The final report is over 600 pages with an entire chapter (although only comprising 2 percent of the report) on ethics and morality in sport.

The same month this study was completed the trustees of the Knight Foundation in the United States created a Commission on Intercollegiate Athletics and directed it to propose a reform agenda for intercollegiate athletics (specifically NCAA schools). In doing so, they expressed concern that abuses in athletics had reached proportions threatening the very integrity of higher education. The Commission spent more than a year in study and debate and took advice and suggestions from more that 80 experts. The report was completed and published in March of 1991.

It appears that from these reports we may have a blueprint for action for reform in amateur sport. We are at a critical juncture. The reports clearly spell out the nature of the problems. As Charles Dubin (1990) concludes, the problem is not educational, not economic, and not social—but moral.

Permit me to briefly summarize these reports as they relate to ethics and morality. Let us view ethics as a science of conduct, as the principles of right (or justice), morals, and standards of conduct, including integrity.

Knight Foundation and Dubin Reports

Many problems with intercollegiate sport are identified, but Report 7 states that at the root of the problem is a great reversal of ends and means; there is a lack of direction. It asks the question, "If the university is not itself a model of ethical behavior, why should we expect such behavior from students or from the larger society?" Problems are so deep-rooted and longstanding they are thought to be systemic and can no longer be swept under the rug. "This is not an athletics problem," suggests Jack Lengyel, athletic director at the U.S. Naval Academy. "This is a mission problem where the institution has not accepted the athletics program as part and parcel of the educational objectives of the university." The report suggests that intercollegiate athletics and higher education must reclaim the high moral ground by showing "respect for the dignity of the young men and women who compete and the conviction that they occupy a legitimate place as students on our campuses. If we can get that right, everything else will fall into place. If we cannot, the rest of it will be all wrong" (Knight Foundation 1991, 7). It was clear to the Commission that a "realistic solution would not be found without a serious and persistent commitment to the fundamental concept that intercollegiate athletics must reflect the values of the university" (11).

In concluding his report it is clear too that Chief Justice Charles Dubin of Ontario anticipated some opposition to his recommendations:

> There will be those who say that this view of sport and its purposes is idealistic and out-of-date, that I have taken too high a moral tone, that the modern world of sport has progressed beyond the point where the original amateur ideals of fair play, honest striving to do one's best, camaraderie, and wholesome competition have any meaning or validity. If that is indeed the view of Canadians (and I do not accept that it is) then there is no justification for government support and funding of sport. (1990, 524)

I would agree with the Chief Justice and further suggest that we have been presented with a "window of opportunity." With both the Knight Commission and the Dubin Inquiry calling for ethical action, the ball has been thrown, the baton passed. Will we as leaders, and especially Christian leaders, take up the challenge? Will we be prime movers and shakers as in the past through the playground movement and the development of the YMCA and so forth? Christians have been leaders in sport in the past, and we have an opportunity now to regain our lost foothold. But, we need a model for ethical or right action in sport.

Ethical Action in Sport: A Model

We must have a new set of marching orders, a new or clean road map or blueprint to follow if we are to "save sports' soul." Our intentions must be founded on solid standards and principles. For the Christian this benchmark or reference point must be scripturally and spiritually based. For too long Christians have been culture followers rather than "culture formers" (Walsh and Middleton 1984) or "culture transformers" (Hoffman 1991). We have a cultural mandate to tend the garden of sports in our society, to be actively involved in shaping competitive athletics. In defining our mandate we must constantly ask ourselves, "What would Jesus do?" James Sire suggests that we all need a "starting place, a place to stand, a ground zero. Ground zero is a terra firma, a rock which doesn't shift but stays put" (1990, 80–81). In sport, we need to get back on the solid rock and regain a solid footing.

At the same time "we cannot marginalize (or compartmentalize) God or push him to the edge of our minds when we are involved in sports. He must be the hidden premise of all our work" (Sire, 48). As physical educators, our view of competitive sports must be consistent and coherent with our faith. Hiebert (1983) declares that we can no longer identify unequivocally with sport in its present form. Christians' attitudes toward sports should be much different from non-Christians. Tragically, this intention has not been fruitful. Christian hockey and basketball teams often resemble secular teams expressing no commitment to the greater glory of God. The Jekyll and Hyde syndrome of Christian teams must cease.

One possible model as presented by Fox (1991) is comprised of at

---

FIGURE 1

COMPONENTS OF ETHICAL ACTION

FOLLOW THROUGH
|
INTENTION
|
JUDGEMENT
|
SENSITIVITY

---

least four components: 1) ethical sensitivity, 2) ethical judgment, 3) intention, and 4) follow through. Unethical behavior is likely to result if there is a deficiency in any of the components. The model can be viewed as a ladder where we begin climbing at the bottom and progress upward from one rung to the next.

The first component is *ethical sensitivity, discernment,* or *awareness* that an ethical issue exits. As we have noted, the evidence is overwhelming that ethical issues exist in sport. One way to help clarify issues is proposed by Ken Blanchard (1988) in the book *The Power of Ethical Management,* where he suggests using three "ethics check" questions:

1. *Is it legal?* Does it violate the law or organizational policy?

2. *Is it balanced?* Is it fair to all concerned in the short term as well the long term? Does it promote win-win relationships?

3. *How will it make me feel about myself?* Will it make me proud? Would I feel good if my decision was published in the newspaper? Would I feel good if my family knew about it? (27)

We need to recognize that if we avoid or ignore confronting an ethical issue we are basically giving our silent consent to it.

The second component is *ethical assessment* or *judgment* which involves gathering information and opinions. Some feel it is a stage for analysis, reasoning, and reflection before making decisions or charting a course of action. The two reports previously highlighted have certainly assisted us in an indepth appraisal of particular elements of sport. Judgment has also been passed with a clear mandate to correct past errors.

The third rung of the ladder model is the *intention to act* ethically. This, to me, is the key component because it relates to our purpose, our predetermination, our resolve, our raison d'etre, our commitment to our mission. Somewhere we got sidetracked and forgot or allowed some of the basic principles on which competitive sport was founded to become mutated by expediency, the need to win at all costs. It is time to "get back to the basics," to redefine the athletic experience and to revise old mission statements.

Frey and Massengale suggest that we socialize and educate athletes, coaches, the media, and spectators in a dysfunctional manner. "Selected actions, behaviors, and traits are often taught, reinforced, and then rewarded" (1988, 42), even though these actions are not reflective of desirable social values. "For example: How often is blind obedience taught in place of the courage of conviction? How often is intimidation taught under the guise of tenacity? How often is manipulation and deliberate rule violation taught as strategy? How often are sports evaluated on the basis of the budget, not the value of participation? This list could go on forever" (43).

If sport is to be seen as an ethical pursuit for Christians, then we need to examine the ingredients that we put into the mix. We all carry culturally shaped equipment, based on our upbringing and life experiences which have shaped our values and ethics. Our ground zero must be scripturally based. While the Bible does not forbid psychologically intimidating your opponent, it does offer solid life principles that must be carried into the sport arena. The principles need to be blended together in developing a sport ethic that would be God-glorifying.

Following is a list of scriptural themes and principles that should be used in developing our intentions or mission in sport and woven into the fabric of ethical action. If time permitted we could examine each principle, but listing them must suffice for now. We can begin by considering 2 Timothy 2:5: "an athlete competes according to the rules."

Other scriptural principles include references to the body as the temple of the Holy Spirit (1 Corinthians 10:31, Colossians 3:17); stewardship of God's precious gifts (1 Corinthians 6:19); use of talents (Matthew 25:15); control of the tongue (Proverb 21:23, James 3:2); demonstrating the fruits of the spirit in our lives (Galatians 5); forgiving others (Ephesians 4:32); personal discipline (1 Corinthians 9:26–27); servant leadership according to the model of Christ (Gospels); humility (Proverbs 16:2, 18); and being slow to become angry (Proverbs 16:32). Perhaps these principles could provide the fabric and thread to weave the banners of Christian Signals and Sentiments that Shirl Hoffman (1991) feels should fly high in our stadiums.

Finally, to complete the model there is the *follow-through* stage, the persistence, determination, and courage to follow through on our intentions. At this level we attempt to implement our choices and strategies. Our mission will not be realized if it sits on a shelf. Dubin said now is the time to act and to act quickly. The Knight Foundation Commission reports that "a great nationwide effort is required to move reform from rhetoric to reality" (1991, 25). Individual action is needed but the "lone ranger" approach that focuses on the leadership of a few people such as Hoffman, Flynn, or Hiebert needs to be supplemented. We need to gather together a posse, not a lynch mob, to rescue sport and restore its tarnished image.

In closing, allow me to quote from Fox regarding the challenge we face:

We need to create a concept of group ethical action where each individual conceives of him/herself as a "stakeholder." It is in collaboration, support and collective projects where we the group develop strength, persistence, and courage. . . . We must not underestimate the difficulty of pursuing a course of ethical action. Such a course takes practice and the perseverance to overcome many obstacles and mistakes. It is the process that is crucial—that we continue to struggle and choose the ethical channels. (1991, 30)

References

Blanchard, K. 1988. *The power of ethical management.* New York: Pocket Books.

Croakley, J. 1990. *Sport in society* (4th ed.). St. Louis: Times Mirror/Mosby.

Crawford, S. 1986. Values in disarray: The crisis of sport's integrity. *Journal of Physical Education, Recreation and Dance* 57 (9): 41–44.

Dubin, C. 1990. *Commission of inquiry into the use of drugs and banned practices intended to increase athletic performance.* Ottawa: Can. Gov't. Publication Centre.

Fair Play. 1990. Commission for Fair Play. Minister of State, Fitness and Amateur Sport, Government of Canada.

Figler, S. and Whitaker, G. 1991. *Sport and play in American life.* Dubuque: Wm. C. Brown.

Fox, K. 1991. Environmental ethics and the future of parks and recreation. *Recreation Canada* 49(2): 28–31.

Frey, J. and Massengale, J. 1988. Enriching social values through restructuring. *Journal of Physical Education, Recreation and Dance* 59(6): 40–44.

Gwynn, P.H. 1953. Why not teach social ethics? *High School Journal* 37, 54.

Heibert, D. 1983. Sanctified sports, *His* 43, 1, 4.

Hoffman, S. 1991. The expressive and impressive faces of sport and leisure. A paper presented at the Symposium on Christianity, Sport, and Leisure. Symposium conducted at Calvin College, Grand Rapids, Michigan.

Holmes, A. 1983. *Contours of a world view.* Grand Rapids: Eerdmans.

Knight Foundation (Commission on Intercollegiate Athletics). 1991. *Keeping faith with the student-athlete: A New Model for Intercollegiate Athletics.* Charlotte, NC.

Kretchner, S. 1990. Moral "callouses" in sport. *Strategies* 4 (10): 5, 27

McIntosh, P. 1979. *Fair play.* London: Heinemann.

Michner, J. 1976. *Sports in America.* New York: Random House.

Ogilvie, B. and Tutko, T. 1971. Sport: If you want to build character try something else. *Psychology Today* 5 (5): 61–63.

Ostro, H. 1987. Ethical values: Does the rhetoric exceed the practice? *Scholastic Coach* 56 (7): 4, 6, 8, 10.

Roberts, R. 1989. *Winning is the Only Thing*. Baltimore: John Hopkins University Press.

Roos, R. 1986. Do rough games hinder kids' moral growth? *The Physician and Sports Medicine* 56 (12): 31–32, 34.

Sire, J. 1990. *Discipleship of the mind: Learning to have God in the ways we think*. Downers Grove: InterVarsity.

Walsh, B. and Middleton, R. 1984. *The transforming vision: Shaping a Christian world view*. Downers Grove: InterVarsity.

SECTION FIVE

Leisure and Culture

The study of leisure in the North American context has traditionally been associated with sport and physical education. Leisure studies and recreation departments have been placed in the same faculties as departments of physical education and kinesiology. The close association of sport and leisure is even evident in this volume with seven chapters in the previous section on Play, Sport, and Athletics and only three in this final section on Leisure and Culture. A number of papers on Play, Sport, and Athletics were presented at the first three Symposiums on Christianity and Leisure. However, not until the fourth symposium, which focused on the theme "Leisure, Sport, and Popular Culture" was a paper presented on a topic related to leisure and culture. All three papers in this section were presented at the fourth symposium.

Historically, leisure has been associated with culture and not just with sport. In Greek society leisure was seen as being essential for attaining the ideals of the culture. The classical view of leisure was articulated by Aristotle who viewed leisure as a state of being in which activity is performed for its own sake or as its own end. For Aristotle two activities were worthy of the name leisure—music and contemplation. Both of these activities were not as limited as we might expect. For the Greeks music was almost a synonym for culture—it could include music, poetry, social interaction with friends and the exercise of the speculative faculty. All these activities had value for the cultivation of the mind. Contemplation was prized above all other activities and was understood as being very similar to leisure.

In this century Joseph Pieper (1963) revived this classical concept of leisure. For Pieper leisure is a mental or spiritual attitude which is linked closely to contemplation. Pieper considered leisure to be the primary basis of any culture in the past, present, or future. Culture, according to Pieper, is dependent on leisure for its very existence, and leisure in turn is only possible if it has a strong and vital link with divine worship.

In our society we do not associate culture with contemplation but rather with the performing and visual arts such as theatre, ballet, opera, museums, symphony, and art galleries. However, there is far greater leisure time participation in mass media consumption than attending the arts (e.g., theatre, concert and museum going). As Quentin J. Schultze points out in his chapter in this section, television viewing is the most predominant leisure activity in the United States.

Each of the three chapters in this section explores the relationship between leisure and a dimension of culture: storytelling, humor and drama. In Chapter 18, Schultze argues that North American leisure is dominated by storytelling of one form or another. He believes that television is the most popular leisure time activity because it tells tales. When other storytelling activities such as reading and conversation are grouped together with television viewing, then the prevalence of storytelling as a leisure activity is apparent. Schultze concludes that the vast majority of leisure-time in North America is devoted to the consumption of mass-produced, mass-distributed entertainment products.

Schultze's conclusion is echoed by Russell Heddendorf in the next chapter (19). Heddendorf believes that a contemporary "culture of fun" has developed which revolves around the mass media and technologies which offer a new language of visual images. Noting that humor is a powerful social and cultural force that shapes us, Heddendorf examines the cultural meaning of humor as it is manifest in leisure-time activities. He concludes that humor, as an integral part of the leisure ethic, has developed the contemporary "culture of fun."

In the final chapter (20), Gwen Wright urges us to expand our understanding of leisure beyond that of sports and physical activities. Wright encourages a definition of leisure similar to the classical view articulated by Aristotle and Pieper, one in which "being" as well as "doing" is recognized, one in which leisure is seen as a process and a way of becoming, one in which openness and contemplation helps us develop an awareness of God, ourselves and creation. The focus of Wright's paper is on improvisational theatre and how it can help us develop this receptive attitude of leisure.

Paul Heintzman

References

Pieper. J. 1963. *Leisure: The basis of culture*. New York: Random House.

Chapter Eighteen

From the Super Bowl to Worship: The Roles of Story in Work and Leisure

QUENTIN J. SCHULTZE

Several years ago I drove to suburban Chicago with my two pre-teen-age children and my wife to show them the neighborhood of my youth. It was a combination vacation and nostalgia trip. My son and daughter wanted to know more about where I had grown up and what my child-hood was like. Above all, I think they wanted assurance that I had indeed once *been* a child like them—that I had a fun-loving child hidden deep in my adult heart, if only the kids could tap into it. As parents go, I am fairly serious. In short, my children sought to know about their father's past as a way of reaching deeper into their father's present. This was to be a vaca-tion with a special purpose.

So we took off for the Windy City in our silver minivan, the pride of many yuppies, to see whether or not Thomas Wolf was right—that you can never go home again. Along the way we patronized a few service stations and toll booths, proving that if you can go home, it's not a free ride. Eventually we left the highway for the main street of my youth. We moved slowly as I tried to reacquaint myself with the buildings and shops along the way while avoiding possible accidents. The closer we got to the center of the old suburb, the more disoriented I became. It seemed like I was a mere tourist in someone else's culture. Almost nothing was the same—the people were totally unrecognizable, the autos were all differ-ent, store facades were transformed, some buildings were gone, and even the street lights and stop signs looked different. My minivan could have been traveling through any American city.

I pulled into a parking space to contemplate my next move. How could I bring to life my childhood for my own offspring when the setting had completely changed? I could lament the loss of the past by describing the old sights, sounds, and smells—like the Prince Castle ice cream and hamburger joint that once existed right across the street from our parking spot. For a few moments I recalled the exotic, castle-like building with turrets on either side—the Middle Ages as interpreted by a fast-food franchise company in the early 1960s. Then I remembered the sultry summers, when my gym shoes got stuck on gum that careless kids had spit out on the sizzling asphalt in front of the restaurant. I also recalled the strange, cube-like ice cream scoops, the colorful patterns produced by piling various cubes of sherbet flavors on a sugar cone, the smell of chocolate ice cream melting on the cement sidewalk just outside the front doors of the castle, the whir of stainless steel malt mixers . . . it all started coming back to me. But there was no place to show my children. Only my memories were left, and they may have been so infused with the romance of youth that they were little more than suburban fairy tales.

If nothing else, the drive and the memories made me hungry. And I had promised to show the kids the first McDonald's franchise restaurant in the country. Actually, the visit to McDonald's was the one activity that both of my children had requested; they wanted to see this relic of past civilizations, as if it were an exhibit at the Smithsonian or the Natural History Museum. After all, my hometown McDonald's didn't even have inside seating.

Sure enough, the old McDonald's was still there. And the kids' curiosity was not misguided; the restaurant had been turned into a museum—a tribute to the golden days of the golden arches, when McDonald's had no competition, before the "franchisation" of the Western World, and when life was supposedly less complicated, more moral, and more fun. Unfortunately, the museum was closed and the entire lot was fenced and gated to keep suburban interlopers off the grounds.

As luck or providence would have it, the company had erected a large McDonald's across the street to make a few bucks on the tourists who were naive enough to visit this mecca of Americana. I muttered a few things about how I contributed personally to the growth of a global, commercial empire, and then we all jaywalked toward the grease on the other side of the street. The kids had a great time consuming their burgers, fries, and shakes. They congratulated me on a terrific childhood and marveled at how their dad was part of true cultural progress. I sat listlessly on the plastic bench, trying to figure out what the family pilgrimage had become. My childhood existed only in my memory. My parents were both gone. And my brothers were so much older than I that they knew little of my childhood. But the loss of my youth mattered little to my kids, who could relate to cheeseburgers and golden arches. In their eyes the trip home was a success because it let them experience another expression of the same culture of their youth. *They* had gone home, while *I* had discovered that Wolf was right.

I began this academic paper with a personal story as an illustration of the major points I wish to make: that human beings are storytellers, and that stories are probably the most important form of human communication. To give away my thesis regarding recreation and leisure, I would add that most of our discretionary time is taken up with storytelling of one form or another. We tend to contextualize our personal and collective lives as narratives. So do the purveyors of mass media products, in game shows, sports, news, and, of course, drama. My trip home was an ill-fated attempt to recreate the story of my life for my children. It actually back-fired creating the tale that life for me as a child was essentially the same as it is now for my children. I was simply not ready or not equipped to take my offspring on a more accurate journey through my life. But even though the *places* were not the same, the old stories of my youth persisted in my memory. I could take my children to those tales without a minivan.

Theology of Narrative

I believe that humankind's narrative capacity is fundamental to its cre-atedness. Unlike other creatures, we are natural makers of tales, fictional and non-fictional. Because of our symbolic capacity, especially human-kind's miraculous use of language, we make layers of meaning and sig-nificance which are like lenses through which we view the world. Perhaps it is helpful to think of us as image-bearers of God who are constantly "re-creating" the symbolic webs of life called "culture." As T.S. Eliot once put it in *Notes Towards the Definition of Culture* (1949), humankind is inher-ently cultural, spinning entire ways of life. And we are gifted storytellers not merely for our own enjoyment, though that is part of it, but more precisely to take care of and to develop the Creation.

Certainly it is not enough to say that human beings are linguistic, cul-tural image-bearers of God. We must add, based on our own experience of the Creation as well as on the scriptures, that a great deal of our sym-bolic activity is invested in using stories. I mean by "story" a series of events with an apparent beginning, middle, and end. We use such tales to think about our past, to navigate the present, and to ponder the future.

Stories are often the form that our introspection and retrospection take. Thus, stories contextualize human experience, thereby giving the present a sense of past and future.[1]

It might be that this use of stories is precisely why God, in His infinite wisdom and through the work of the church in history, eventually communicated the scriptures in a narrative form, from Genesis (the beginning) to Revelation (the eternal end). Our lives, then, are to be "found" in God's story of Creation, Fall, Redemption, and Second-coming. God's story is our story: He is our author, and we are players in His cosmic drama, regardless of whether or not we acknowledge it as the truth. Both the individual human creature and the body of believers will find their scripts in the Biblical story. The theological depth of this truth is largely beyond human grasp, but the magnificent outlines of the biblical narrative are lucid and compelling.

These theological truths about human narrative capacity are worked out in a myriad of ways by various cultures. It is obvious to those of us of "The Book" that religious faith is narrative in character. Worship, for instance, is partly the body of Christ being reminded whose it is and who it is in the story of the scriptures. Even apparently secular cultures use narratives in this way as a means of giving life meaning and direction. Stories contextualize our experience in powerful ways that mere facts and disconnected events cannot. As I have argued elsewhere, it is possible to speak of any culture's most popular stories as its "sacred text." Art historian Gregor Goethals put it this way, "Today our friezes, the visual narratives of grandeur and perfection, may be found in popular art. Our mythological dramas, heroes and heroines, and ideological visions are produced through the contemporary forms of soap operas, sit-coms, commercials, news and sports" (1990, 162).

Story in Leisure

Before addressing the various ways that story relates to recreation and leisure, I would like to comment briefly on the overall importance of narrative within leisure time. There is no question that North American leisure is dominated by obvious forms of storytelling, especially mass media narratives. Years ago this may have been significantly less true, but I have not been able to find data to support such a conclusion. My guess is that narrative has always dominated people's discretionary time. The differences between today and, say, one hundred years ago, are likely related more to the media available and to spendable income than to storytelling per se ("The Evolution of Media," 1987).

The single largest leisure activity in the United States is television viewing. No other activity comes even close. In November of 1991, for instance, adults viewed 4 hours and 40 minutes daily; teens watched 3 hours and 14 minutes daily; kids saw about 3 hours and 20 minutes each day. The "average" home had the set on for 7 hours and 26 minutes *every day* ("Average Daily Viewing," 1992). Incidentally, viewing tends to go up with the addition of new technologies, such as the VCR and cable TV. In 1990, for instance, households with pay-cable service watched an average of over 13 hours per week more than families without cable ("Hours of Cable," 1990). According to the University of Maryland study of "American's Use of Time" in 1985, television viewing accounted for over one-third of adults' leisure time and was five times larger than the next-largest activity, traveling (Kane 1992). Similarly, Decision Research Corporation's study in the mid 1980s found that "at-home entertainment," including watching TV or movies on a VCR and listening to the radio, records, or tapes, was the most frequent leisure activity among Americans with household incomes of $25,000 or more (Hall 1988).

Rather than overemphasizing the significance of television as a leisure activity, I would prefer to look at the astounding role of story in leisure. The tube is so popular, in part, because it tells tales. If we add other obvious story-related activities, such as reading and conversation, the full significance of narrative as a leisure activity begins to become apparent. Leisure is not only dominated by the tube, but more tellingly by a variety of narrative activities. As I will suggest shortly, even sports can be viewed from a *narrative* paradigm. Television's enormous popularity is more a result of the way the medium turns practically all of its programming into stories than it is any other aspect of the medium.

Human Uses of Story

Undoubtedly the most intriguing question related to our storytelling capacity is one that only God can answer with absolute certainty: Why were human beings created as narrative users? Again, I believe the scriptures and everyday life in God's creation point to some likely answers. As I indicated earlier, stories help us to accomplish the "Cultural Mandate" to take care of and to develop the Creation. Also, storytelling enables us to communicate to others the truths of God's redemptive acts in history. After all, the Good News is the narrative of God's works and humankind's responses, especially in the shed blood of Christ, who himself often used parables to capture deep spiritual truths. Biblically speaking, the metaphors of "cultivating" and "broadcasting" are the major human activities in the world, and each of them is substantially a process of narrative communication.

When we turn to our everyday lives, however, we capture some of the more specific narrative purposes behind cultivating and broadcasting. I am convinced that there are at least five functions of storytelling, and we shall eventually see that each of them has implications for recreation and leisure. Each of them is "neutral" in the sense that it is neither inherently good or inherently evil. In a few minutes I will suggest how we might contextualize the narrative functions in order to make judgments about their value and goodness.

Pleasure

One function of narratives is the *pleasure* derived simply from the telling of stories. I'm convinced that people enjoy stories, regardless of whether the tales are comedic or tragic. If a story is well-told, it can grab an audience, pull them vicariously into the tale, and lead them along with anticipation. And if the ending truly creates a sense of completeness, the audience's pleasure is especially evident. This effect is true for children as well as adults.

Could it be that this type of narrative pleasure is behind much of our enjoyment of seemingly non-narrative forms of leisure, especially our appetite for competitive sports events? Suppose we consider a collegiate basketball game as a story. The players and coaches are the principle characters in the tale. Let's go a step further and pretend we're talking about a playoff game for a national title. The spectators arrive and begin watching the players practicing on the court. The spectators have a sense, more or less, of each team's strengths and weaknesses, and they also have their own hopes and fears about what might happen after the opening jump. In fact, each of the teams is like a collective "character" in the unfolding drama of the story of that team, its history, and its opportunity. The game is the story of two excellent teams doing battle on a collegiate court. If played well (if told well) it will please the audience, regardless of which team wins. That would be the sheer pleasure of a game well-told.

A game such as the Super Bowl takes on virtually mythic proportions as a narrative. In fact, it is interesting to note that the "pleasure" of this annual event is often derived not from the game itself but from the narrative hoopla surrounding the event. Sports "spin doctors," publicists, coaches, and commentators create the "story of the Super Bowl," beginning weeks before the broadcast. Sometimes the actual game is a disappointment in the face of expectations about the football tale that will be told on Super Bowl night.[2] In other words, the more mythic the sports event, the more impact that media can create by "narrating" the event long before it is held. I've often wondered if all of the media speculation about defense and offense, player-to-player matches, regional advantages, and momentum are not just one gigantic tale that becomes more real than the eventual game.

Instruction

Stories can also *teach* humankind. This truth is obvious in Protestantism, which often emphasizes the lessons to be learned from sermons and Biblical stories. And it's clear in parenting, which relies extensively on children's actions as a basis for admonition and correction: "Remember the time you forgot to let the dog out after school and the new carpet was ruined?" Most learning from narratives derives from the capacity we have as humans to generalize from specific tales to similar situations.

Again, consider a basketball game. Both the team that loses and the one that wins will likely try to learn something from the finished playoff competition. What was done well? Poorly? What lessons can we learn? Day in and day out, our recreational activities, as stories, frequently become opportunities for teaching ourselves and others about the fish that got away, the walk that was so refreshing, the game of trivial pursuit that embarrassed us, and so forth.

Amusement

Third, stories can *amuse* human beings. Instead of generalizing reflective thought, narratives often divert our attention from the real world toward a fictional world of amusement. Much popular comedy does this, including most television sitcoms, comedic films, humorous novels, and newspaper comics. Television critic and educator Neil Postman (1985) decries this type of programming because he believes it makes citizens thoughtless and ill-informed about matters of great public significance.

Regardless of whether or not he is correct about the impact of televisual amusement, the use of narratives for amusement certainly predates modern mass communications and would not disappear even if we eliminated electronic technologies. It seems that humankind finds some type of value in resting the mind with largely mindless narratives—narratives that tickle the funny bone while allowing us to escape from the troubling aspects of our everyday lives.

Amusement is likely the dominant use of stories in contemporary Western society. Amusement requires little of the "consumers" of mass-produced stories; it demands neither critical response nor moral judgment. We should not be surprised, then, that leisure time is loaded with amusing activities, from sharing humorous tales about our children's escapades (like the time a son or daughter asked an overweight supermarket cashier if she was so fat because she worked there) to television game shows, church talent nights, and an occasional game of golf by a true duffer. (One of the most humorous stories I tell about my brothers is a game of golf on a redwood-infested course in Northern California, where the fairways became an enormous pin-ball machine as the balls repeatedly ricocheted around us, over us, and through us like horizontally-flying hailstones; the harder my brothers tried to overcome the enormous redwood obstacles, the more dangerous and humorous the game became. By the time we reached the sixth hole, the competitive edge of sibling rivalry was transformed into a real-life tale of human insanity. There were times when the three of us were doubled over with laughter as we had been as children when something extraordinarily silly had happened.)

Obviously not all amusement is either humorous or narrative, but I believe that most of it is. Competitive sports can be a serious activity for players and spectators. And as I discussed earlier, the seriousness is often instructional as well as narrative in character. However, the day-to-day rituals of backyard football, driveway basketball, seasonal ice-skating, horseback riding, and hiking are probably forms of amusement that relieve boredom at the least and can offer such benefits as physical exercise, human interaction, and personal refreshment. Also, it might be that the amusement derived from such simple and common activities has at least somewhat of a narrative impulse, namely, to make and participate in a personal story whose outcome is unknown but positively anticipated.

Confirmation

Another significant function of storytelling is *confirmation*. We frequently make new narratives or use existing ones in order to confirm what we already believe and value about ourselves, our families, our religious communities, our enemies or antagonists, our favorite sports teams, or places. Humans as a rule are skeptical of narratives that conflict with existing beliefs, and they greatly prefer to participate in or use stories that affirm their views of the world. This is why the most effective propaganda does not attempt to change existing values and beliefs, but rather tends to direct those beliefs toward particular ends.

If confirmation sounds too cognitive or intellectual for a leisure activity, then modern propaganda has worked its magic. Confirmation is probably the most underestimated function of storytelling in contemporary mass marketing of leisure-time stories. In a market system where the audience is more or less king and where manufacturers seek to exploit those audiences, narratives must confirm as well as amuse.[3] To put it differently, the thematic content of popular stories will almost invariably tell people what they already believe or want to believe, not necessarily what they should believe. For this reason Hollywood moguls rely on secret screenings of movies to gauge viewers' responses and, when necessary, to change the content, especially endings.

The importance of confirmatory leisure narratives might help to explain the way recreational choices are sometimes made. For example, we might select a particular television program or film because of its happy ending—a kind of secularized Romans 8:28 ("All things work together for good . . .").

Similarly, we might arrange a family vacation to a particular location because we believe that such a trip will create the positive stories we wish to tell ourselves and others (the TV program "The Love Boat" was a boon to cruise vacations). Also consider how significant confirmation is in professional sports spectator-ship; attendance and viewership normally decline when a team is consistently losing, while they often skyrocket when a team is headed for a championship. A team's annual "story" for the season puts competition into a soap-opera-like context, with each game being part of the overall seasonal narrative; games are "episodes" in the season's tale. Finally, consider how critical some fans are of professional sports commentators whose interpretations of the team's narratives are at odds with their own. A commentator may be publicly opinionated, but such opinions should be in general agreement with the fans if he or she expects to be popular. Howard Cosell was, in my judgement, disliked more for his opinions than for his repertorial style. He seemed to enjoy exposing the weaknesses of cherished sports heroes, a treat that endeared him only to those who shared his frank opinions.

Illumination

The last major function of narrative found regularly in leisure activities is *illumination*. This involves using stories to discover truths about life and the human condition, or at least to see humankind in a different light.

For example, I know movie buffs who greatly prefer to view the types of artsy foreign films that raise questions about the nature of evil, the reality of existence, and the attributes of God. I similarly know adults who truly enjoy reading provocative novels and wandering through museums displaying esoteric modern art. These individuals are not after moralistic lessons or simple confirmation of their values and beliefs. Nor are they usually seeking amusement or pleasure. They like to be challenged intellectually as much as others might like to cultivate a vegetable garden or collect unusual beer cans.

Clearly, illumination is a relatively intellectual goal that presumes the value or at least enjoyment of a particular kind of mental activity. But for many of these types of individuals it is very much a recreational activity, not just a vocation. Just as some people might enjoy silly laughs, the person who seeks illumination might appreciate the laughs deriving from satire or irony. Whereas amusement is typically humorous in a comedic sense, illumination is often humorous in a tragic sense.

Implications and Lessons

This short tour of narrative functions was meant to capture some of the scope of storytelling in human life. Let me frankly admit that not all leisure activities fit nicely into narrative form. Competitive sports follows narrative form largely because it takes on clearly dramatic elements, where the teams or individuals are in conflict (drama) and where anticipation builds towards a necessary ending or series of endings. Similarly, television and movies are greatly open to narrative uses. Moreover, seemingly non-narrative activities, such as family vacations and gardening, can take on narrative significance because of the human tendency to contextualize life in story form. In one sense it seems silly to speak of an afternoon walk as a "story," but from an experiential perspective we do this all of the time with many similar activities. I would argue that our createdness naturally moves us to think of much recreational activity as narrative.

So what are the implications of this narrative view of leisure and recreation? Is it merely an academic theory or does the narrative paradigm have practical implications? What kind of new understanding can we gain?

I see two fairly obvious implications, and there are probably more. These implications stem from two questions arising out of narrative theory: (1) Who shall create the narratives that we use? and (2) How shall we assess the relative importance of the five functions of narrative discussed earlier?

The first question, regarding the authority to create narratives, is fundamentally a recreational issue. All narratives belong to someone who has created or recreated them. This ownership of stories must come from somewhere, and in Western society, especially North America, the ownership is primarily corporate and commercial. The vast majority of leisure time in the United States and Canada is dedicated to the individual consumption of mass-distributed entertainment products. And the overall effect of this is to turn recreation into mere consumer consumption, or "consumerism." Perhaps the major result is an implicit disenfranchisement of many people from the process of their own recreation.

I am not arguing that mass entertainment is inherently evil or that it is always and entirely disempowering. However, we have to admit that when recreational narratives are largely consumed by people who do not make them, there is the possibility that culture will be dictated by some people for other people. In other words, the "couch potato" becomes a metaphor for all recreational activity, and not just television viewing. Surely recreation ought not to be reduced to mass-mediated entertainment, no matter how edifying, uplifting, or enjoyable the entertainment might be. A sole recreational diet of mass-produced instruction or illumination would surely not be healthy.

Therefore, I would suggest the importance of balance in recreational uses of narrative—a balance between those stories produced by others, usually professionally, and those produced by our own minds and bodies. This balance would effectively help us to escape the consumerist trap. Such balance would also help guarantee that local, even familial narratives are not eclipsed by the national and international storytellers. Without such balance I don't see how it would be possible to enable individuals and groups or organizations to have their own identities. Locally told stories are essential for a vibrant sense of self and self-worth. Biblically speaking, Christians' responsibility to take care of and develop the Creation is the opposite of consumerism. Should not recreation be under the same mandate?

The second question, regarding the relative worth of the various functions of narrative, is for me also an issue of balance. I am not persuaded by elitists, for instance, who argue that amusement is bad or unrefined, while illumination is the mark of real civilization. Nor do I like the tendency in modern, middle-class society to equate amusement with culture. Similarly, the moralistic do-gooders who seem to evaluate all narratives merely in terms of moral lessons are, in my view, sadly unbalanced. Lest I leave the advocates of "pure pleasure" or market-driven confirmation off the hook, let me simply say that these two uses of story are also made into virtual idols by their own constituencies. Arguments about the superiority of narrative uses often say more about the preoccupations and cultural idiosyncracies of their advocates than they do about the relative value of various stories.

I conclude that one of the significant implications of narrative theory for recreation is that we have a paradigm for living a balanced life. Instead of arguing about the value of Shakespeare over the "Beverly Hillbillies," or the relative value of backyard football over jogging (at least in terms of narrative function), we can concentrate on how balanced our narrative recreational lives are. Do we overindulge in amusement and show little interest in illumination? Do we tend to turn our recreational narratives into intellectual work, namely illumination? Have we developed the capacity to enjoy stories simply because they are well-told?

The often delicate balance among narrative functions is especially important in our world. It is so easy for all of us to turn work into leisure, to approach worship as if it were amusement, to make leisure activities have some pecuniary value, and so forth. All of these types of modern tendencies are issues not only of appropriateness, but of balance as well.

When I drove to Chicago with my two children, I had a strong tendency not to see or enjoy the trip as a pleasurable excursion—as a self-created story of grace that allowed a family some time together. Instead of a pleasurable adventure, the story expectations for me were wrapped around the illumination I expected for my offspring. I sought their illumination about me and about the past that created me. Because of that narrowness of vision, I nearly missed an opportunity at McDonald's to share with my children the fact which they implicitly realized: that some experiences of children are common to nearly all kids, and one of them is a cheap meal together, complete with laughs, burps, and puns. Ironically, I took my children to the Windy City to learn about me, but the story worked its own, unexpected magic. I learned more about being a better father, especially when I realized that the trip itself was something I rarely experienced with my own father. And that unexpected realization, more than my planned instruction, was part of the grace of recreation that we shared with greasy fries and milk shakes.

Notes

1. The literature on "narrative theory" has expanded rapidly in the last twenty years. Among the studies on narrative and theology are Stanley Hauerwas, "Story and Theology," *Religion in Life* 45 (Autumn 1976): 339–350; John Narone, *The Jesus Story: Our Life as Story in Christ* (Collegeville, MN: Liturgical Press, 1979); John Dominic Crossan, *The Dark Interval: Towards a Theology of Story* (Nile, IL: Argus Communications, 1975); Wesley A. Kort, *Narrative Elements and Religious Meaning* (Philadelphia: Fortress Press, 1975); John Narone, *Towards a Theology of Story* (Slough: St. Paul Publications, 1977): Michael Goldberg, *Theology and Narrative: A Critical Introduction* (Nashville: Abingdon Press, 1982): John Shea, *Stories of Faith* (Chicago: The Thomas More Press, 1978).

2. Michael Real calculated that only 3 percent of one Super Bowl broadcast was actual live play-action. See Michael R. Real, *Mass-Mediated Culture* (Englewood Cliffs, NJ: Prentice Hall, 1977), 94.

3. This "mythopoetic" function of popular culture is now widely recognized by scholars of television. See R. Silverstone, *The Message of Television: Myth and Narrative in Contemporary Culture* (London: Heinemann Educational Books, 1981); G. Goethals, *The TV Ritual* (Boston: Beacon, 1981); Q. J. Schultze, *Redeeming Television* (Downers Grove: InterVarsity, 1991); J. W. Carey, ed., *Media, Myths and Narratives: Television and the Press* (Newbury Park, CA: Sage, 1988); D. Thorburn, "Television as an Aesthetic Medium," *Critical Studies in Mass Communication* 4 (June 1987): 161–173.

References

Average daily viewing in November. 1992. *Electronic media,* 20. February 10.

Eliot, T.X. 1949. *Notes towards the definition of culture.* New York: Brace.

Goethals, G. 1990. *The electronic golden calf.* Cambridge, MA: Cowley.

Hall, T. 1988. Why all those people feel they never have any time. *New York Times,* 8. January 2.

Hours of cable TV usage per week by households. 1990. *Electronic Media,* 41. November 19.

Kane, M. 1992. Researchers say we have more free time than ever. *Grand Rapids Press,* Dl. October 16.

Postman, N. 1985. *Amusing ourselves to death.* New York: Viking.

The evolution of media as entertainment. 1987. *Communication Research Trends* 8 (1): 12.

Chapter Nineteen

From Faith to Fun: Humor as Invisible Religion

RUSSELL HEDDENDORF

The Problem

There is nothing new in thinking of humor as a social lubricant. The ability to see the funny side in difficult or embarrassing moments has long been recognized as a way to resolve tension. At such times, humor acquires a halo effect that sanctifies its appearance, and the ability to laugh in such circumstances is recognized as a gift.

What is new in our time is the increasing tendency to encourage the use of this gift in social situations when, traditionally, its use might have been questioned. The presidential use of humor, for example, is a fine art that king-makers encourage. Laughter is also considered now to be a form of exercise that's good for the mind and body. In business, humor is encouraged for the improvement of relationships and, ultimately, to increase productions and profits. Even in times of war, humor is recognized as a potentially important survival tool. On this micro level, humor is a desirable and even necessary means for adjusting to the threats of modern life.

But humor doesn't exist only on the individual or psychological levels. In fact, humor is a powerful social and cultural force that influences all of us in subtle ways. Even when we laugh for our personal benefit, some residue of humor may have another effect on others. When I laugh at a fallen skier, for example, because it reduces my fear of skiing, I must ask what effect my laughter might have on the one who has fallen. Will the skier agree that his or her fall was, indeed, funny?

Laughter is the key to moving humor from the individual level to the social level, from the micro to the macro level of social life. Laughter not only defines what is funny but it also lends weight to that definition; others also agree that the skier's fall was, indeed, funny. Laughter defines a form of social reality which influences our ways of thinking as well as behaving. But in our modern world, much of this power to define has been taken from the individual and given to the mass media. On this macro level of social life, humor acquires a cultural value as it shapes the meaning that life might have for us.

My concern in this paper is with this cultural meaning of humor, especially as it is manifest in our leisure time activities where the tendency is to encourage humor as a social palliative. In this context, I'm especially concerned with the effect humor has had on the traditional way of defining the world and the reality we find there. It is in this context, too, that humor may be something of a curse, not a cure, a social problem and not a social palliative.

Humor as Worldview

Understanding humor, Wittgenstein believed, was similar to understanding philosophy; what is needed is "the right point of view" from which to "see" a joke or some philosophical conclusion. Anyone who doesn't "get a joke" doesn't share the cultural understanding behind its meaning. Wittgenstein states it more simply: "Humour is not a mood but a way of looking at the world" (1980, 78). In German, the phrase "looking at the world" is translated *Weltanschauung* or "worldview" by Wittgenstein.

But not all people share the same worldview or humor, especially when it is applied to a specific incident. As Wittgenstein states,

> What is it like for people not to have the same sense of humor? They do not react properly to each other. It's as though there was a custom among certain people for one person to throw another a ball which he is supposed to catch and throw back; but some people, instead of throwing it back, put it in their pocket. (1980, 83)

What we keep in this pocket is a worldview, some perspective on life that helps us to explain the world as it is experienced. The first task of a worldview "is to overcome bafflement" and to make sense of a world that is otherwise confusing and even paradoxical. The second task is to provide some help in relieving pain and oppression. A worldview helps us deal with the desire for freedom. Finally, a worldview helps us to understand how justice will ultimately win out in a world of corruption and deceit (Roberts 1990). But as Wittgenstein suggests, not all people share the same perspective on these tasks. In any culture there is a dominant point of view of the world held by the majority of the people who catch the ball and throw it back. Others hold to a different point of view and put the ball in their pocket.

Gordon Allport describes humor as a perspective that is in contrast with the world.

> Humor in one respect . . . is like religion. By setting up a frame of reference that is at variance with the ordinary mundane frame of reference, both have the peculiar ability of precipitating the ordinary worries and mischances of life into new and sure patterns. Humor, like religion, shatters the rigidity of literal mindedness. . . . In humor things are not all earnest or purposive, but pompous and out of step; in religion there is no such thing as incongruity. Thus, in setting up novel standards, both religion and humor, albeit in different ways, bring perspective. (*Context*, 1991, December 1)

Luckmann (1967) describes something of this same process in his explanation of invisible religion as an emerging worldview. In modern society, religiosity is changing as people create their own meaning systems which are less eternal and less compelling. Drawing on a wide range of popular philosophies, people seek to derive a new sense of meaning for their lives. This meaning provides an "invisible" form of religion that gives the person some new and often subversive religious feeling about the meaningfulness of life. Consequently, humor may provide a religiosity that bears little resemblance to traditional forms.

Arguing that worldview is an elementary social form of religion, Luckmann makes two assumptions: "that the worldview performs an essentially religious function and that it is part of socially objectivated reality" (1967, 55). Since language is basic for the establishment of a worldview, this elementary form of religion is being formed whenever people use symbols to convey meaning about everyday life. There is always some element of choice in a worldview which finds indirect expression in specific representations implying some ultimate significance. Put more simply, when we choose to laugh at some social situations symbolized by a joke, we give assent to an implicit worldview and the ultimate religious meaning it suggests.

Luckmann argues that everyday life may be either unproblematic or problematic. At the least problematic level of worldview, we approve of those descriptions of the world which are generally unquestioned; traditionally, for example, children were "seen and not heard." But as new problematic areas of life are encountered, new worldviews may be needed to interpret those areas. In the case of contemporary patterns of leisure, traditional worldviews are not adequate. Leisure activities are often on the margin of everyday life as it has been traditionally experienced. Consequently, a new worldview, one which helps to interpret the meaning of contemporary leisure activities, is needed.

For Luckmann, then, there is a distinct difference between trivial and unproblematic forms of social reality and those which benefit from the ultimate—meaning in a worldview. It is the latter form of everyday life that may gain a sacred quality as defined by some transcendent domain. While separated, these two domains, the secular and the sacred, are, nevertheless, related in some manner. By means of language, especially the worldview objectivates meaning, secular or sacred, and shapes it into what Luckmann calls a "sacred cosmos" which provides meaning for an otherwise problematic situation (1967, 59). Consequently, the worldview serves "to legitimate conduct in the full range of social situations" (61).

In traditional society, traditional religion serves to legitimate those problem areas needing interpretation. But with rapid social change, traditional religious views are limited and new worldviews may be needed to interpret emerging problem areas in modern life. These problem areas are limited here to the following three: the problem of meaning and the need to interpret the paradox surrounding it; the problem of freedom and the need to escape the restraints limiting it; and the problem of ultimacy and the need to overcome the realities of modern life. Each of these areas takes on a new dimension in modern life, a dimension that calls for a new worldview that either supports or subverts traditional religious attempts to deal with these problems.

Humor contributes to the religious worldview when it supports the traditional religious worldview. As one authority states, "The fact is that laughter is indivisible from the most sacred notions created by man. The laughing, humorous element is sometimes even called the echo of the sacred" (Zelvys 1990, 326). But humor may also subvert that traditional worldview by mocking it. And in that process of subversion, a new worldview is being shaped, one that becomes an invisible religion in modern society.

The Problem of Paradox

"Paradox is the reverse of what, properly perceived, would be synthesis" (Lubac 1987, 9). In that sense, paradox is entropic and characterizes modern life. "As each truth becomes better known, it opens up a fresh area for paradox" (10). Although paradox has always existed, it flourishes with "the provisional expression of a view which remains incomplete"

(9). In an earlier time, religion reconciled and integrated those incomplete views. Indeed, Weigert defines religion as "those institutionalized modes of behavior, feelings, rules, and sets of intentionalities by which humans contain ambivalence within a symbolic order that ultimately reconciles opposites" (1987, 9). In modern society, paradox increasingly defies traditional religious reconciliations and responds only to new symbolic orders.

Something of this religious paradox is found in the account of Abraham and Sarah and the birth of Isaac. While God is faithful in fulfilling His promise of a child to Abraham and Sarah at their advanced ages, the parents-to-be laugh at this paradox. First, it is the laughter of ridicule and mockery as Abraham laughs at the thought of Isaac's birth (Genesis 18:12–15). When the child is born, he is named Isaac or "laughter" as commanded by God. Sarah again laughs but not in a mocking tone. Instead, it is with a spirit of joy as she says, "God hath made me to laugh; everyone that heareth will laugh with me" (Genesis 21:6).

Lacking appropriate faith, Abraham and Sarah resort to mocking laughter as a way of making sense of the paradox. It is only after the birth of Isaac that the true meaning of laughter is expressed as joy that is to be shared by "everyone that heareth." As an expression of humor, laughter may subvert faith when it doesn't take it seriously. But laughter may also support faith when it is used as expression that takes seriously what the faith is seeking. Put differently, humor may either support or subvert religious faith.

In the New Testament, parables are used by Jesus to communicate truths that are incomplete in meaning. The believer will understand if there is hearing with the eyes of faith. Synthesis comes not from Jesus' words but from the interpretation provided by the hearer. Like Abraham and Sarah, one who hears a parable and interprets it with faith can laugh with joy at the paradox now reconciled as promise.

Today, paradox is a cultural problem in modern daily life. Making this observation, Toffler states, "Our present is exploding with paradox. . . . Systematic research can teach us much. But in the end we must embrace—not dismiss—paradox and contradiction, hunch, imagination and daring (though tentative) synthesis" (1980, 128–129). Because of the rapidity of social change, then, science is limited in its capacity to deal with modern paradox which becomes the kind of problematic social reality described by Luckmann as in need of a new worldview.

In a sense, attempts to resolve modern paradox will be futile and only complicate the problem. As Weigert states, "The cultural solution of contradictory feelings, in other words, has now become the problem. . . . *Modern culture does not effectively resolve ambivalence but increasingly generates it. . . .* In this modem condition, secondary ambivalence arises. People experience culturally induced contradictory feelings toward the same object" (1987, 21). Stated differently: "Culture was the solution; it is not part of the problem" (52). In fact, "modern culture has constructed ambivalence as a social object" (158). Moderns are condemned, not so much to be free as to be ambivalent. The hero system needs to face up to the great reversal; Charlie Brown, who has a hard time deciding what to do, is the archetypal cultural hero. Faced with this fact, a reasonable response to modern paradox is to live with it. Culturally, paradox "may be redefined as a modern virtue . . . (and) such a handy redefinition could be part of an informed worldview" (158).

The Problem of Freedom

If freedom is a problem in the modern world, it was hardly less so in biblical times. Throughout scripture, people seek freedom from old restraints. The Israelites wanted to be free of the Mosaic law. The disciples wanted Jesus to destroy the oppression of Roman rule. Jesus offered the people a new interpretation of the legalism of the Pharisees. In each case, faith was needed to accept the interpretation of the problem offered by God. Lacking such faith, humor could be relied on as a substitute for it.

In his study of the subversion of Christianity, Ellul explains how language is distorted as he describes the encounter of the Hebrews with neighboring cultures. Rather than separate themselves completely from these cultures, the Hebrews chose to use reorientation, the process of "taking a text and giving its objective sense a new turn so as to make it say something else" (1986, 16). In such a case, "even though the phrases remain the same, the meaning is radically broken" (16). It was by breaking the meaning that the Hebrews sought freedom from the authority of God.

Humor was one of the ways used to accomplish this reorientation. Distorting language by changing words or even letters, new meaning was given to phrases and sentences. Canaanite gods, which would not have been accepted in the original language, were included into Hebrew culture when subtle changes were made in the meaning of words. It was thought that ridiculing a foreign culture would render it harmless because it would not be taken seriously. In fact, Hebrew culture was gradually corrupted with the erosion of its language and the meaning system it referred to.

In our society, we find this same tendency to bring two meaning systems together and to change the meaning of one by changing the language of the other. Often this is done in the context of humor as seen in a recent publication that gave an issue over to the fifty most beautiful people in the world. A caption read, "Virtue is nice but beauty's a lot more fun." The lead article described a beautiful person as illustrative of "the whole creation just hit(ting) the jackpot. Exceptional people offer a glimpse of paradise. You're towed into heaven on their tan lines" (*People Weekly Extra,* 1991, 22).

Offered in a light-hearted manner, these words distort the meaning of "heaven," "paradise," and "creation." Hyers suggests that "such acts of profanation, frequently having comic overtones, [produce] a reversal . . . through which certain necessary and healthy functions are performed: psychological release is given to pent up emotional forces" (1969, 16). But if that psychological release is gained through the mass media, as it is in this case, there is also a cultural effect which implies, at the least, that religion is not to be taken seriously in society.

Throughout history, fun has been associated with freedom. The comic fool, for example, represented a free spirit opposing the majority. In modern society, this association has shown the new and deviant ways that humor may creatively resist the way things ought to be. Freud and Bergson, for example, saw humor as the breakdown of control and routine in life. Resisting predictability, humor supplied the opportunity for unpredictability and freedom.

The rapidity of social change in modern society is so diverse and broad that restraint appears to be ubiquitous. Whole new areas of life are seen as constraining. Bergson, for example, saw technological development as a major force to be resisted with humor. Patterns of social mobility produced changes which threatened the class structure, encouraging the use of ethnic humor. As women have become more free from traditional restraints, new forms of gender humor have developed to explain these changes and encourage gender equality. Similarly, the trend to greater sexual freedom has been accompanied by new patterns of sexual humor that explain and justify this freedom.

In each case, the traditional system has been seen as flawed or incomplete. Logic and rational thought are no longer adequate to explain the changes that have occurred. In an earlier day, society would call for a return to faith as the means to interpret what has become paradoxical or constraining. But these problems have become so pervasive and threatening in modern society that faith is no longer adequate. For one thing, the use of faith in a secular society by the masses is no longer plausible. For another, the problems are so threatening that they cannot be taken seriously. Only a new and radical worldview, including humor, can reorder the social structure.

In a traditional society, the minority and deviant perspective offered by humor could not have challenged the logic of serious thought. As Mulkay suggests, once serious discourse is deemed ineffective and is discarded, humor appears consistent and even logical. Consequently, "paradoxes appear to be problematic only in so far as we insist on judging the humorous domain by the criteria of serious discourse" (1988, 219). But once humorous and not serious discourse is considered the norm in society, humor is deemed an acceptable response to paradox and restraint.

Faced with the dilemma of sustaining orderliness on a daily basis, the modern person needs to find new meaning in life, a new worldview. Humor offers such an explanation with its consistent inconsistency. As Mulkay states,

> If what we now call the humorous mode *were dominant*, it would have become the serious mode. In this new world, the criteria of semantic adequacy would be radically different. In particular, genuine claims about the nature of the world would not be acceptable *unless* they generated inconsistency, incongruity, or paradox, or in some way revealed or acknowledged the multiplicity of the world. (1988, 221)

The Problem of Ultimacy

In this new world of consistent inconsistency, any system that satisfactorily explains paradox would challenge old worldviews and raise itself to a place of preeminence. As an invisible religion, it would replace the Christian worldview that relied on faith to explain the paradox of miracle. It would also replace science which challenged faith and established its own worldview based on fact to explain the inconsistency in a world that remained, for the most part, logical and open to serious discourse. In short, such a worldview would redefine much of what we have come to know as "true."

Ultimately, then, humor mocks truth as we have known it in western society. All those traditional paradoxes that made no sense except through faith can now be explained with humor; they are not to be taken seriously. As in the past, pockets of meaning may still be provided by faith, accompanied by fun. Increasingly, however, the two worldviews represented by faith and fun have separated and now oppose each other in the attempt to interpret the modern world.

In an earlier day, God's world had meaning and made sense to the serious observer who approached that world with occasional amusement. Even the resurrection of Jesus, it has been suggested, was joyous because Jesus had the last laugh. But that world has been reshaped by modernity and appears senseless to the modern observer. In such a world "the devil laughs because God's world has meaning" (Donnelly 1992, 385).

It could be argued that life could be taken too seriously if all incongruities were to be approached with logic. Reinhold Niebuhr would seem to agree:

> Laughter is our reaction to immediate incongruities and those which do not affect us essentially. Faith is the only possible response to the ultimate incongruities of existence which threaten the very meaning of our life. . . . Man's very position on the universe is incongruous. That is the problem of faith, and not of humor. (as quoted in Hyers 1981, 31)

But if humor is a worldview, an invisible religion competing with Christianity in its attempt to explain the paradoxes of modern life, wouldn't laughter be a reaction to an ultimate incongruity which may acquire a sense of ultimacy when the only reaction to them is laughter with its implicit religious meaning? Since laughter is a cultural phenomenon, it may be just as important to ask why we laugh at something as to ask only what we laugh at.

Much of the mass media would have us laugh at reality itself. Following the tendency of humor to make "the inconsistent consistent," reality is distorted so that it cannot be taken seriously. Beginning with animation and the creation of Mickey Mouse, a watershed was reached in the production of "Who Framed Roger Rabbit." In this film, the sensible world of humans was juxtaposed against the nonsensical world of the animated Toons, so that it is difficult to know what is true. In effect, the world of animation is viewed as equal to the world of God's creation.

Reality denial has become such a common theme in the movies that it is found in a wide range of films, all relying on some form of humor. In the "Back to the Future" series, the reality of time is denied. The heroes have the freedom to transcend time, always in a paradoxical and humorous fashion. Horror movies have developed their own form of paradox in the use of "horror humor" at the point of horror or murder. With the use of one liners, the reality of brutality and sadism is denied with laughter. In effect, violence and murder are not to be taken seriously.

These are not the "immediate incongruities" that Niebuhr would have us respond to with laughter. These are those "ultimate incongruities of existence" that should be approached with faith. Reality denial has moved from the denial of the mundane to those realities thought to be of religious concern. In this process, the comic image has emerged triumphant as a portrayal of reality. Presented as a device to stimulate laughter, the image of, say, Roger Rabbit, stereotypes the humanity of people as human beings. The comic image has now become reality itself and "masks the fact that there is no basic reality" (Denzin 1991, 5).

As an invisible religion, humor encourages laughter as a ubiquitous response to the problems of modern society. It acquires a transcendent quality that denies the reality of even the most human and eternal dilemmas that people can face. "Fun" replaces "fact" and even "faith" as an element in a worldview entrusted to deal with the paradoxes and restraints of everyday life. Instead of posing as a minority or deviant view of the world, humor now provides us with a dominant, majority perspective that increasingly functions as a religion. In an increasingly secularized society, humor successfully competes with traditional religion and gradually replaces it.

Conclusion

Traditional culture has been under attack from the forces of modernization for some 100 years. It is only within the past fifty years or so that this attack has taken the direction often referred to as Postmodernism and has redefined the traditional boundaries of lifestyle patterns. Included in these redefinitions is the shift in emphasis from our traditional work ethic, which had been the dominant worldview, to the modern leisure ethic which is replacing it. As an integral part of the leisure ethic, humor has taken its place as a dynamic, creative force, redefining the nature of reality in modern society.

As an invisible religion replacing the traditional "culture of faith," humor has developed a contemporary "culture of fun." Much of this fun culture revolves around the mass media and technologies that offer a new language of visual images. This new language changes the nature of the person and his or her relationship to traditional notions of the world. By suggesting that this world is not to be taken seriously, the fun culture offers the alternative view—that the world God has created has no meaning. As an invisible religion, the fun culture provides, at best, a mere reflection or distortion of that created world. At worst, it destroys any assurance that reality can exist. Such a religion mocks not only God's creation; it mocks God Himself.

References

de Lubac, H. 1987. *Paradoxes of Faith.* San Francisco: Ignatius Press.

Denzin, N. 1991. *Images of postmodern society: Social theory and contemporary cinema.* London: Sage Publications.

Donnelly, D. 1992. Divine folly: Being religious and the exercise of humor. *Theology Today* 45 (4): 385. January

Ellul, J. 1986. *The subversion of Christianity.* Grand Rapids: William B. Eerdmanns.

Hyers, C. 1969. *Holy laughter: Essays on religion in the comic perspective.* New York: Seabury.

Hyers, C. 1981. *The cosmic vision and the Christian faith.* New York: The Pilgrim Press.

Luchmann, T. 1967. *The invisible religion.* New York: Macmillan.

Mulkay, M. 1988. *On humor.* Oxford: Basil Blackwell.

People Weekly Extra. 1991. Table of contents and 22. Summer.

Roberts, K. 1990. *Religion in sociological perspective* (2nd ed.). Belmont, CA: Wadsworth Publishing.

Toffler, A. 1980. *The third wave.* New York: Bantam Books.

Weigert, A. 1987. *Mixed emotions.* Albany: State University of New York Press.

Chapter Twenty

Leisure, Drama, and Christianity

GWEN LAURIE WRIGHT

The scene: The Women's Restroom at an eastern College

The year: A Friday evening, April 1983

A conversation between two women:

> A. I have never in my life felt so invigorated; it's so much fun to feel so alive!
>
> B. Yeah, isn't it great?
>
> A. Un–hm. I'm 68 years old, and I've never done movement and acting and being creative! I think every adult should have this opportunity. I feel wonderful!

This conversation took place at a workshop on "The Arts and Spirituality." The workshop was part of a conference which included lectures and experiential learning in which I used many of the exercises that I use in improvisational theatre classes. The connections between drama and spirituality which this woman found exhilarating will be further described in this paper.

Leisure, drama, and Christianity doesn't affirm leisure—does it? In this paper, I would like to describe leisure and work, and to suggest a different definition of leisure than the one commonly held in Western society. I also want to demonstrate how drama, particularly improvisational theatre, can expand our awareness of God and our relationship to God, and our awareness of ourselves and of other people.

Let's look at our definitions of work and leisure. Those of us in the Protestant churches often believe, as Max Weber states in *The Protestant Ethic and the Spirit of Capitalism*, that "one lives to work" (1958, 171); or, as Robert Lee states, "Americans are working, sweating people" (1964, 19). In California, as well as in other parts of the country, people work seven days a week. They do, however, stop to smell the roses as they jog along in a marathon, but they make that "work," too; we stop only when exhausted. We do not have a different rhythm on days off; we still work in some way.

In American society, leisure is often viewed as "time off from work" which means time for more activities, such as participating in sports (playing in little league, jogging marathons, sailing races). Are these "work activities" or activities that re-create us? Let me state that I am not against competition, it is good to push oneself to do something well and to excel, because that enhances our sense of well-being as humans. The question remains as to whether our work and activities are good for us or whether they take away some of our humanness. (See Schumacher 1979 or Dorothee Soelle 1984 for a consideration of a theology of work.)

What I am suggesting is that most of us need to have a varied rhythm to our lives—competitive sports are good for us, whether done as our main kind of work or whether done in leisure time—but most of us also need to have a time of "being" as well as a time of "doing." I am indebted to Robert Wilson for his definition of leisure in the sense of becoming. He states,

> Leisure is identified as a process rather than a state; as a willing surrender of the whole self to experience rather than a parceling-out of some one or few of the individual's faculties. (1981, 285)

In other words, Wilson's definition suggests continuous development involving changes, rather than a static state, and a letting the whole self experience an idea, an action, another person, or a situation. Wilson further explains leisure as an "openness to the world," a willingness to let things happen, rather than to plan things; and letting go of tight boundaries around the self (285).

When considering Wilson's definition of leisure, one can ask—isn't this idea of leisure antithetical to our Protestant, and especially our Reformed, faith? Certainly the Protestant work ethic stresses rest from the work that earns us money—rest on Sunday, that is; but for some Sunday is a different kind of work, or rather activities: Sunday School, church attendance, a big dinner that at least the women have worked to produce, and in the afternoon we often have church ball games, potlucks, and other activities.

We keep busy, because idleness has been frowned upon. As Dorothee Soelle explains in *To Work and to Love*, "In the minds of the Reformers, human work was the antidote to idleness, which was considered the breeding ground of sin. Because work helped people resist temptations and worldly pleasures, it was essential for salvation" (1984, 65). Josef Pieper further points out in *Leisure: The Basis of Culture* (1963) that idleness has been viewed with suspicion by many Protestants; leisure is equated with idleness. Pieper elucidates this idea by saying that idleness is feared, because if one is not busy, one might lose control of oneself; one might lose control of emotions and actions. People fear losing control, because they fear being overwhelmed by those emotions, and they are afraid that their actions also might get out of control.

Before describing the ways in which improvisational theatre (or "improv" for short) can facilitate the kind of leisure that Wilson proposes, let us look at some of the Biblical basis for redefining leisure as a process that helps us develop more awareness of God, ourselves, and the rest of creation. In Genesis, we read that men and women are created in the image of God, and a few verses later God blesses the human beings, and says that all of the creation is good (Genesis 1:27–31). The Hebrew word *tov*, which means good, also means beautiful. Do we see ourselves as good *and* our bodies as not only good but also beautiful?

Along with the Garden being a place to *enjoy* and to care for is the idea in the first question and answer of the Westminster Confession of Faith that the chief end of men and women is to glorify God and to enjoy God forever. We are supposed to "Sing to the Lord with *cheerful* voice, serve God with *mirth*" (*Presbyterian Hymnal*, 1990, No. 220). Sometimes we forget to take delight in what God has created, and we do not have time to enjoy God as much if we are busy all the time. Enjoyment is a process we need to let develop in a time of leisure.

A new definition of leisure that can be developed through improvisational theatre has been suggested. This kind of theatre is drama in which the actors improvise or make up the actions and dialogues as they go along, rather than using a previously written script. In improvisational acting, one learns to be more expressive with emotions, movements, and dialogue, using all of one's body. As Paul says in 1 Corinthians 6:19: "Your body is a temple for the Holy Spirit." To me, this means having healthy bodies that are comfortable with emotions and with movement, so that we can praise God with our bodies as well as with our minds.

In Christian growth retreats I have led, we often do Body Prayer using the whole body to express our petitions to God. In acting classes, we do exercises that free the body to move.

Getting in touch with the actor within also enables the person to express emotions, and enables one to use all of one's body for expression. It sounds frightening to suggest doing something that many Christians suspect or believe to be wrong, because it means letting go of control.

However, improvisation taught by a teacher skilled in theatre techniques and one who has had some psychological training can enhance one's growth as a whole person. Psychological training is necessary, so that the "improv" teacher knows the difference between acting and therapy, which this is not. Knowing the difference means the teacher will strive to prevent the participants from getting hurt emotionally. If anyone in the group seems to have gotten in touch with painful past experiences in the scenes being acted out, the teacher needs to know how to guide the class in a different direction, and the teacher has a responsibility to talk with the person privately and to make a referral to a therapist, if that seems appropriate. These warnings are necessary, because improvisational theatre does cause people to get in touch with painful as well as joyful parts of the self; that experience is part of the process of letting the actor within emerge. In improv groups, I ask the participants to express only as much emotion as they are comfortable with, and I do not push emotional expression.

In improvisational theatre we learn to let our emotions emerge and to let our bodies be more expressive. Movement helps to free emotions; for example, we do exercises where the entire class shouts; they show anger with the whole body. No one is embarrassed when *all* are doing it. The class also chooses characters that allow them to express various emotions and conflict between characters—an area that Christians are sometimes uncomfortable with; however, Jesus certainly got involved in conflicts many times. (Confrontations with the Pharisees are an example.)

We also do exercises to learn how to be better listeners, and to see, that is, to notice what is happening. All of the senses are heightened in improv groups. This brings us to the sense of touch. In a dramatic scene touching frees people, because the more they do it, the more comfortable they feel with it, and often they will come back to class the next week stating that. They have also discovered, in the world outside the class, that touching can be a show of affection, and that it doesn't necessarily imply sexual attraction. Thinking of Jesus' life, he touched the blind man to heal him (John 9:6), and he let others touch him (Luke 7:36–50).

To return to Wilson's definition of leisure, he states that leisure as process is a way of becoming, of developing that encourages openness and letting life happen—attitudes also necessary for play and creativity, close human relationships, and religious contemplation. How can improv help us become playful? Playfulness is that ability to be spontaneous, to "seize the moment," to have childlike (not childish) wonder, innocence in the sense of being non-judgmental and accepting. Freeing emotions and the body are childlike activities. It is also true in improvisational theatre that there are few negative judgments made about what the actor can say or do, because there are no preconceived scripts and directions. Acting exercises that encourage play are hopping, skipping, jumping, humming, and children's games. It is interesting that when someone in one of my classes chooses an age to act out in a scene, many choose to be a small child under eight years old. Perhaps the reason is that of unconsciously wanting to regain the sense of wonder and of innocence in the sense of not having to be responsible. Letting go, even momentarily, of the cares of adulthood frees a person, because the constraints that keep us from being spontaneous have disappeared temporarily.

An attitude of leisure is necessary for play, and second, for close relationships. Whether traditional or improvisational acting, theatre is the enactment of scenes based on life. Improvisational theatre by its very nature teaches us various ways to relate to another character on stage. How the scene progresses depends on what comes forth from each of our inner selves. Furthermore, working together in scenes involving humans both as actors and as real persons creates community; if community does not result, the scene will fail to communicate what was intended to the audience. Participants in improvisational acting classes discuss the exercises and scenes they do; many people learn not only to "act" but also to discern what it feels like in daily life to be another person through trying out a character different from themselves or through what happens spontaneously in a scene. Since leisure, as defined by Wilson, allows one to let go of tight boundaries, so too does improvisational acting enable one to learn how to let go, because there is no right way to do a scene. Tight boundaries help us control emotions; improv helps us express our emotions. Tight boundaries help us plan our actions; improv enables us to let our actions happen. Improv allows our boundaries to be fluid, to change, to expand. By allowing fluid boundaries, improv helps us be more spontaneous in our relationships. All the knowledge about human relationships that emerges in improv is, to my way of thinking, enabling us to become more of the persons God is calling us to be.

God sent Jesus to show us the way, and one of the ways Jesus did this in his life was to redraw the boundaries. First, he said that the law was made for men and women, not that humans were made for the law. An example was that he said it was acceptable for his disciples to pick corn on Sunday, which was against the law, because they needed to eat (Mark

2:23–28). Jesus also redrew the boundaries by becoming friends with all kinds of undesirable people—tax collectors, prostitutes, the woman who had five husbands—thus showing that we too can reach out to people and expand our human relationships.

The third area where an attitude of leisure is necessary is for religious contemplation, which is not often part of Protestant faith and practice. Dorothee Soelle states that "the Protestant work ethic eschewed contemplation and upset the balance between contemplation and work by stressing the dignity of work" (1984, 64). As Protestants, many of us tend to study and think about our Christian faith more than we practice contemplation. Protestants are, however, re-discovering the "art of contemplation"—that is, praying in a way that allows one to be still, to be open to thoughts and emotions coming from God, instead of talking so much in our praying that we fail to "listen" with all our senses. Contemplation is praying with Scripture by taking a passage and letting thoughts, images, and feelings emerge so that we sense what that particular passage is saying to us right now in our lives. Besides praying with Scripture, we might contemplate the Cross, a painting, or a musical selection. Practicing contemplation is a way of allowing our boundaries to be fluid; it allows God to show us possibilities, to present us with a different vision.

We have looked at reasons for developing an attitude of leisure—an openness in play, close human relationships, and religious contemplation. One additional function of improvisational theatre is that it fosters expansion of the imagination. Since we do not have a logical progression of events and speeches to learn, we must let our *imaginations* take over during a scene. When I give a person a character to be, whatever happens in the scene often triggers something deep within called imagination, that is, creativity, emotions, actions that we would not have "thought" of. When imagination is triggered, so is insight—again something makes sense that didn't before, but it is not something we thought out; imagination triggers intuition; we risk and take a leap of faith; we assume that something is true or meaningful, and that is insight. When we take this leap of faith, we trust in possibilities, because we let imagination, creativity, words, actions happen, which is what occurs in improvisational theatre. We need to learn to accept some things or people or happenings as gift, and realize we can *trust* that process.

We have examined the connection between improvisational theatre as a means of developing an attitude of leisure, of openness that will help us grow as Christians. In improvisational theatre, there are no losers; people win, because they learn in their own ways, and what is right for one may not be right for another. If we view leisure as a process of learning to become more open to what happens in our lives, as I have suggested, then we will see a different way of viewing the Sabbath. This day then becomes not just a day for more activities, although these are certainly important, but, as Pieper suggests, the Sabbath can be not only rest from work, but a day to regain one's dignity as a human being through celebration and worship of the Divine Creator. This attitude of leisure as openness to the world prepares us for Sunday worship of the Divine Creator, because it prepares us to truly hear, see, feel, and express ourselves with dignity in all our fullness as humans; it helps us remember who we are—the People of God (1963, 42–45). Regaining our dignity enables us to be renewed to love and to work, and by work I mean not only gainful employment but also work toward justice and dignity for other humans.

An attitude of letting life happen means we will also be open to letting God happen in our lives; we will be more sensitive to God's word to us, especially in worship. We of the Reformed faith often have worship that is mostly from the mind, although today that is changing in some places. What we need, I want to suggest, is a more holistic worship that includes not only well-planned sermons, but also the opportunity to listen in the silences, to express emotions, and yes, to be dramatic. As Walter Wangerin writes, "Although the church is often scared of drama, the whole concept of drama is integral to worship" (1992, 28). There were valid reasons for expelling drama from the church in the Middle Ages: it had become lewd. Not only that, but during Reformation times, Protestants wanted to get rid of the vestiges of masses in a language not understood by the people, of sacred space for the clergy only, of symbols and actions that were little understood and therefore not meaningful to most people. At the time of the Reformation, Protestants deemed these decisions as necessary; however, the "drama" of the liturgy was also obliterated.

Today many Presbyterians, for example, feel the need to restore some of the ritual (the acting out) to worship. But first we need to develop an attitude of leisure as preparation for the Sabbath. Development of our imaginations through improvisational theatre helps us see the possibilities—to accept different ways of worship. Traditionally we sit in pews taking our cues from the leaders at the front, and much of what the congregation does is passive. In the instances where the congregation does act out some of the worship, the Spirit moves in unexpected ways. In St. John Presbyterian Church in Berkeley, California one Sunday, Carla de

Sola, a liturgical dance leader, led the People of God (clergy and laity) in moving prayerfully through a labyrinth painted on a large canvas on the floor. Those who at first looked askance at praying with movement soon joined the others, quietly moving to the music. People who had a grievance stopped to reach out with a hand. The Spirit moved the People of God into closer communion.

When we Christians have developed into whole persons—with thinking, emotional, and intuitive functions operating—we are more able to hear, to see, to feel, to intuit God's word energized through the Holy Spirit. As more sensitive persons, the words and actions of Jesus will speak to us at this moment in ways that help us grow. As sensitive whole persons, we will be more in tune with the rhythm of our lives and of the whole creation. When we are alive emotionally and physically, we are connected to others and to all of God's creation. As theologian Jurgen Moltmann says, ours is a God who communicates with us, not by powerful actions, but through love (1985, 75–76). That love is often communicated to us in imaginative ways through our seeing, tasting, smelling, touching, and hearing. Improvisational theatre helps us develop these senses; in the words of English professor and artist, Mary Caroline Richards, the arts wake us up to life (1964, 15). The arts enable us to become whole in mind and body—a wholeness centered in God, revealed in Jesus Christ, and kept alive by the Holy Spirit. The arts help us rediscover the creativity given to us by God, a creativity that heals us. As healed persons, everyone that breathes can praise God. As healed persons, we can receive the Holy Spirit with our entire beings as we move through the dance of life.

References

Cox, H. 1969. *The feast of fools: A theological essay on festivity and fantasy.* Cambridge, MA: Harvard.

Ellis, M.H. 1981. *Peter Maurlin: Prophet in the twentieth century.* New York: Paulist.

Huizinga, J. 1955. *Homo Ludens: A study of the play element in culture.* Boston: Beacon.

Kern, M.R. 1977. Class on "Genesis." Findlay, Ohio: Winebrenner Theological Seminary. Fall.

Lee, R. 1964. *Religion and leisure in America.* New York: Abingdon.

Moltmann, J. 1985. *God in creation: An ecological doctrine of creation.* London: SCM Press.

Pieper, J. 1963. *Leisure: The basis of culture.* New York: Pantheon.

Richards, M. C. 1964. *Centering in pottery, poetry, and the person.* Middletown, CT: Wesleyan University.

Schumacher, E. F. 1979. *Good work.* New York: Harper and Row.

Soelle, D. 1984. *To work and to love: A theology of creation.* Philadelphia: Fortress.

The Presbyterian Hymnal. 1990. Louisville, KY: Westminster/John Knox.

Wangerin, W., Jr. 1992. The divine drama in human experience. *Radix* 20 (4): 8–11, 28.

Weber, M. 1958. *The Protestant ethic and the spirit of capitalism.* New York: Scribner's.

Wilson, R. N. 1981. The courage to be leisured. *Social Forces,* 60. December.

CPSIA information can be obtained at www.ICGtesting.com
Printed in the USA
LVOW080451081212

310268LV00002B/79/A